Patricio Galeas

Using Search Term Positions for Determining Document Relevance

Patricio Galeas

Using Search Term Positions for Determining Document Relevance

Südwestdeutscher Verlag für Hochschulschriften

Impressum/Imprint (nur für Deutschland/ only for Germany)
Bibliografische Information der Deutschen Nationalbibliothek: Die Deutsche Nationalbibliothek verzeichnet diese Publikation in der Deutschen Nationalbibliografie; detaillierte bibliografische Daten sind im Internet über http://dnb.d-nb.de abrufbar.

Alle in diesem Buch genannten Marken und Produktnamen unterliegen warenzeichen-, marken- oder patentrechtlichem Schutz bzw. sind Warenzeichen oder eingetragene Warenzeichen der jeweiligen Inhaber. Die Wiedergabe von Marken, Produktnamen, Gebrauchsnamen, Handelsnamen, Warenbezeichnungen u.s.w. in diesem Werk berechtigt auch ohne besondere Kennzeichnung nicht zu der Annahme, dass solche Namen im Sinne der Warenzeichen- und Markenschutzgesetzgebung als frei zu betrachten wären und daher von jedermann benutzt werden dürften.

Verlag: Südwestdeutscher Verlag für Hochschulschriften GmbH & Co. KG
Dudweiler Landstr. 99, 66123 Saarbrücken, Deutschland
Telefon +49 681 37 20 271-1, Telefax +49 681 37 20 271-0
Email: info@svh-verlag.de
Zugl.: Marburg, Philipps-Universität Marburg, Diss., 2010

Herstellung in Deutschland:
Schaltungsdienst Lange o.H.G., Berlin
Books on Demand GmbH, Norderstedt
Reha GmbH, Saarbrücken
Amazon Distribution GmbH, Leipzig
ISBN: 978-3-8381-2422-3

Imprint (only for USA, GB)
Bibliographic information published by the Deutsche Nationalbibliothek: The Deutsche Nationalbibliothek lists this publication in the Deutsche Nationalbibliografie; detailed bibliographic data are available in the Internet at http://dnb.d-nb.de.

Any brand names and product names mentioned in this book are subject to trademark, brand or patent protection and are trademarks or registered trademarks of their respective holders. The use of brand names, product names, common names, trade names, product descriptions etc. even without a particular marking in this works is in no way to be construed to mean that such names may be regarded as unrestricted in respect of trademark and brand protection legislation and could thus be used by anyone.

Publisher: Südwestdeutscher Verlag für Hochschulschriften GmbH & Co. KG
Dudweiler Landstr. 99, 66123 Saarbrücken, Germany
Phone +49 681 37 20 271-1, Fax +49 681 37 20 271-0
Email: info@svh-verlag.de

Printed in the U.S.A.
Printed in the U.K. by (see last page)
ISBN: 978-3-8381-2422-3

Copyright © 2011 by the author and Südwestdeutscher Verlag für Hochschulschriften GmbH & Co. KG and licensors
All rights reserved. Saarbrücken 2011

Abstract

The technological advancements in computer networks and the substantial reduction of their production costs have caused a massive explosion of digitally stored information. In particular, textual information is becoming increasingly available in electronic form.

Finding text documents dealing with a certain topic is not a simple task. Users need tools to sift through non-relevant information and retrieve only pieces of information relevant to their needs [14]. The traditional methods of information retrieval (IR) based on search term frequency have somehow reached their limitations, and novel ranking methods based on hyperlink information are not applicable to unlinked documents.

The retrieval of documents based on the positions of search terms in a document has the potential of yielding improvements, because other terms in the environment where a search term appears (i.e. the neighborhood) are considered. That is to say, the grammatical type, position and frequency of other words help to clarify and specify the meaning of a given search term [98]. However, the required additional analysis task makes position-based methods slower than methods based on term frequency and requires more storage to save the positions of terms. These drawbacks directly affect the performance of the most user critical phase of the retrieval process, namely query evaluation time, which explains the scarce use of positional information in contemporary retrieval systems.

This thesis explores the possibility of extending traditional information retrieval systems with positional information in an efficient manner that permits us to optimize the retrieval performance by handling term positions at query evaluation time.

To achieve this task, several abstract representation of term positions to efficiently store and operate on term positional data are investigated. In the Gauss model, descriptive statistics methods are used to estimate term positional information, because they minimize outliers and irregularities in the data. The Fourier model is based on Fourier series to represent positional information. In the Hilbert model, functional analysis methods are used to provide reliable term position estimations and simple mathematical operators to handle positional data.

The proposed models are experimentally evaluated using standard resources of the IR research community (Text Retrieval Conference). All experiments demonstrate that the use of positional information can enhance the quality of search results. The suggested models outperform state-of-the-art retrieval utilities.

The term position models open new possibilities to analyze and handle textual data. For instance, document clustering and compression of positional data based on these models could be interesting topics to be considered in future research.

Kurzfassung

Die technologischen Fortschritte bei Rechnernetzen und die erhebliche Senkung ihrer Produktionskosten haben ein gewaltiges Wachstum von digital gespeicherten Daten verursacht. Besonders die Verfügbarkeit von Textinformationen im Internet nimmt ständig zu.
In dieser Situation ist das Finden von relevanten Informationen keine einfache Aufgabe mehr. Benutzer brauchen ständig effizientere Werkzeuge, um relevante Dokumente aus dem riesigen Datenbestand zu extrahieren. Da traditionelle Algorithmen im Bereich des Information Retrieval (IR) in der Regel nur auf Worthäufigkeiten basieren, haben sie mittlerweile ihre Leistungsgrenzen erreicht. Auf der anderen Seite können die neuesten Methoden aktueller Suchmaschinen, die auf Hyperlink-Informationen zurückgreifen, nur in verlinkten Dokumenten verwendet werden. Alle Dokumente, die keine Hyperlink-Informationen enthalten, können meistens nur mit traditionellen (Wort-Häufigkeits-) Methoden ausgewertet werden.

IR-Methoden, die Informationen über die Positionen von Suchbegriffen in Dokumenten berücksichtigen, haben das Potenzial, bessere Ergebnisse als Standard-Methoden zu liefern. Der Grund ist, dass positionsbasierte Methoden die Suchbegriffe in ihrem Kontext bzw. ihrer Nachbarschaft innerhalb eines Dokumentes betrachten. Das heisst, die Position eines Wortes hilft, die Bedeutung eines anderen Wortes abzuklären. Allerdings bedeutet die Auswertung von räumlichen Informationen auch aufwändige Berechnungen, was die positionsbasierten Algorithmen langsamer und platzraubender machen. Solche Nachteile wirken sich unmittelbar auf die Performanz der wichtigsten Phase des Retrieval-Prozesses aus: der Auswertung einer Anfrage eines Benutzers. Aus diesem Grund werden heutzutage positionsbasierte Algorithmen in Suchmaschinen selten verwendet.

Diese Doktorarbeit untersucht die Möglichkeit, ein traditionelles IR-System mit positionsbasierten Informationen auf eine neue Weise zu erweitern und durch die Auswertung dieser Informationen die Performanz des Systems zur Anfragezeit zu verbessern.

Um dieses Ziel zu erreichen, werden unterschiedliche Darstellungen von Wortpositionen in einem Dokument untersucht. Im Gauss-Modell werden Methoden deskriptiver Statistik verwendet, weil sie für die typischen Unregelmässigkeiten und Ausreisser in den positionsbasierten Daten geeignet sind. Das Fourier-Modell basiert auf Fourierreihen zur Repräsentation positionsbasierter Informationen. Im Hilbert-Modell werden Methoden der Funktionalanalysis für das Speichern und Bearbeiten von Wortpositionen eingesetzt.

Alle vorgeschlagenen Modelle werden mit Standard-Datenbeständen der IR-Gemeinschaft (Text Retrieval Conference) evaluiert. In den Experimenten wird gezeigt, dass die Verwendung von positionsbasierten Informationen die Qualität der Suchergebnisse

erhöht und die Leistung von aktuellen Ansätzen übertrifft.
Die positionsbasierten Modelle eröffnen neue Möglichkeiten zur Analyse von textuellen Daten. Zum Beispiel sind die Clusterung von Dokumenten und die Komprimierung von positionsbasierten Daten basierend auf diesen Modellen interessante Themen für die zukünftige Forschung.

Acknowledgements

I would like to thank my supervisor Prof. Dr. Bernd Freisleben. Without his guidance, this research would not have been possible.

I want to thank my family. Mamá, papá, and especially my wife have always been there for me and supported me.

Contents

1	**Introduction**	**1**
	1.1 Motivation	1
	1.2 Research Contributions	2
	1.3 Publications	2
	1.4 Organisation of the Thesis	3
2	**Information Retrieval**	**5**
	2.1 Introduction	5
	2.2 Information Retrieval History	5
	2.2.1 The Dawn of IR	5
	2.2.2 The Period 1945-1960	6
	2.2.3 The Period 1960-1970	8
	2.2.4 The Period 1970-1980	8
	2.2.5 The Period 1980-1990	9
	2.2.6 The Period 1990-today	9
	2.3 Definition of an Information Retrieval System	10
	2.4 Information Need	12
	2.5 The Document	14
	2.6 The Role of the Index	17
	2.7 Semantic Noise	17
	2.8 Information Retrieval Models and Strategies	18
	2.8.1 Introduction	18
	2.8.2 Classical Information Retrieval	19
	2.8.3 Alternative Models	29
	2.8.4 Structured Text Retrieval Models	31
	2.9 Retrieval Utilities	33
	2.9.1 Document Pre-Processing	33
	2.9.2 Inverted Index	34
	2.9.3 Relevance Feedback	36
	2.9.4 Automatic Relevance Feedback	38
	2.9.5 Passage-based Retrieval	45
	2.10 Information Retrieval Evaluation	48
	2.10.1 Recall and Precision	48

	2.10.2 Document Collections	52
	2.10.3 The DARPA TIPSTER Project	54
	2.10.4 The TREC Collection	55
2.11	Information Retrieval Software	58
	2.11.1 The Expansion Analyzer	59
	2.11.2 Apache Lucene	60
	2.11.3 Terabyte Retriever - Terrier	61
2.12	Summary	61

3 Related Work   **63**

- 3.1 Introduction 63
- 3.2 General Approaches Using Contextual Information 63
- 3.3 Term Proximity 65
  - 3.3.1 Shortest-Substring Model 65
  - 3.3.2 Fuzzy Proximity Model 71
  - 3.3.3 A Proximity Weighting Model 75
  - 3.3.4 Arbitrary Passage Retrieval 77
  - 3.3.5 Proximity and Relevance Feedback 80
- 3.4 Fourier Domain Scoring 82
  - 3.4.1 FDS Methodology 82
  - 3.4.2 Words Position Representation 83
  - 3.4.3 Weighting Bins 84
  - 3.4.4 Applying the Discrete Fourier Transform 85
  - 3.4.5 The Score Calculation 86
  - 3.4.6 Further Assumptions 89
- 3.5 Summary 89

4 The Gauss Model   **91**

- 4.1 Introduction 91
- 4.2 Term Distribution Analysis 91
  - 4.2.1 Descriptive Statistics and Document Semantics 92
  - 4.2.2 The Document Relevance Estimator 93
  - 4.2.3 The Semantic Distance Estimator 93
- 4.3 Implementation Issues 94
  - 4.3.1 Index, Search and Ranking 94
- 4.4 Experimental Results 95
  - 4.4.1 The Dispersion Runs 95
  - 4.4.2 The Query Expansion Runs 98
- 4.5 Summary 99

5 The Fourier Model   **101**

- 5.1 Introduction 101
- 5.2 Term Distribution Analysis Using Fourier Series 101
- 5.3 Comparing Term Distributions 103

	5.3.1	Comparing the Term Distribution Functions	104
	5.3.2	Relevance Ranking Optimization	105
	5.3.3	Query Expansion	107
5.4	Experimental Results		107
	5.4.1	Objective Function Runs	108
	5.4.2	Query Expansion Runs	110
5.5	Summary		111

6 The Hilbert Model — 113

- 6.1 Introduction ... 113
- 6.2 Analyzing Term Positions ... 113
  - 6.2.1 Expansions in Hilbert Spaces ... 114
  - 6.2.2 Truncated Expansions of Term Distributions ... 116
  - 6.2.3 The Semantic Interaction Range ... 117
- 6.3 Applications ... 119
  - 6.3.1 Ranking Optimization ... 119
  - 6.3.2 Query Expansion ... 120
  - 6.3.3 Cluster Analysis of Terms in Documents ... 120
- 6.4 A Suitable Index Implementation ... 122
- 6.5 Implications Regarding the Document Length ... 123
- 6.6 Experimental Results ... 126
  - 6.6.1 Software ... 126
  - 6.6.2 Experiment 1: Varying the Query Expansion Parameters ... 127
  - 6.6.3 Experiment 2: Using Fixed Query Expansion Parameters ... 129
  - 6.6.4 Experiment 3: Comparing the Query Expansion Terms ... 129
  - 6.6.5 Experiment 4: Objective Function with Term Position Models ... 131
- 6.7 Summary ... 131

7 Conclusions — 139

- 7.1 Summary ... 139
  - 7.1.1 Term Position Models ... 139
  - 7.1.2 Query Expansion ... 140
  - 7.1.3 User Objective Functions ... 140
  - 7.1.4 Document Length ... 141
- 7.2 Future Work ... 141
  - 7.2.1 Document Structure ... 141
  - 7.2.2 Index Size ... 141
  - 7.2.3 Other Applications ... 142
  - 7.2.4 Clustering ... 142
  - 7.2.5 Software Platform ... 142

1
Introduction

1.1 Motivation

Due to the constant improvements in the capture, transmission and storage of digital information and the need for managing this enormous amount of data, many tools and services for information search and retrieval have been developed. One of the most popular are *search engines* that currently serve as widespread universal interfaces to information, transcending user categories and geographic regions. Thus, the advances in Information Retrieval (IR), the underlying technology of search engines, has become a topic of interest of any online user.

Search engines contend with the basic question of information retrieval: how to estimate the relevance of a document for a user's information need and how to present only the most relevant documents to the user.

The main criterion to measure the relevance of documents in a collection is based on the frequency of search terms in the document. This criterion has been used in the origins of information retrieval and it is still the most important approach in the IR community. With the development of the World Wide Web (WWW), a new paradigm to determine the relevance of documents arose. Algorithms such as HITS [84] and PageRank [17] extend the original citation ranking of research papers to the hyperlink structure of the WWW, bringing the use of popularity rankings to the masses. Nevertheless, popularity rankings have some drawbacks: (a) they do not always reflect the real content of the documents, (b) relevance values can be manipulated to unjustly get some pages ranked higher or to push others further down [115, 66], and (c) they cannot be applied to document collections without hyperlink information.

Collections without hyperlink information are common in enterprise scenarios, where textual information is disseminated throughout a company without any logical association. In this environment, keyword based IR systems are not replaceable. However, in such systems, term-frequency models still predominate, and no substantial advances have been made in the last years.

One way to improve the performance of keyword based IR models is to consider the positions of the search terms in the document, regarding the environment (neighborhood) where they appear. This means, the positions of other terms help to specify the meaning of a given term. However, the required effort to process this positional information make such algorithms unsuitable to be applied at query evaluation time.

Thus, the goal of this thesis is to find new methods of extending traditional relevance models by exploiting positional information of search terms efficiently to improve the quality of search results.

1.2 Research Contributions

This thesis proposes novel models of representing term positions in documents to improve relevance estimation in the information retrieval process. Like other text retrieval methods, retrieval is performed by locating the appearances of the query terms in each document of a given set of documents. But unlike other text retrieval methods, the document information is mapped into the functional domain and the similarity between documents and a user query is estimated using simple mathematical operators.

The main concepts applied in the proposed models stem from three different areas: (a) descriptive statistics (b) signal processing, and (c) functional analysis. Descriptive statistics are used to estimate term positional information, because they minimize outliers and irregularities in the data. Concepts of signal processing (Fourier series and orthogonal polynomials) are used to generate an abstract representation of term positions in documents. Metrics of functional analysis (Hilbert spaces) are used to develop a criterion for matching a user's information need and the relevance of search results.

This novel form of representing term positions shifts the complexity of analysis to the non time-critical phase of the retrieval process, permitting us to exploit the term positional information at query evaluation time.

Two popular open source retrieval software tools are extended to implement the proposed models and to estimate their performance using document collections and evaluation software available in the information retrieval community.

Apart from the improvements in information retrieval, the proposed models also open new ways of exploring content disposition in documents, e.g. in related areas such as cluster analysis in textual data.

1.3 Publications

The research contributions of this thesis have been published in the following papers:

1. Patricio Galeas, Bernd Freisleben: *Word Distribution Analysis for Relevance Ranking and Query Expansion*, Proceedings of the 9th International Conference on Computational Linguistics and Intelligent Text Processing, Haifa, Israel, vol. 4919 of Lecture Notes in Computer Science, pages 500-511, Springer-Verlag, 2008.

2. Patricio Galeas, Ralph Kretschmer, Bernd Freisleben: *Document Relevance Assessment via Term Distribution Analysis Using Fourier Series Expansion*, Proceedings of the 2009 ACM/IEEE-CS Joint International Conference on Digital Libraries, Austin, USA, pages 277-284, ACM Press, 2009.

3. Patricio Galeas, Ralph Kretschmer, Bernd Freisleben: *Information Retrieval via Truncated Hilbert Space Expansions*, Proceedings of the 9th IEEE International Conference on Computer and Information Technology, Bradford, UK (*accepted for publication*), IEEE Computer Society, 2010.

1.4 Organisation of the Thesis

Chapter 2 provides an overview of where information retrieval has been and where it is currently at, including some historical topics, such as user information need, document processing, indexing, and a short introduction into the most important IR models and utilities. In the final part, a standard infrastructure for the evaluation of IR systems is outlined.

Chapter 3 defines the scope of this thesis and discusses different models related to positional information retrieval and term proximity described in the literature.

Chapters 4, 5 and 6 present the three newly proposed models to represent and manage term positional information in a document collection: the Gauss model, the Fourier model and the Hilbert model. Apart from the corresponding description, each model includes sections with experimental results.

Chapter 7 summarizes the thesis and outlines directions for future work.

2
Information Retrieval

2.1 Introduction

In the last fifty years, the size of electronic information and online databases appears to be growing exponentially [30, 31], and the task of finding relevant information gets more difficult. In one study of inexperienced searchers [16], one-quarter of the subjects were unable to pass a benchmark test of minimum searching skill. Even experienced searchers could improve their search results [46].

However, the heart of the problem does not concern size, but rather it concerns meaning. That is to say, there have been a number of hardware solutions to the problem of data size, but the major difficulties associated with the information retrieval problem remain, namely, the identification of content, the problem of determining which of two items of data is "closer" in meaning to a third item, the problem of determining whether or not (or to what degree) some document is *relevant* to a given request.

In order to estimate the relevance of documents, it is necessary to establish various measures of closeness of meaning, and an approach to this semantical problem is via statistics. The models presented in this chapter define various measures of closeness between documents and between requests for information so that given an arbitrary request, a machine can automatically elaborate upon a search in order to retrieve relevant documents that otherwise would not have been selected [98].

2.2 Information Retrieval History

2.2.1 The Dawn of IR

The *index* concept (originally called Cataloging), one of the most critical aspects in Information Retrieval (IR) [86], dates back to the ancient Rome. There, when used in relation to literary works, the term index was used for the little slip attached to papyrus scrolls on which the title of the work (and sometimes also the name of the author) was written so that each scroll on the shelves could be easily identified without having to pull them out for inspection [157].

The Romans also developed the usage of index for the title of books, which was later (1st century A.D.) extended to a table of contents or a list of chapters (sometimes with a brief abstract of their contents) and hence to a bibliographical list or catalog.

However, indexes in the modern sense, giving exact locations of names and subjects in a book, were not compiled in antiquity and only very few seem to have been made before the age of printing around 1450 [105].

In 1545, Conrad Gesner published Bibliotheca Universalis, in which he listed alphabetically all of the authors who had written in Greek, Latin, and Hebrew, with a listing of all their books printed up to that time. Three years later, Gesner published the second part containing a classification system with about 20 functional groups [87]. For this contribution, Gesner was recognized as the father of modern bibliography.

In 1751, Diderot and D'Alembert began publishing the Encyclopedia, a systematic relationship of all branches of knowledge.

2.2.2 The Period 1945-1960

The popularization of the idea of information retrieval started in 1945, with Vannevar Bush's article [22], where he predicted fast access to the contents of the world's libraries.

The tremendous explosion of scientific literature during and after World War II overwhelmed existing indexing and retrieval methods. New methods, including machines to search for and store information, were needed. A new research phase in information began.

Between 1950 and early 1960, pioneers such as James W. Perry, Calvin Moore, and Mortimer Taube published the first ideas of modern information retrieval:

James Whitney Perry, considering a major influence in automatic indexing and information retrieval systems using punched card machines, developed in 1945 his ideas on improving library literature searching and methodology. His experience dealing with the literature in chemistry demonstrated to him that the efficiency of the library and document retrieval needed to be brought up to speed [111]. In the late 1940s he was charged with developing punch card systems of organizing chemical information [162]. While exploring these information issues in the sciences, Perry became interested in difficulties of information retrieval in many other disciplines, including law, medicine, and metallurgy [111].

In 1950, the mathematician Calvin Mooers established the concept of information retrieval. Mooers set out to explore the use of digital processes and mathematics to impose control on the MIT technical reports (COSATI system). At MIT, Mooers discussed his ideas with J. W. Perry, and few months later, Perry arranged a meeting at the American Chemical Society to present Mooers's ideas on the development of a machine capable of Boolean searching. In his paper, Mooers advocated that chemists should be involved in the development of such a machine (Zatocoding) [33].

In 1950, the computer scientist Hans Peter Luhn developed a prototype of the Luhn Scanner for IBM. (see Figure 2.1). Its technology is based on IBM punched cards, run

2.2 Information Retrieval History

Figure 2.1: Hans Peter Luhn demonstrating a mock-up of an IBM card used in his scanner (1952).Courtesy of IBM.

vertically through a specially adapted scanner, using photo-electric cells. It does not require fixed-field searching.

In 1951, Derwent Publications, Ltd. (Great Britain), begins patent abstracting services with Central Patents Index. Punched cards are used to construct the indexes.

In 1952, Mortimer Taube with the foundation of his company Documentation, Inc. took a leadership role in the documentation field. He developed Uniterm, a system of coordinate indexing [148], and helped to establish its use as a major tool in library and documentation work. Taube's writings provoked considerable discussion in the library press, and contributed to his international recognition.

In 1954, the US Naval Ordnance Test Station, China Lake, CA, developed the first subject search ever made by a digital computer [65], consisting of a retrieval system using the Taube Uniterm system on an IBM 701 calculator on a file of 15,000 documents. It mimics a manual search of a Uniterm card file. Users can add new information, delete information on discarded documents, match search requests against a master file, and produce a printout of document numbers. It was only able to do Boolean and search strategy [161]. The same year (in France), Jacques-Emile Dubois does initial work on the DARC (Description, Acquisition, Retrieval, and Correlation) system.

In 1958, Hans Peter Luhn developed the concepts of Key Words In Context (KWIC) indexing and Selective Dissemination of Information (SDI), establishing many of the basic techniques now standard in information science.

On May 27, 1958, IBM unveiled Luhn's ideas for business intelligence or selective dissemination system (SDI). In the International Conference on Scientific Information held the same year, Luhn introduced his new equipment and illustrated the practical results by producing the KWIC indexes for the conference program. Two new Luhn inventions, the 9900 Index Analyzer and the Universal Card Scanner, and the new Luhn Keyword-in-Context (KWIC) indexing technique were introduced. Following the conference, newspapers all over USA carried stories about auto-abstracting and auto-indexing [142].

2.2.3 The Period 1960-1970

In 1958, the Western Reserve University developed a searching selector for a bibliographic database of metals, and the same year the U.S. Patent Office and National Bureau of Standards developed the experimental HAYSTAQ (Have You Stored Answers to Questions) system using a Standards Electronic Automatic Computer (SEAC) for use in searching patent files.

In 1959, IBM built batch retrieval system for Strategic Air Command, three years later the University of Pittsburgh developed full-text legal information retrieval system.

In 1960, Eugene Garfield's Institute for Scientific Information (ISI) introduced the first citation index for papers published in academic journals. ISI was the first information retrieval organisation with commercial interests [26]. It started with the Science Citation Index (SCI), and later expanded to produce the Social Sciences Citation Index (SSCI) and the Arts and Humanities Citation Index (AHCI).

In 1963, more than 1,500 abstracting and indexing services existed. The Library of Congress initiated a study on the computerization of bibliographic surrogates, while the Institute for Scientific Information published the first issue of Genetics Citation Index (GCI) and the prototype of Science Citation Index (SCI), relying on computer indexing.

The same year, MEDLARS (Medical Literature Analysis and Retrieval System), an off-line batch service, begins operation from the National Library of Medicine.

In 1964, C. Meyer and M. Kessler of Massachusetts Institute of Technology, developed Technical Information Project (TIP), an experimental online searching system.

Gerald Salton, another classical author in information retrieval published in 1965 his Vector model [134], were documents and queries are compared in a n-dimensional vector space. Simultaneously, NASA developed the earliest commercial catalog system DIALOG, and began to develop the Canadian Geographic Information Systems (CGIS).

Between 1966-1968, the Library of Congress ran its MARC I pilot project. MARC (MAchine Readable Cataloging) standardized the structure, contents and coding of bibliographic records.

In 1969, ERIC and the first databases in Canada and Europe went online. The U.S. Department of Defense implemented ARPANET (Advanced Research Projects Agency NETwork) to demonstrate how communications between computers could promote cooperative research among scientists. The Japanese Information Center for Science and Technology began an online service of its database. The NASA began offering the online search service RECON (REmote CONsole) to NASA facilities. In 1969, the MARC system became operational.

2.2.4 The Period 1970-1980

In 1970, further organizations from many branches offered information services, over 300 online databases were available.

In 1971, MEDLARS went online as MEDLINE. The OCLC (Online Computer Library Center) went online with 54 participating libraries.

In 1973, as outgrowth of the collaboration between U.S. Air Force and Ohio Bar As-

2.2 Information Retrieval History

sociation the Lexis Legal Retrieval System went online. The ABI/Inform system becomes first business-oriented online database.

In 1974, the NY Times InfoBank became the first online newspaper abstracting and indexing service. The Patents index and Dow Jones went online.

In 1976, Bibliographic Retrieval Services (BRS) were founded and the ISI's SciSearch went online.

2.2.5 The Period 1980-1990

In 1980, over 600 databases were online with a growth rate about 100% pro year. In the 1990s, the significant reduction in cost of processing power and memory in modern computers allowed information retrieval systems to implement the previously theoretical functions introducing a new information retrieval paradigm [86]. Full text indexing techniques were applied, and free-text search systems were used routinely.

The first sites appeared on the world wide web and earliest modern search engines such as Altavista and Google started.

2.2.6 The Period 1990-today

On the Web, manual linking is coming back. As we have learned how to handle text, information retrieval is moving on to projects in audio, image, video and other types of multimedial data.

Given the current progress, Bush's dream of the *Memex* (Memory Extender) device [22], "in which an individual stores all his books, records, and communications, and which is mechanized so that it may be consulted with exceeding speed and flexibility could soon be achieved.

Nowadays, storage, sensor, and computing technology have progressed to the point of making *Memex* feasible and even affordable. Indeed, we can now look beyond *Memex* at new possibilities. In particular, while media capture has typically been sparse throughout a lifetime, one can now consider continuous archival and retrieval of all media relating to personal experiences in a Human Digital Memory (HDM) [61].

Information can be captured from a myriad of personal information devices including desktop computers, PDAs, digital cameras, video and audio recorders, and various sensors, including GPS, Bluetooth, and biometric devices [56].

A device capable of registering such types of information is the SenseCam [72], a wearable digital camera that archives multimedia data without user intervention (see Figure 2.2). The SenseCam also contains a number of different electronic sensors for light intensity, temperature and a multiple-axis accelerometer. It is planned for the next versions to incorporate audio level detection, audio recording and GPS location sensing.

Diverse collections of personal information are potentially very valuable, therefore new models have to be developed to efficiently store and retrieve this highly heterogeneous and unstructured data.

The chronology of Figure 2.3 summarizes some of the most significant milestones in information retrieval history.

2 Information Retrieval

  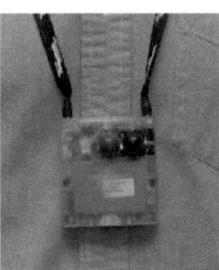

Figure 2.2: The SenseCam

2.3 Definition of an Information Retrieval System

An Information Retrieval (IR) system is a system capable of storing, retrieving, and maintaining information [86]. In this case, information can be composed of text, image audio, video and other types of multimedia data. Furthermore, an IR system is a software program that supports the user to satisfy his information needs.

The quality of an IR system is delimited by how effectively the properties and the characteristics of a person's information need [55] will be determined. Additionally, Kowalski [86] proposes that the gauge of success of an IR system consists in how well it can minimize the overhead for a user to find the needed information. Defining overhead as the time required to satisfy the information need, i.e. query construction, search execution, and reading non relevant items (documents).

In information retrieval, the term "relevant" item is used to represent an item containing the needed information. In reality, the definition of relevance is not a binary classification but a continuous function [86]. From a user perspective, information "relevant" and "needed" are synonymous.

The two major measures commonly associated with information systems are *precision* and *recall*. When a user starts a search process looking for information on a topic, the total document collection is logically divided into four groups: relevant retrieved, relevant not retrieved, non-relevant retrieved and non-relevant not retrieved.

Relevant items are those documents that contain information that helps the searcher in answering his question. Non-relevant items are those items that do not provide any directly useful information. There are two possibilities with respect to each item: it can be retrieved or not retrieved by the user's query. Precision and recall are defined as:

$$Precision = \frac{Number\ of\ Retrieved\ Relevant}{Number\ of\ Total\ Retrieved} \quad (2.1)$$

$$Recall = \frac{Number\ of\ Retrieved\ Relevant}{Number\ of\ Possible\ Relevant} \quad (2.2)$$

where $Number\ of\ Possible\ Relevant$ are the number of relevant items in the collec-

2.3 Definition of an Information Retrieval System

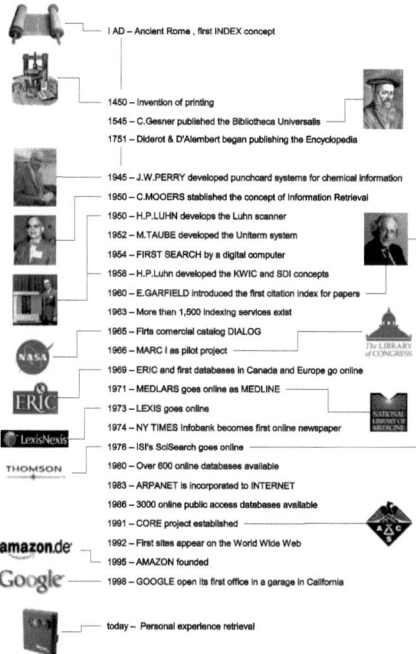

Figure 2.3: The information retrieval chronology.

tion. *Number of Total Retrieved* is the total number of items retrieved from the query. *Number of Retrieved Relevant* is the number of items retrieved that are relevant to user's search need.

As depicted in the Figure 2.5, a typical IR system contains three basic components: queries, processor and output [153].

Input (documents and queries) : The main difficulty here is to obtain a suitable representation for the computer logic. Computer based retrieval systems store only a reduced representation of documents or queries which means that the text of such items is partially lost once they have been processed. For example, a document representation could be a list of extracted relevant words representing the content of the document.

Processor : On the one hand, the processor deals with the structuring of the information in some appropriate way, such as classifying it. On the other hand, it will also involve

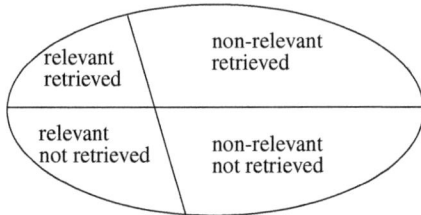

Figure 2.4: Effects of search on the whole document collection

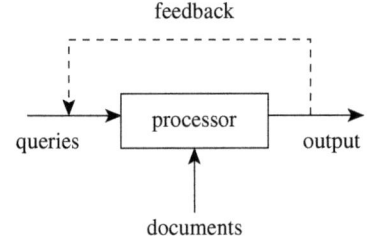

Figure 2.5: A typical Information Retrieval System.

performing the actual retrieval function [153], i.e. executing the search strategy in response to a query.

Output : Is usually a set of ranked documents.

Feedback : Considering the cyclic characteristics of the IR process, it is possible that the user change his request during one search session, hoping to improve the results in the subsequent retrieval cycle.

One can observe from the definitions above that the "information need" concept and its counterpart the "documents" play an fundamental role in the IR model. In the next sections, their characteristics, representations and relationships are described.

2.4 Information Need

The psychologists define Information Need (IN) as a psychological state of an individual which is sensed to be a kind of "dissatisfaction" or "discomfort" [121]. It is information that permits one to successfully adapt to the environmental conditions [55]. Moreover, a living system (human being) needs to search constantly for information about the state of the external environment. The more information the system has, the more chances it has to survive.

2.4 Information Need 13

Table 2.1: Examples of *concrete information needs* (CIN) and *problem oriented information needs* (POIN):

CIN
1. How many federal states has Germany?
2. What was the unemployment rate in Germany in 1990?
3. When became Poland as members of the European Union?
POIN
1. How can the information need be satisfied?
2. How can malignant tumors be treated?
3. How can I drive from Cologne to Berlin?

Table 2.2: Comparative characteristics of CIN and POIN

CIN	POIN
1. The thematic boundaries are clearly defined.	1. The thematic boundaries are not defined
2. The request is put into exact words, i.e., it corresponds exactly to the CIN thematic limits.	2. As a rule, the request does not conform to the POIN.
3. To satisfy a CIN, only one good document is needed.	3. As a rule, the POIN cannot be satisfied, even with all good documents existing in the system.
4. As soon as the good document is found, the CIN disappears.	4. As soon as good documents are delivered, the thematic limits of POIN itself remain for a long time.

According to Frants and Brush [54], IN can be classified in two types: *a concrete information need* (CIN) and a *problem oriented information need* (POIN).

Some examples of CIN and POIN are presented in the Table 2.1.

The characteristics given in the Table 2.2 describe the differences between the two types of IN.

Lancaster [90] studied the relationship between a query and a need. He noted that the lack of precise thematic boundaries not only hampers the formulation of a query, but also may lead to situations in which the formulated query does not coincide with the thematic boundaries of POIN. Either the query does not intersect with POIN, or it coincides with POIN only partially, or it is entirely included in the POIN, or it exceeds the thematic boundaries oh the POIN by including it entirely. Thus, the same query generated by different users can represent different POINs. Figure 2.6 illustrates these relationships.

Furthermore, it is not unusual that two different users having exactly the same POIN, express their IN with different queries or set of queries.

It is also interesting to mention the relation between IN and information. It is possible to classify different types of information related to a specific type of IN. Information can be represented in different forms: a scientific article, a table, a dictionary, in a form of a graphic, etc., which leads to different type of documents. Thus, for different types of IN,

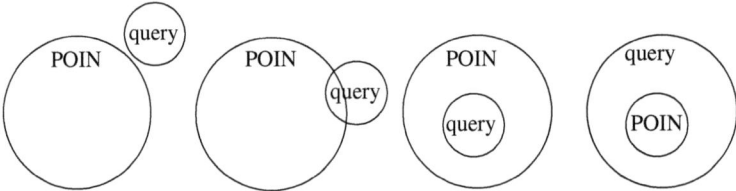

Figure 2.6: Possible relationships between need and query.

different types of document will be required (see Figure 2.7).

The types of information have a definite set of properties which limit their representation. For example, it is impossible to represent the information of this chapter graphically or in the form of a dictionary.

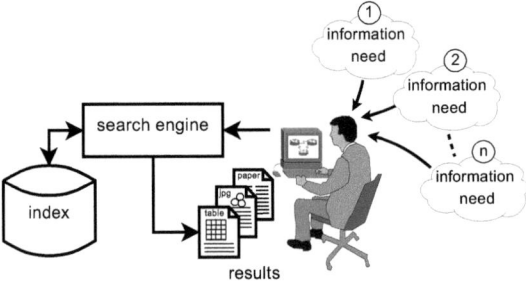

Figure 2.7: The information need process

Finally, the IN process described in Figure 2.7 is cyclic, as soon as some are satisfied, new INs arise [54].

2.5 The Document

The *document* concept appears with the creation of writing, and can be defined as a *material carrier with information fixed on it* [55]. Written documents satisfy an important function for the society: the transmission of information in time and space.

We use the term *document* to denote a single unit of information, typically text in a digital form, but it can also include other media. Furthermore, with respect to its physical representation there are documents in a form of a file, an email, a Web page, etc.

The creator of a document expresses in it "something" that is information from the creator's point of view, which can be interpreted as the creator's IN.

2.5 The Document

As mentioned earlier, different types of INs influence the existence of different document types.

From the user's point of view, the document represents a potential object to satisfy an arising INs, and due to that, the extraction of information from the document has an individual character, i.e. different users can extract different information from the same document [55].

With regard to the user's knowledge level, his ability to perceive information and specially the faced task (whose solution requires the searched information), the same document can be useful for one user and useless to another, depending on whether or not the user satisfied his IN with the help of this document.

As depicted in Figure 2.8, the main elements characterizing a documents are: syntax, structure, semantics, representation style, and meta data [8].

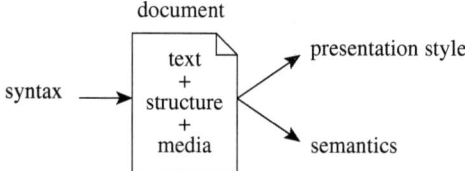

Figure 2.8: Characteristics of a document

The syntax of a document can express structure, presentation style, semantics, or even external actions, where one or more of these elements could be implicit or given together. For instance, a structural element (e.g., a section) can have a fixed format style. The syntax of a document can also implicit in its content or implicit in a declarative language such as the typesetting system TEX.

Due to the disability of computers to understand natural language, the trend is to use a language which provides information on the document structure, format, and semantics so that they are readable by humans as well as computers. One example of such a language is the Standard Generalized Markup Language (SGML) including all document characteristics mentioned above.

Documents in a collection are normally represented through a set of keywords or index terms. Such terms might be extracted directly from the text of the document or might be specified by a human subject. Regardless of the extraction mechanism (automatically or manually), they provide a *logical view of the document* [8]. When the document is represented with its full set of words, we say that the retrieval system adopts a *full text* logical view of the documents. But due to the storage and performance limitations of processing large collection of documents, the set of representative word might be reduced [8]. This reduction can be accomplished applying some text operations:

stopword elimination : *stopwords* are terms considered relatively meaningless in regards to the document relevance. Such terms have a grammatical function and reveal nothing about the content of the document [158]. Stopwords represent approximately

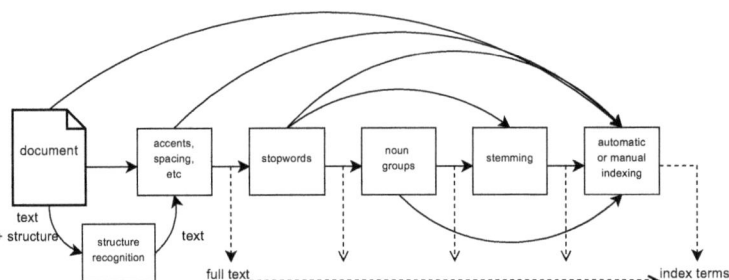

Figure 2.9: Logical view of a document: from full text to a set of index terms.

40% of the document collection [53], and normally are not stored in the IR system [64]. For example, the information provider DIALOG uses for the English language only nine terms: *an*, *and*, *by*, *for*, *from*, *of*, *the*, *to*, and *with* [68]. Traditionally, stopwords or stoplists are supposed to have included the most frequently occurring words. However, some frequently occurring words are important depending on the document collection features. For example, some of the most frequent words in a database of English literature are: *time*, *war*, *home*, *life*, *water*, and *world*. On the other side, a computer literature collection will contain many stopword candidates (*computer*, *program*, *source*, *machine*, and *language*) which are not frequent in the English literature database [51].

stemming : *stemming* reduces distinct words to their common grammatical root. The stem is the portion of a word which is left after the removal of its prefixes and suffixes. For example, the words *fishing*, *fished*, *fish*, and *fisher* could be reduced to the root word, *fish*. The Porter [125] and Lovins [95] approaches are traditionally the most used stemming algorithms. More sophisticated algorithms such as KSTEM [89] use dictionaries to ensure that any generated stem will be a valid word.

identification of noun groups : eliminates adjectives, adverbs, and verbs. This technique is practically an extension of the stopword list. In [53], a list of 425 stopwords derived from the Brown corpus is proposed.

compression : text compression is about finding ways to represent the text in fewer bits or bytes. Applying such techniques, the space to store text on computers can be significantly reduced. The more conventional compression approach for IR is word-based compression, where symbols to be compressed are words and not characters. Furthermore, new word-based compression algorithms allow random access to words within the compressed text which is a critical issue for IR systems.

There are two general approaches to text compression: *statistical* and *dictionary* based.

Despite of the benefits applying text operations, their use implicate some considerable drawbacks. A counterexample to the use of stopword removal occurs when a query requests a phrase that only contains stop words (e.g. "to be or not to be"). Documents containing *Hamlet*'s citation will not be found.

Despite arguments supporting stemming seems sensible, there is controversy in the literature about the benefits of stemming for retrieval performance [8]. Furthermore, empirical studies on potential performance benefits in IR do not deliver a satisfactory conclusion [51].

Due to these difficulties, many Web search engines consider a full-text document representation and do not adopt any stemming algorithm in the IR system [8].

2.6 The Role of the Index

An index to a document acts as a tag by means of which the information content of the document in question may be identified. The index consists normally of a set of terms that identify the content of each document. The terms that constitute the allowable vocabulary for indexing documents in a library form the common language that bridges the gap between the information in the documents and the information requirements of the library users.

In principle, an indexer reads an incoming document, selects one or several of the index terms from the "library vocabulary", and then coordinates the selected terms with the given document. Thus, the assignment of terms to each document has a binary character, for each term either it applies to the document in question or it does not.

Furthermore, the process of indexing information and that of formulating a request for information are symmetrical in the sense that, just as the subject content of a document is identified by coordinating to it a set of index terms, so also the subject content of a request must be identified by coordinating to it a set of index terms. Thus, the user who has a particular information need identifies this need in terms of a library request consisting of one or several index terms or a logical combination thereof [98].

Then, given a set of indexing terms that describe a request for information, and a set of indexing terms identifying the content of each document, the problem of automatic searching resolves itself to that of searching for and matching terms or a combination thereof.

The set of index terms representing the whole document collection will be normally encoded and stored in a digital form, and searched automatically.

2.7 Semantic Noise

The correspondence between the content of a document and its set of indexes is not exact because it is extremely difficult to specify precisely the subject content of a document by means of one or several index words. If we consider the set of all index terms on the one hand, and the class of subjects that they denote on the other hand, then we see that there is no strict one-to-one correspondence between them. It turns out that given any term there are many possible subjects that it could denote, and, conversely, any particular subject of knowledge usually can be denoted by a number of different terms. This situation may be characterized by saying that there is "semantic noise" in the index terms. In the same way, the correspondence between a user's request, as formulated in terms of one or many index terms, and his real information need is not exact. Thus, there is a semantic noise in both the document indexes and in the request for information [98].

One of the reasons that the index terms are noisy is due to the fact the meaning of these terms are a function of their settings. That is to say, the meaning of an isolated term is often quite different when it appears in an environment (sentence, paragraph, etc.) of other words. The grammatical type, position and frequency of other words help to clarify and specify the meaning of a given term. Furthermore, individual word meanings vary from person to person because, the meaning of words are a matter of individual experience. This is all to say when words are isolated and used as tags to indexing documents it is difficult to pin down their meaning, and consequently it is difficult to use them to accurately index documents or to accurately specify a request.

There are many attempts that try to reduce the semantic noise in indexing. Some of the most popular are the use of specialized index systems and the logical combination of index terms. In the first case, an indexing tailored to a particular type of documents would be less noisy than it would be the case otherwise. The idea is to apply the principle of an ideoglossary, as it is used in machine language translation, to remove semantic ambiguity. In spite of a careful work in the developing of a "best" set of index terms for a particular library , the problem of the semantic noise and its consequences remain, albeit, to a lesser extent.

Another attempt to remove the semantic noise in request formulations is the use of logical combinations of index terms. That is to say, if two or more terms are joined conjunctively (intersection), it helps to narrow or better specify a subject. On the other hand, the same set of terms connected disjunctively (union) broadens the scope of the request. Thus, using logical combinations of index terms, one would hope to either avoid the retrieval of irrelevant material or avoid missing relevant material. However, although a request using index terms joined conjunctively does decrease the probability of obtaining irrelevant documents, it also increases the probability of missing relevant documents.

The fact that conventional searching consists in matching noise index terms implies that the results of a search provides documents that are irrelevant to the real information need, and, even worse, some of the really relevant documents are not retrieved. Thus, in spite of specialized indexing systems and the use of logical combinations of index terms, the major problem is still that of properly identifying the subject content of both documents and request.

2.8 Information Retrieval Models and Strategies

2.8.1 Introduction

Conventional information retrieval systems use index terms to index and retrieve documents. An index term is considered as a keyword (or group of related words) that has some meaning of its own. In general, an index term is simply a word that appears in the text of a document in the collection. Retrieval based on index terms adopts the idea that the semantics of the document and of the user information need can be naturally expressed through

2.8 Information Retrieval Models and Strategies

sets of index terms [8]. The idea behind the term frequency was formulated in the very beginning of information retrieval research by Luhn [96]:

> *"It is here proposed that the frequency of word occurrences in an article furnishes a useful measurement of word signicance. It is further proposed that the relative position within a sentence of words having given values of signicance furnishes a useful measurement for determining the signicance of sentences. The signicance factor of a sentence will therefore be based on a combination of these two measurements."*

Evidently, this is a considerable oversimplification of the problem because important semantic information in a document or user request is lost when we replace its text with a set of words. For this reason a matching between each document and the user request using the space of index terms could be very imprecise. Thus, it is possible that the documents retrieved in response to a user request expressed as a set of keywords are irrelevant.

Clearly, document relevance estimation is the fundamental problem in information retrieval systems. Such a relevance calculation defines the model logic of the implemented search algorithm, ordering the retrieved document in a ranking. Documents appearing at the first ranking positions will be considered as more relevant.

2.8.2 Classical Information Retrieval

Whereas the information retrieval domain as a computer science research field is as old as computers themselves, and that thousands of experiments were conducted, there is no agreement on a unique model of information retrieval. In every text book about information retrieval, a chapter is dedicated to the models and each of them proposes, at least in its table of content, a taxonomy of the models. While there is not a complete consensus on the classification of these models, the one proposed by Baeza-Yates and Ribeiro-Neto [8] is quite common. As depicted in Figure 2.10, these authors consider three classic models, namely the Boolean model, the vector model and the probabilistic model. Each of these three models is refined in i) Probabilistic models (Inference Networks and Belief Networks), ii) Algebraic models (Generalized Vector, Latent Semantic Indexing, and Neural Networks), iii) Set Theoretic models (Fuzzy and Extended Boolean models).

Boolean Model

The Boolean model is based on set theory and Boolean algebra. Due to the simplicity of the set concepts, the Boolean model provides a simple framework of an IR system. The queries are specified as Boolean expressions which have precise semantics. Given its inherent simplicity, the Boolean model has had great popularity in the past years and was adopted by many of the early commercial bibliographic systems, one of the best known of these is Dialog[1]. Others include search services provided by newspapers such as *The New York Times* and *Visual Recall* (Xerox Corporation).

---
[1] www.dialog.com

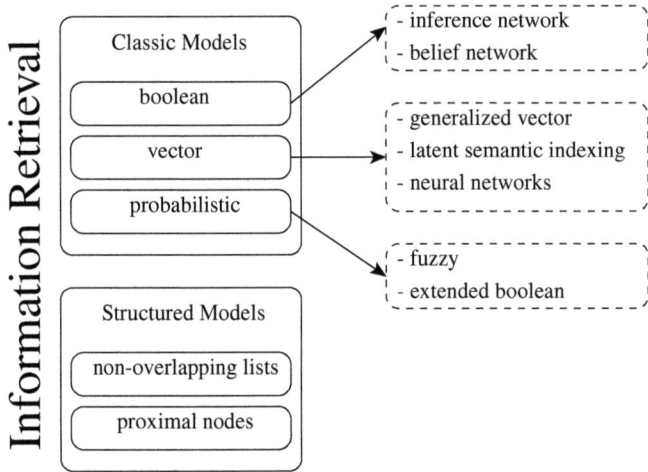

Figure 2.10: The Information Retrieval Taxonomy.

The Boolean model considers that index terms are present or absent in a document. As a result, the index terms are assumed to be all binary. A query q is composed of index terms linked by three operators: *not*, *and*, *or*. Thus a query is essentially a conventional Boolean expression that can be represented as a disjunction of conjunctive vectors (i.e., in *disjunctive normal form* DNF) [8]. For example, the query $[q = k_a \wedge (k_b \vee \neg k_c)]$ can be written in DNF as $[\vec{q}_{dnf} = (1,1,1) \vee (1,1,0) \vee (1,0,0)]$, where each of the components is a binary weighted vector associated with the tuple (k_a, k_b, k_c). These binary weighted vectors are called the conjunctive components of $\vec{q}_{dnf}$.

Definition 1 *For the Boolean model, the index term weight variables are all binary i.e., $w_{i,j} \in \{0,1\}$. A query q is a conventional Boolean expression. Let $\vec{q}_{dnf}$ be the disjunctive normal form for the query q. Further, let $\vec{q}_{cc}$ be any of the conjunctive components of $\vec{q}_{dnf}$. The similarity of a document d_j to the query q is defined as*

$$sim(d_j, q) = \begin{cases} 1 & \text{if } \exists\, \vec{q}_{cc} \mid (\vec{q}_{cc} \in \vec{q}_{dnf}) \wedge (\forall\, k_i,\ g_i(\vec{d_j}) = g_i(\vec{q}_{cc})) \\ 0 & \text{otherwise} \end{cases}$$

If $sim(d_j, q) = 1$ the Boolean model predicts that the document d_j is *relevant* to the query q. Otherwise, the prediction is that the document is *non-relevant*, not considering a partial match to the query conditions.

Unfortunately, the Boolean model suffers from major drawbacks:

2.8 Information Retrieval Models and Strategies

1. It is based on a binary decision criterion, i.e. a document is predicted to be either relevant or non-relevant without any intermediate scales, which hinder a good retrieval performance [8].

2. While the lack of an adequate weighting mechanism results in queries that are less than optimal, the second problem with the Boolean queries is the probability of a misstated query [85]. This problem involves incorrect interpretation of the Boolean operators AND an OR. People who are not experienced with logical conventions tend to misuse these operators in certain situations. For example, a person seeking "Saturday night entertainment" may specify an interest in (*dinner* AND *sports* AND *symphony*). The choices of events that are simultaneously dinner and sports and symphony is limited; most probably the person means (*dinner* OR *sports* OR *symphony*), or perhaps (*dinner* AND (*sports* OR *symphony*)). A Boolean retrieval system does not know this, however, and will misinterpret the query. In fact, most users find the representation of their queries in terms of Boolean expressions difficult and awkward, restricting the formulation to quite simple expressions [8].

3. A third problem with Boolean retrieval systems lies in the order of precedence for the logical connectives. Two different standards for the order of precedence are followed. Both rely on parentheses to group terms together: The combination within parentheses is evaluated as a unit before the terms outside the parentheses. In one type of systems, NOT is applied first within the parentheses, followed by AND, followed by OR, with a left-to-right precedence among operators of the same kind. Other systems, however, follow a strict left-to-right order of precedence without regard of the operators.

Various modifications of Boolean query systems permit some finer grading of the set of retrieved documents. Consider, for example, the query A OR B OR C. This is satisfied by any document containing one of the terms, while others will contain two or all three. Thus, the retrieved set can be graded by how many of the three terms each document contains and even by the specific terms, thus separating the documents with the term A and B but not C from those with the terms A and C but not B, and both of these sets from the documents containing all three terms.

Vector Space Model

As deficiencies in Boolean retrieval systems became apparent, alternative models of retrieval were developed.

The vector model took shape due to the work of Luhn [97], Salton [134, 129, 130], Salton and McGill [136], and van Rijsbergen [123, 153]. Among the earliest successful systems based on this model was the SMART system [135], originally developed at Harvard University. Continued development of this system by Salton and his students at Cornell University has kept it a vital force in experimental information retrieval today [85].

The vector space model calculates a measure of similarity by defining a vector $\vec{d}$ representing the terms on each document, and a vector $\vec{q}$ that represents the terms on the query

[138]. The model is based on the idea that the meaning of a document is contained by the words used. If one can represent the words in the document by a vector, it is possible to compare documents with queries to determine how similar their content is [64].

If a query is considered to be related to a document, a similarity coefficient (SC) between a document and a query can be computed. This similarity measure has the following three basic properties:

- It is usually normalized (i.e., it takes on values between 0 and 1).
- Its value does not depend on the order in which the query and the document are considered for comparison purposes (symmetry or commutativity).
- It is maximal, i.e., equal to 1, when the query and the document vectors are identical (reflexivity).

Documents whose content is most closely to the content of the query are judged to be most relevant.

The traditional method to measure the closeness (similarity) of these two vectors is the cosine measure [153, 160], defined by the cosine of the angle (θ) between the vectors (Figure 2.11). In mathematical terms this is the *inner product* of the document and query vectors, normalized by their lengths.

$$similarity(\vec{d}, \vec{q}) = cos(\theta) = \frac{\vec{d} \cdot \vec{q}}{|\vec{d}| \times |\vec{q}|} \qquad (2.3)$$

where $|\vec{d}|$ and $|\vec{q}|$ are the norms of the document and query vectors.

The cosine measure levels the playing fields by dividing the computation by the length of the document vector. The assumption used in the cosine measure is that document length has no impact on relevance. Without normalization factor, longer documents are more likely to be found relevant simply because they have more terms which increases the likelihood of match. Dividing by the document vectors removes the size of the document from consideration [64].

A simple example is given in Figure 2.12. Using a language with a two word vocabulary (only "A" and "I" are valid terms), all queries and documents can be represented in a two-dimensional space. A query and three documents are given along with their corresponding vectors and a graph of these vectors.

The similarity coefficient between the query q and the documents can be computed as the distance from the query to the two vectors. In this example, one can see that document d_1 is represented by the same vector as the query so it will have the highest rank in the result set.

It is important to remark that not all terms are equally useful for describing the document contents. In fact there are index terms which describe better the document content than others, and deciding on the importance of terms for summarizing the contents of a document is not a trivial issue. A simple method to determine such term properties is to measure the frequency of terms in the whole collection. For example, considering a collection of one thousand documents, a word which appears in each of the one thousand documents is

2.8 Information Retrieval Models and Strategies

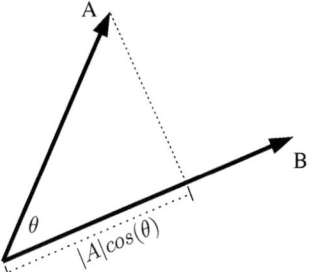

Figure 2.11: The inner product between two vectors : $a \cdot b = |a||b| \cos \theta$

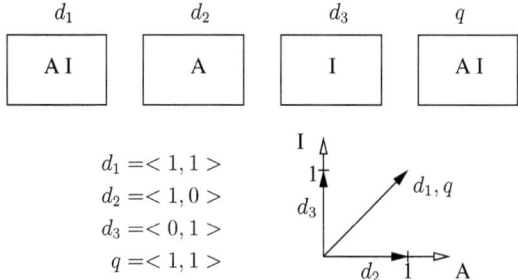

Figure 2.12: Vector Space Model with a two term vocabulary

completely useless as an index term because it does not give us information to differentiate which document is potentially better for the user. On the other side, a word that appears only in few documents is quite useful because it restricts the space of documents that may be of interest for the user. Thus, it should be clear that distinct index terms have varying relevance when used to describe document contents. This effect is captured through the assignment of numerical *weights* to each index term of a document. These weights are computed using the *inverse document frequency* (*idf*) corresponding to a given term.

One of the most effective term-weighting approaches is related to the basic principles that support clustering techniques [8]. Given a collection C of objects and a *vague* description of a set A, the goal of a simple clustering algorithm might be to separate the collection C of object into two sets: a first one that is composed of objects related to the set A and a second one that is composed of objects not related to the set A. Vague description here means that we do not have enough information for deciding precisely which objects are and which are not in the set A. More sophisticated clustering algorithms might attempt to separate the objects of a collection into various clusters (or classes) according to their properties.

The IR case considers only the simple version of the clustering problem (i.e., the one that considers only two classes) because all that is required is a decision on which documents are predicted to be relevant and which ones are predicted to be not relevant (with regard to a given query). In this clustering problem, two main issues have to be resolved:

- First, one needs to determine what are the features that better describe the objects in the set A.

- Second, one needs to determine what are the features that better distinguish the objects in the set A from the remaining objects in the collection C.

The first set of features provides for quantification of *intra-cluster* similarity, while the second set of features provides for quantification of *inter-cluster* dissimilarity. The most successful clustering algorithms try to balance these two effects.

In the vector model, intra-clustering similarity is quantified by measuring the raw frequency of a term k_i inside a document d_j. This term frequency is usually referred to as the *tf factor* and provides one measure of how well that term describes the document contents. Furthermore, inter-cluster dissimilarity is quantified by measuring the inverse of the frequency of a term k_i among the documents in the collection. This factor is usually referred to as the *inverse document frequency* or the *idf factor*. The motivation for using the idf factor is that terms which appear in many documents are not very useful for distinguishing a relevant document from a non-relevant one.

Definition 2 *Let N be the total number of documents in the system and n_i be the number of documents in which the term k_i appears. Let $freq_{i,j}$ be the raw frequency of term k_i in the document d_j. Then, the normalized frequency $tf_{i,j}$ of term k_i in document d_j is given by*

$$tf_{i,j} = \frac{freq_{i,j}}{\max_l freq_{l,j}} \qquad (2.4)$$

where the maximum is computed over all terms that are mentioned in the text of the document d_j. If the term k_i does not appear in the document d_j, then $f_{i,j} = 0$.

Further, let idf_i, the inverse document frequency for k_i, be given by

$$idf_i = log\frac{N}{n_i} \qquad (2.5)$$

The best known term-weighting schemes use weights which that are given by

$$w_{i,j} = tf_{i,j} \times log\frac{N}{n_i} \qquad (2.6)$$

or by a variation of this formula [133], where the author tries to avoid the negative effect of high frequency single terms:

2.8 Information Retrieval Models and Strategies

$$w_{i,j} = \frac{(log\ tf_{ij} + 1.0) \cdot idf_i}{\sum_{i=1}^{t}[(log\ tf_{ij} + 1.0) \cdot idf_i]^2} \qquad (2.7)$$

Such term-weighting strategies are called *tf-idf* schemes.

Vector Calculation - An Example. The following example [60], originally proposed by David Grossman [64], shows a detailed term vector calculation, consisting of a case insensitive query Q and a document collection consisting of the documents D_1, D_2, D_3.

Q : "gold silver truck"

D_1 : "Shipment of gold damaged in a fire"

D_2 : "Delivery of silver arrived in a silver truck"

D_3 : "Shipment of gold arrived in a truck"

In this collection, there are three documents, so $d = 3$. Applying the expression (2.5), if a term appears in only one of the three documents, its idf is $log\frac{d}{df_j} = log\frac{3}{1} = 0.477$. Similarly, if a term appears in two of the three documents, its idf is $log\frac{3}{2} = 0.176$, and a term that appears in all three documents has an idf of $log\frac{3}{3} = 0$.

Since eleven terms appear in the document collection, an eleven-dimensional document vector is constructed. The retrieval results are summarized in the following table.

Table 2.3: Term Vector Model based on $w_i = tf_i \cdot IDF_i$

Terms	Q	D1	D2	D3	df_i	D/df_i	idf_i	Q	D1	D2	D3
a	0	1	1	1	3	3/3=1	0	0	0	0	0
arrived	0	0	1	1	2	3/2=1.5	.176	0	0	.176	.176
damaged	0	1	0	0	1	3/1=3	.477	0	.477	0	0
delivery	0	0	1	0	1	3/1=3	.477	0	0	.477	0
fire	0	1	0	0	1	3/1=3	.477	0	.477	0	0
gold	1	1	0	1	2	3/2=1.5	.176	.176	.176	0	.176
in	0	1	1	1	3	3/3=1	0	0	0	0	0
of	0	1	1	1	3	3/3=1	0	0	0	0	0
silver	1	0	2	0	1	3/1=3	.477	.477	0	.954	0
shipment	0	1	0	1	2	3/2=1.5	.176	0	.176	0	.176
truck	1	0	1	1	2	3/2=1.5	.176	.176	0	.176	.176

The columns header row also includes grouped headers: "Counts,tf" over Q/D1/D2/D3 and "Weights, $w_i = tf_i \cdot idf_i$" over Q/D1/D2/D3.

The Columns 1 - 5 : Determine the term counts tf_i for the query and each document D_j.

The Columns 6 - 8 : Contain the document frequency df_i for each document. Since $idf_i = log\frac{D}{df_i}$ and $D = 3$, this calculation is straightforward.

The Columns 9 - 12 : Contain the $tf \cdot idf$ products and the term weights. These columns can be viewed as a sparse matrix in which most entries are zero.

Here, the weights are treated as coordinates in the vector space, effectively representing documents and query as vectors. To find out which document vector is closer to the query vector, we use the traditional method proposed in equation (2.3). For each document and query, all vector lengths are computed:

$$\begin{aligned}
|\vec{D}_1| &= \sqrt{0.477^2 + 0.477^2 + 0.176^2 + 0.176^2} &= \sqrt{0.517} &= 0.719 \\
|\vec{D}_2| &= \sqrt{0.176^2 + 0.477^2 + 0.954^2 + 0.176^2} &= \sqrt{1.200} &= 1.096 \\
|\vec{D}_3| &= \sqrt{0.176^2 + 0.176^2 + 0.176^2 + 0.176^2} &= \sqrt{0.124} &= 0.352 \\
|\vec{Q}| &= \sqrt{0.176^2 + 0.477^2 + 0.176^2} &= \sqrt{0.290} &= 0.538
\end{aligned}$$

Now, the dot products are computed:

$$\begin{aligned}
\vec{Q} \cdot \vec{D}_1 &= 0.176 \cdot 0.176 &= 0.031 \\
\vec{Q} \cdot \vec{D}_2 &= 0.477 \cdot 0.954 + 0.176 \cdot 0.176 &= 0.486 \\
\vec{Q} \cdot \vec{D}_3 &= 0.176 \cdot 0.176 + 0.176 \cdot 0.176 &= 0.062
\end{aligned}$$

And finally, the similarity values are computed:

$$\begin{aligned}
sim(\vec{D}_1, \vec{Q}) &= cos(\theta_{\vec{D}_1, \vec{Q}}) &= \frac{\vec{Q} \cdot \vec{D}_1}{|\vec{Q}| \times |\vec{D}_1|} &= \frac{0.031}{0.538 \cdot 0.719} &= 0.080 \\
sim(\vec{D}_2, \vec{Q}) &= cos(\theta_{\vec{D}_2, \vec{Q}}) &= \frac{\vec{Q} \cdot \vec{D}_2}{|\vec{Q}| \times |\vec{D}_2|} &= \frac{0.486}{0.538 \cdot 1.096} &= 0.825 \\
sim(\vec{D}_3, \vec{Q}) &= cos(\theta_{\vec{D}_3, \vec{Q}}) &= \frac{\vec{Q} \cdot \vec{D}_3}{|\vec{Q}| \times |\vec{D}_3|} &= \frac{0.062}{0.538 \cdot 0.352} &= 0.327
\end{aligned}$$

Sorting and ranking the documents in descending order according to the similarity values, we obtain:

Rank 1: D_2 = 0.8246
Rank 2: D_3 = 0.3271
Rank 3: D_1 = 0.0801

Other similarity measures. Two other commonly used measures are the Jaccard and the Dice similarity measures [153]. Both change the normalizing factor in the denominator to account for different characteristics of the data: the denominator in the cosine formula is invariant to the number of terms in common and produces very small numbers when the vectors are large and the number of common terms is small.

In the Jaccard similarity measure (2.8), the denominator becomes dependent upon the number of terms in common. As the common elements increase, the similarity value quickly decreases, but is always in the range -1 to +1:

$$sim_{jaccard}(q, d_i) = \frac{\sum_{j=1}^{t} w_{qj} d_{ij}}{\sum_{j=1}^{t} (d_{ij})^2 + \sum_{j=1}^{t} (w_{qj})^2 - \sum_{j=1}^{t} w_{qj} d_{ij}} \quad (2.8)$$

The Dice measure (2.9) simplifies the denominator of the Jaccard measure and introduces a factor 2 in the numerator. The normalization in the Dice formula is also invariant to the number of terms in common:

$$sim_{dice}(q, d_i) = \frac{2 \sum_{j=1}^{t} w_{qj} d_{ij}}{\sum_{j=1}^{t} (d_{ij})^2 + \sum_{j=1}^{t} (w_{qj})^2} \quad (2.9)$$

2.8 Information Retrieval Models and Strategies

The main advantages of the vector model are: (a) its term-weighting scheme improves retrieval performance; (b) its partial matching strategy allows retrieval of documents that *approximate* the query conditions; (c) its cosine ranking formula sorts the documents according to their degree of similarity to the query.

For its flexibility, simplicity and good performance with general collections, the vector model is one of the most popular models nowadays.

Probabilistic Model

The basic assumption in the probabilistic model is that given a document and a query, it should be possible to calculate the probability that the document is relevant to the query. The concept was first introduced by Maroon and Kuhns [98]; it later became known as the *binary independence retrieval* (BIR) model.

The model attempts to capture the IR problem within a probabilistic framework. The fundamental idea is as follows. Given a user query, there is a set of documents that contain exactly the relevant documents and no others. This set of documents is called the *ideal answer set* (R). Given the description of this answer set, we would have no problems in retrieving its documents. Thus, the querying process can be defined as the process of specifying the properties of an ideal answer set.

The problem is that we do not know exactly what these properties are. All we know is that there are index terms whose semantics should be used to characterize these properties. Since these properties are not known at query time, an effort has to be made at initially guessing what they could be. This initial guess allows us to generate a preliminary probabilistic description of the ideal answer set which is used to retrieve a first set of documents. An interaction with the user is then initiated with the purpose of improving the probabilistic description of the ideal set. This interaction could proceed as follows.

The user takes a look at the retrieved documents and decides which ones are relevant and which ones are not. The system uses this information to refine the description of the ideal answer set. By repeating this process many times, it is expected that such a description will evolve and become closer to the real description of the ideal answer set. Thus, one should always have in mind the need to guess the description of the ideal answer set at the beginning. Furthermore, a conscious effort is made to model this description in probabilistic terms [8].

The probabilistic model is based on the following fundamental assumption:

Given a user query q and a document d_j in the collection, the probabilistic model tries to estimate the probability that the user will find the document d_j relevant. The model assumes:

- the probability of relevance only depends on the query and the document representations.

- there is a subset of all documents which the user prefers as the answer set (R) for the query q.

- R should maximize the overall probability of relevance to the user.

- Documents in the set R are predicted to be relevant to the query.

- Documents not in R are predicted to be non-relevant.

This assumption is quite problematic because (a) it does not state explicitly how to calculate the probabilities of relevance and (b) it does not give a sample space that is to be used for defining such probabilities.

In the probabilistic model, each document d_j is assigned with the ratio

P(d_j is relevant to q) / P(d_j is not relevant to q)

as a measure of similarity. This ratio gives the probability of the document d_j being relevant to the query q [8].

Definition 3 *For the probabilistic model, the index term weight variables are all binary i.e., $w_{i,j} \in \{0,1\}, w_{i,q} \in \{0,1\}$. A query q is a subset of index terms. Let R be the set of documents known (or initially guessed) to be relevant. Let $\bar{R}$ be the complement of R (i.e., the set of non-relevant documents). Let $P(R|\vec{d_j})$ be the probability that the document d_j is relevant to the query q and $P(\bar{R}|\vec{d_j})$ be the probability that d_j is non-relevant to q. The similarity $sim(d_j, q)$ of the document d_j to the query q is defined as the ratio:*

$$sim(d_j, q) = \frac{P(R|\vec{d_j})}{P(\bar{R}|\vec{d_j})} \qquad (2.10)$$

Using Bayes' rule,

$$sim(d_j, q) = \frac{P(\vec{d_j}|R) \times P(R)}{P(\vec{d_j}|\bar{R}) \times P(\bar{R})} \qquad (2.11)$$

where $P(\vec{d_j}|R)$ stands for the probability of randomly selecting the document d_j from the set of relevant documents (R), $P(R)$ is the probability that a document randomly selected from the entire collection is relevant. $P(\vec{d_j}|\bar{R})$ and $P(\bar{R})$ are the corresponding complements.

Since $P(R)$ and $P(\bar{R})$ are the same for all the documents in the collection, we can redefine the similarity value as:

$$sim(d_j, q) \sim \frac{P(\vec{d_j}|R)}{P(\vec{d_j}|\bar{R})} \qquad (2.12)$$

Assuming independence of index terms,

$$sim(d_j, q) \sim \frac{\prod_{g_i(\vec{d_j})=1} P(k_i|R) \times \prod_{g_i(\vec{d_j})=1} P(\bar{k_i}|R)}{\prod_{g_i(\vec{d_j})=1} P(k_i|\bar{R}) \times \prod_{g_i(\vec{d_j})=1} P(\bar{k_i}|\bar{R})} \qquad (2.13)$$

where $P(k_i|R)$ is the probability that the index term k_i is present in a document randomly selected from the set R, $P(\bar{k_i}|R)$ is the probability that the index term k_i is not present in a document randomly selected from the set R.

2.8 Information Retrieval Models and Strategies

Taking logarithms, recalling that $P(k_i|R) + P(\bar{k}_i|R) = 1$, and ignoring factors that are constant for all documents in the context of the same query, we can write finally:

$$sim(d_j, q) \sim \sum_{i=1}^{t} w_{i,q} \times w_{i,j} \times \left(log \frac{P(k_i|R)}{1 - P(k_i|R)} + log \frac{1 - P(k_i|\bar{R})}{P(k_i|\bar{R})} \right) \quad (2.14)$$

which is the key expression for ranking computations in the probabilistic model [8].

Since we do not know the set R a the beginning, it is necessary to define a method for the initial calculations of $P(k_i|R)$ and $P(k_i|\bar{R})$. There are many alternatives for such computations. For example, in the very beginning (i.e., immediately after the query specification), there are no retrieved documents, Thus, one has to make some simplifications: (a) assume that $P(k_i|R)$ is constant for all index terms k_i (typically, equal to 0.5) and (b) assume that the distribution of index terms among the non-relevant documents can be approximated by the distribution of index terms among all the documents in the collection, that is $P(k_i|R) = 0.5$ and $P(k_i|\bar{R}) = \frac{n_i}{N}$, where n_i is the number of documents that contain the index term k_i and N is the total number of documents in the collection. Given this initial guess, we can then retrieve documents that contain the query terms and provide an initial probabilistic ranking for them. After that, this initial ranking is improved as follows.

Let V be a subset of the documents initially retrieved and ranked by the probabilistic mode. Such a subset can be defined, for example, as the top r ranked documents where r is a previously defined threshold. Further, let V_i be the subset of V composed of the document in V that contain the index term k_i. For simplicity, V and V_i will be used to refer the number of elements in these sets. For improving the probabilistic ranking, the guesses for $P(k_i|R)$ and $P(k_i|\bar{R})$ will be improved, which can be accomplished with the following assumptions : (a) one can improve $P(k_i|R)$ by the distribution of the index term k_i among the document retrieved so far. (b) one can approximate $P(k_i|\bar{R})$ by considering that all the non-retrieved documents are not relevant. Using these assumption, one can write, $P(k_i|R) = \frac{V_i}{V}$ and $P(k_i|\bar{R}) = \frac{n_i - V_i}{N - V}$.

Repeating this process recursively, it is possible to improve the guesses of the $P(k_i|R)$ and $P(k_i|\bar{R})$ probabilities, without human assistance. However, one can also use assistance from the user for the definition of the subset V as originally conceived.

The last formulas for $P(k_i|R)$ and $P(k|\bar{R})$ present some problems for small values of V and V_i (for example $V = 1$ and $V_i = 0$). To prevent this situation, an adjustment factor (0.5) is often added: $P(k_i|R) = \frac{V_i + 0.5}{V + 1}$ and $P(k_i|\bar{R}) = \frac{n_i - V_i + 0.5}{N - V + 1}$. In the case of unsatisfactory results, the constant 0.5 can be replaced with the fraction n_i/N.

2.8.3 Alternative Models

Latent Semantic Analysis

Latent Semantic Analysis (LSA) tries to overcome the problem of lexical matching by using statistically derived conceptual indexes instead of individual words for retrieval. It assumes that there is some underlying or latent structure in word usage that is partially obscured by variability in word choice [12].

LSA maps documents as well as terms to a representation in the so-called latent semantic space, using $\vec{M}$, a (high dimensional) vector space representation of documents based on term frequencies as a starting point, and applies a dimension reducing linear projection. The specific form of this mapping is determined by a given document collection and is based on a Singular Value Decomposition (SVD) of the corresponding term/document matrix.

$$\vec{M} = \vec{K}\vec{S}\vec{D}^t \tag{2.15}$$

The matrix $\vec{K}$ is the matrix of eigenvectors derived from the term-to-term correlation matrix given by $\vec{M}\vec{M}^t$. The matrix $\vec{D}^t$ is the matrix of eigenvectors derived from the transpose of the document-to-document matrix given by $\vec{M}^t\vec{M}$. The matrix $\vec{S}$ is an $r \times r$ diagonal matrix of singular values where $r = min(t, N)$ is the *rank* of $\vec{M}$.

Considering that only the s largest singular values of $\vec{S}$ are kept along with their corresponding columns in $\vec{K}$ and $\vec{D}^t$ (i.e. the remaining singular values of $\vec{S}$ are deleted). The resulting $\vec{M}_s$ matrix is the matrix of rank s which is closest to the original matrix $\vec{M}$ in the least square sense [8]. This matrix is given by

$$\vec{M}_s = \vec{K}_s\vec{S}_s\vec{D}_s^t \tag{2.16}$$

where s, $s < r$, is the dimensionality of the reduced concept space.

The selection of a value s attempts to balance two opposing effects:

1. s should be large enough to allow fitting all the structure in the real data.

2. s should be small enough to allow filtering out all non-relevant representational details, present in the original matrix.

The relationship between any two documents in the reduced space of dimensionality s can be obtained from the $\vec{M}_s^t\vec{M}_s$ matrix given by

$$\vec{M}_s^t\vec{M}_s = (\vec{K}_s\vec{S}_s\vec{D}_s^t)^t\vec{K}_s\vec{S}_s\vec{D}_s^t = \vec{D}_s\vec{S}_s\vec{K}_s^t\vec{K}_s\vec{S}_s\vec{D}_s^t = \vec{D}_s\vec{S}_s\vec{S}_s\vec{D}_s^t = (\vec{D}_s\vec{S}_s)(\vec{D}_s\vec{S}_s)^t \tag{2.17}$$

In the above matrix, the (i, j) element quantifies the relationship between documents d_i and d_j.

To rank documents with regard to a given user query, one can simple model the query as a pseudo-document in the original $\vec{M}$ term-document matrix. Assume the query is modeled as the document with number 0. Then, the first row in the matrix $\vec{M}_s^t\vec{M}_s$ provides the ranks of all documents with respect to the query.

Since the matrices used in the latent semantic model are of rank s, $s << t$, and $s << N$, then form an efficient indexing scheme for the documents in the collection. Further, they provide for elimination of noise and removal of redundancy.

The general idea in LSA is that similarities between documents or between documents and queries can be more reliably estimated in the reduced latent space representation than in the original representation. The rationale is that share frequently co-occurring terms will

2.8 Information Retrieval Models and Strategies

have a similar representation in the latent space, even if they have no terms in common. LSA thus performs a type of noise reduction and has the potential benefit of detecting synonyms, as well as words that refer to the same topic. Although LSA has been applied with remarkable success in various domains, including automatic indexing (LSI) [39, 40], it has a number of deficits that will be mentioned below.

Computational Costs & the Updating Problem: Suppose an LSI generated database already exists. That is, a collection of text objects has been parsed, a term-document matrix has been generated, and the SVD of the term/document matrix has been computed. If more terms and documents have to be added, two alternatives for incorporating the latter currently exist:

- recomputing the SVD of a new term-document matrix or
- folding-in the new terms and documents.

Updating can mean either folding-in or SVD-updating. SVD-updating is the new method of updating developed in [104]. Folding-in terms or documents is a much simpler alternative that uses an existing SVD to represent new information. Recomputing the SVD of a larger term-document matrix requires more computation time and, for large problems, may be impossible due to memory constrains [27]. Recomputing the SVD allows the new terms and documents to directly affect the latent semantic structure by creating a new term-document matrix. In contrast, folding-in is based on the existing latent semantic structure, the current matrix, and hence new terms and documents have no effect on the representation of the pre-existing terms and documents. Folding-in requires less time and memory but can have deteriorating effects on the representation of the new terms and documents [12].

Optimal Dimension of the Concept Space: Determining the optimal number of dimensions in the concept space is another problem encountered with LSI [145]. The original work by Deerwester et al. used trial and error to empirically determine the optimal number of dimensions (they tested between 50-150 dimensions) [91]. Dumais [40] reports using between 200-350 dimensions for TREC-3. Landauer and Littman [91] report using 100 dimensions for cross-language retrieval in English and in French. There does not seem to be a general consensus for an optimal number of dimensions; instead, the size of the concept space must be determined based on the specific collection of documents used.

Document Collection Size and Heterogeneity: When the corpus is large and heterogeneous, LSI's retrieval quality is inferior to methods such as Okapi [127].

2.8.4 Structured Text Retrieval Models

Models Based on Non-overlapping Lists

Burkowski [20, 21] proposes to divide the whole text of each document in non-overlapping text regions that are collected in a *list*. Since there are multiple ways to divide a text in non-overlapping regions, multiple lists can be generated. For example, we can define a list for all chapters in the document, a second list of all sections, and a third list of all subsections. These lists are kept as separate and distinct data structures. While the text regions in the same (flat) list have no overlapping, text regions from distinct lists may overlap [8]. Figure 2.13 shows four separate lists for the same document.

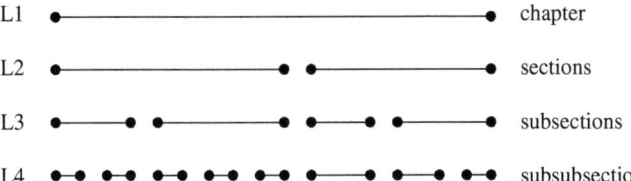

Figure 2.13: Representation of the text structure in a document by four separate indexing lists.

To allow searching for index terms and for text regions, a single inverted file is built in which each structural component stands as an entry in the index. Associated with each entry, there is a list of text regions as a list of occurrences. Moreover, such a list could be easily merged with the traditional inverted file for the words in the text. Since the text regions are non-overlapping, the types of queries that can be asked are simple: (a) select a region containing a given word (and does not contain other regions); (b) select a region A that does not contain any other region B (where B belongs to a list distinct from the list for A); (c) select a region not contained within any other region, etc.

Models Based on Proximal Nodes

Navarro and Baeza-Yates [103] propose a model that allows the definitions of independent hierarchical (non-flat) indexing structures over the same document text. Each of these indexing structures is a strict hierarchy composed of chapters, sections, paragraphs, pages, and lines which are called *nodes* (Figure 2.14). To each of these nodes a text region is associated . Further, two distinct hierarchies might refer to overlapping text regions.

Given a user query that refers to distinct hierarchies, the compiled answer is formed by nodes that all come from only one of them. Thus, an answer cannot be composed of nodes that come from two distinct hierarchies. Notice, however, that due to the hierarchical structure, nested text regions (coming from the same hierarchy) are allowed in the answer set.

Figure 2.14 illustrates a hierarchical indexing structure composed of four levels (chapters, sections, subsections, and sub-subsections of the same document) and an inverted list for the word "everest". The entries in the inverted list indicate all the positions in the text of the document in which the word "everest" occurs. In the hierarchy, each node indicates the position in the text of its associated structural component

The query language allows the specification of regular expressions (to search for strings), the reference to structural components by name (to search for the structural component (e.g. chapter), and a combination of these. In this sense, the model can be viewed as a compromise between expressiveness and efficiency. The somewhat limited expressiveness of the query language allows efficient query processing by first searching for the components which match the specified query string, subsequently, evaluation which of these components satisfy the structural part of the query.

The model based on proximal nodes allows to formulate queries that are more complex than those that can be formulated in the model based on non-overlapping lists. To speed up query processing, however, only nearby (proximal) nodes are looked at which imposes restrictions on the answer set retrieved (all nodes must come from the same hierarchy).

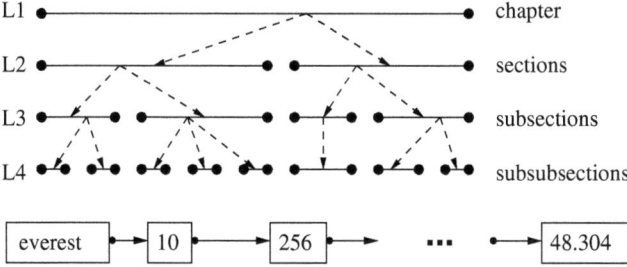

Figure 2.14: Hierarchical index for structural components and flat index for words

2.9 Retrieval Utilities

2.9.1 Document Pre-Processing

Document pre-processing is a procedure that can be divided into five text operations (or transformations):

Lexical Analysis

Lexical analysis treats special characters such as digits, hyphens, punctuation marks, and the case of letters. Some initial rules for lexical analysis are given in [2], but the effect on precision and recall is not discussed. Many TREC papers talk about "cleaning up their parser" and the authors confess to having their own precision and recall results improved by very simple parsing changes. However, we are unaware of a detailed study on single-term parsing and the treatment of special characters, and its related effect on precision and recall [64].

Elimination of Stop Words

Stop words are frequently not stored in the index, because they are considered relatively meaningless with respect to the document relevance, and have a very low discrimination values for retrieval purposes. These terms represent approximately forty percent of the document collection [52] and their elimination reduces index construction, time and storage costs. On the other hand, stop words removal may also reduce the ability to respond to some queries, for instance when a query request a phrase that only contain stop words: "to be or not to be".

Stemming

Stemming removes prefixes and suffixes and allows the retrieval of documents containing syntactic variations of the query terms [113, 95]. For example, if the user includes the term "play" in the query, he can also wish to match "playing", "player", "played", etc. One problem is when two very different terms might have the same stem. A stemmer that removes *-ing* and *-ed* results in a stem of *r* for the terms *red* and *ring*. The KSTEM algorithm [89, 88] uses dictionaries to ensure that any generated stem will be a valid word. Croft et al. [36] use corpus based statistics based on term co-occurrence to identify stems in a language-independent fashion. These stemmers were shown to result in improved relevance ranking over more traditional stemmers [64].

Selection of Index Terms

In this process it is defined which words/stems will be used as index terms. In general, it is related to the syntactic nature of a word. In fact, noun words frequently carry more semantic information than adjectives, adverbs, and verbs.

2.9.2 Inverted Index

An inverted index (or inverted file) is a word-oriented mechanism for indexing a text collection in order to speed up the search task. The inverted file structure is composed of two elements: the *vocabulary* containing all unique terms in the collection, and for each vocabulary-term a *posting list*, with the documents in which the term occurs.

As illustrated in the Figure 2.15, an entry in the list of documents can also contain the frequency of the term $tf_{i,j}$ and the positions of the term $\langle pos \rangle_{i,j}$ in the document (e.g. word, sentence, paragraph, etc.) to facilitate proximity searching [83].

The indexing process requires additional overhead since the entire collection is scanned and substantial input/output operations are required to generate an efficiently represented index for use in secondary storage. Upon receiving a query, the index is consulted, the corresponding posting lists are retrieved, and the algorithm ranks the documents based on the contents of the posting lists [64].

Index Compression

An important topic concerning the efficiency of an IR system is the size of the index. The size of an inverted file can be reduced by compressing the inverted lists. Because the list of document numbers within the inverted list is in ascending order, it can also be considered as

2.9 Retrieval Utilities

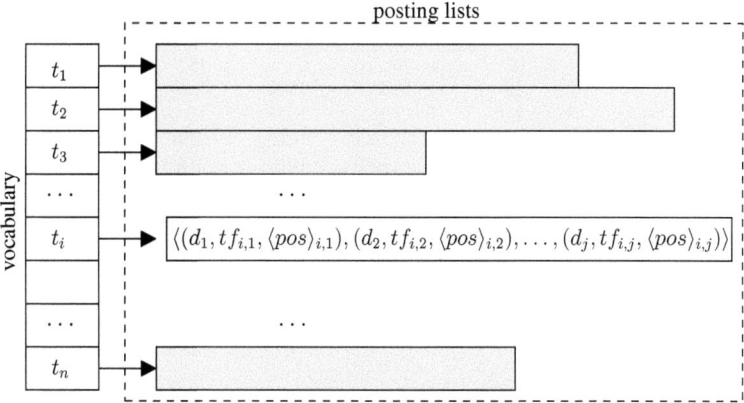

Figure 2.15: An inverted index

a sequence of *gaps* between document numbers. Since processing is usually done sequentially starting from the beginning of the list, the original document numbers can be always be recomputed through sums of the gaps.

By observing that these gaps are small for frequent words and large for infrequent words, compression can be obtained by encoding small values with shorter codes. One possible coding scheme is the *unary code*, in which an integer x is encoded as $(x-1)$ one bits followed by a zero bit, so the code for the integer 3 is 110.

Two alternative methods based on the unary code were proposed by Elias [44]: the Elias-γ code and the Elias-δ codes are variable length coding schemes for integers. In Elias-γ, the number x will be represented as a concatenation of two parts: (1) a unary code for $1 + \lfloor \log x \rfloor$ and (2) a code of $\lfloor \log x \rfloor$ bits that represents the value of $x - 2\lfloor \log x \rfloor$ in binary. For example, the Elias-γ code for $x = 5$ is the unary code for 3 (code 110) with the 2-bits binary number for 1 (code 01) which yields the codeword 11001. The Elias-δ code represents the prefix indicating the number of binary bits by the Elias-γ code rather than the unary code. For $x = 5$, the first part is then 101 instead 110. Thus, the Elias-δ codeword for $x = 5$ is 10101. Golomb [62] presents another run-length coding method for positive integers, which is very effective when the probability of distribution of a gap is geometric, but it requires two passes to be generated.

The Golomb method works as follows. For some parameter b, a gap $x > 0$ is coded as $q + 1$ in unary, where $q = \lfloor (x-1)/b \rfloor$, followed by $r = (x-1) - q \times b$ code in binary, requiring either $\lfloor \log b \rfloor$ or $\lceil \log b \rceil$ bits. That is, if $r < 2^{\lceil \log b \rceil - 1}$ then the number coded in binary requires $\lfloor \log b \rfloor$ bits, otherwise it requires $\lceil \log b \rceil$ bits where the first bit id 1 and the remaining bits assume the value $r - 2^{\lceil \log b \rceil - 1}$ coded in $\lfloor \log b \rfloor$ binary digits. For example, with $b = 3$ there are three possible remainders, and those are coded as 0, 10, and

Gap x	Unary	Elias-γ	Elias-δ	Golomb $b=3$
1	0	0	0	00
2	10	100	1000	010
3	110	101	1001	011
4	1110	11000	10100	100
5	11110	11001	10101	1010
6	111110	11010	10110	1011
7	1111110	11011	10111	1100
8	11111110	1110000	11000000	11010
9	111111110	1110001	11000001	11011
10	1111111110	1110010	11000010	11100

Table 2.4: Example of codes for integers.

11, for $r = 0$, $r = 1$, and $r = 2$ respectively. Similarly, for $b = 5$, there are five possible remainders r, 0 through 4, and these are assigned the codes 00, 01, 100, 101, and 110. Then, if the value $x = 9$ is to be coded relative to $b = 3$, calculations yield $q = 2$ and $r = 2$, because $9 - 1 = 2 \times 3 + 2$ Thus, the encoding is 110 followed by 11. Relative to $b = 5$, the values calculated are $q = 1$ and $r = 1$, resulting in a code of 10 followed by 101. Table 2.4 shows some examples of Unary, Elias and Golomb codes.

Witte, Moffat and Bell [163] present a detailed study of different text collections. For all of their practical work on compression of inverted lists, they use the Golomb code for the list of gaps. In this case, the Golomb code gives a better compression than either Elias-γ or Elias-δ [8].

2.9.3 Relevance Feedback

A popular information retrieval utility is *relevance feedback*. In a relevance feedback cycle, the user is presented with a list of retrieved documents and, after examining them, marks those that are relevant. An alternative is to avoid asking the user anything at all and to simply assume that the top ranked documents are relevant. The main idea consists of selecting important terms, or expressions, attached to the documents that have been identified as relevant by the user, and of enhancing the importance of these terms in a new query formulation. The expected effect is that the new query will be moved towards the relevant documents and away from the non-relevant ones [8].

With the vector space model, the addition of new terms to the original query, the deletion of terms from the query, and the modifications of existing term weights has been done. With the probabilistic model, relevance feedback was only able to re-weight existing terms, and there was not accepted means of adding terms to the original query [64]. The exact means by which relevance feedback is implemented is fairly dependent on the employed retrieval strategy. However, the basic concept of relevance feedback (i.e. run a query, gather relevance information from the user, enhance the query, and repeat) can be employed with any arbitrary retrieval strategy.

2.9 Retrieval Utilities

Relevance Feedback in the Vector Space Model

The application of relevance feedback to the vector model considers that the term-weight vectors of documents identified as relevant (to a given query) have similarities among themselves (i.e., relevant documents are similar). Further, it is assumed that non-relevant documents have term-weight vectors that are dissimilar from the ones for the relevant documents. The basic idea is to reformulate the query that it gets closer to the term-weight vector space of the relevant documents. Rocchio [128] has proposed one of the first relevance feedback approaches for the vector model. The basic assumption is that the user has issued a query q and retrieved a set of documents, where he determines two sets of documents: the set R containing n_1 relevant documents, and the set S containing n_2 non-relevant documents. Rocchio builds the new query q' from the old query q using the vectors of the sets R and S:

$$q' = q + \frac{1}{n_1} \sum_{i=1}^{n_1} R_i - \frac{1}{n_2} \sum_{i=1}^{n_2} S_i \qquad (2.18)$$

R_i and S_i are individual components of R and S, respectively.

The document vectors from the relevant documents are added to the initial query vector, and the vectors from the non-relevant documents are subtracted. If all documents are relevant, the third term does not appear. To ensure that the new information does not completely override the original query, all vector modifications are normalized by the number of relevant and non-relevant documents. The process can be repeated such that q_{i+1} is derived from q_i for as many iterations as desired.

The idea is that the relevant documents have terms matching those in the original query. The weights corresponding to these terms are increased by adding the relevant document vector. Terms in the query that are in the non-relevant documents have their weights decreased. Also, terms that are not in the original query (had an initial component value of zero) are now added to the original query.

In addition to using values n_1 and n_2, it is possible to use arbitrary weights α, β and γ, experimentally calculated and known as the Rocchio weights:

$$q' = \alpha q + \beta \sum_{i=1}^{n_1} \frac{R_i}{n_1} - \gamma \sum_{i=1}^{n_2} \frac{S_i}{n_2} \qquad (2.19)$$

Not all of the relevant or non-relevant documents must be used. By adding the threshold n_a and n_b, one can restrict the number of documents used for the query expansion.

$$q' = \alpha q + \beta \sum_{i=1}^{min(n_a,n_1)} \frac{R_i}{n_1} - \gamma \sum_{i=1}^{min(n_b,n_2)} \frac{S_i}{n_2} \qquad (2.20)$$

Usually, the information contained in the relevant documents is more important than the information provided by the non-relevant ones [136]. This suggests making γ smaller than β. Other common practices are to drop the use of the non-relevant documents (assign zero to γ) or only use the top non-relevant document [74].

The main advantages of the above relevance feedback techniques are simplicity and good results. The simplicity is due to the fact that the modified term weights are computed directly from the set of retrieved documents. The good results are observed experimentally and are due to the fact that the modified query vector reflect a portion of the intended query semantics [8]. The main disadvantage is that *no* optimality criterion is adopted.

2.9.4 Automatic Relevance Feedback

As mentioned before, in a relevance feedback cycle, the user examines the top ranked documents and separates them into two classes: the relevant ones and the non-relevant ones. This information is then used to select new terms for query expansion or query re-weighting. An automatic variant of this procedure involves usually identifying terms that are related to the query terms. Such terms might be synonyms, stemming variations, or terms that are close to the query terms in the text. Two basic types of strategies can be attempted: a global one and a local one.

Automatic Local Analysis

In a local strategy, the documents retrieved for a given query q are automatically examined at query time to determine terms for query expansion. Two different strategies will be discussed, the first strategy proposed by Attar and Fraenkel [7] known as *local clustering* and the second strategy called *local context analysis* corresponds to the work of Xu and Croft [164] which is based on a combination of local and global analysis.

Local feedback strategies are based on expanding the query with terms correlated to the query terms. Such correlated terms are those present in local clusters built from the local documents set. To build these cluster structures, Attar and Fraenkel proposed three basic strategies:

Association Clusters. An association cluster is based on the co-occurrence of *stems*[2] (or terms) inside documents. The idea is that stems that co-occur frequently inside documents have a synonymity association [8]. The association clusters are generated as follows:

Definition 4 *The frequency of a stem s_i in a document d_j, $d_j \in D_l$, is referred to as $f_{s_i,j}$. Let $\vec{m} = (m_{ij})$ be an association matrix with $|S_l|$ rows and $|D_l|$ columns, where $m_{ij} = f_{s_i,j}$. Let $\vec{m}^t$ be the transpose of $\vec{m}$. The matrix $\vec{s} = \vec{m}\vec{m}^t$ is a local stem-stem association matrix. Each element $s_{u,v}$ in $\vec{s}$ expresses a correlation $c_{u,v}$ between the stems s_u and s_v, namely,*

$$c_{u,v} = \sum_{d_j \in D_l} f_{s_u,j} \times f_{s_v,j} \qquad (2.21)$$

The correlation factor $c_{u,v}$ quantifies the absolute frequencies of co-occurrence and is said to be unnormalized. Thus, if we adopt $s_{u,v} = c_{u,v}$, the association matrix $\vec{s}$ is said to be unnormalized. An alternative is to normalize the correlation factor using $s_{u,v} = \frac{c_{u,v}}{c_{u,u}+c_{v,v}-c_{u,v}}$, then the association matrix $\vec{s}$ is said to be normalized.

---
[2] A *stem* is the part of a word that is common to all its inflected variants.

2.9 Retrieval Utilities

Given a query q, we are normally interested in finding clusters only for the $|q|$ query terms. Further, it is desirable to keep the size of such clusters small. This means that such clusters can be computed in query time. A similar procedure can be applied for a non-stemmed version where keywords instead of stems are used. Keyword-based local clustering is equally worthwhile trying because there is controversy over the advantages of using a stemmed vocabulary [8].

Metric Clusters. Associations clusters are based on the frequency of co-occurrence of pairs of terms in documents and do not take into account *where* the terms occur in a document. Since two terms that occur in the same sentence seem more correlated than two terms that occur far apart in a document, it might be worthwhile to consider the the distance between two terms by the computation of their correlation factor. The metric clusters are based in the following definition:

Definition 5 *Let the distance $r(k_i, k_j)$ between two keywords k_i and k_j be given by the number of words between them in the same document. If k_i and k_j are in distinct documents, we take $r(k_i, k_j) = \infty$. A local stem-stem metric correlation matrix $\vec{s}$ is defined as follows. Each element $s_{u,v}$ of $\vec{s}$ expresses a metric correlation $c_{u,v}$ between the stem s_u and s_v namely,*

$$c_{u,v} = \sum_{k_i \in V(s_u)} \sum_{k_j \in V(x_v)} \frac{1}{r(k_i, k_j)} \qquad (2.22)$$

In this expression, as already defined, $V(s_u)$ and $V(s_v)$ indicate the sets of keywords that have s_u and s_v as their respective stems.

The correlation factor $c_{u,v}$ quantifies absolute distances and is said to be unnormalized. Thus, if we adopt $s_{u,u} = c_{u,v}$ the association matrix $\vec{s}$ is said to be unnormalized. An alternative is to normalize the correlation factor. For instance, adopting $s_{u,v} = \frac{c_{u,v}}{|V(s_u)| \times |V(s_v)|}$, then the association matrix $\vec{s}$ is said to be normalized.

Give a local matrix $\vec{s}$, we can use it to build local metric clusters as follows.

Definition 6 *Consider the uth row in the metric correlation matrix $\vec{s}$ (i.e., the row with all the associations for the stem s_u). Let $S_u(n)$ be a function that takes the uth row and returns the set of n largest values $s_{u,v}$, where v varies over the set of local stems and $v \neq u$. The $S_u(n)$ defines a local metric cluster around the stem s_u.*

Scalar Clusters. One additional form to obtain a synonymity relationship between two local stems (or terms) s_u and s_v is by comparing the sets $S_u(n)$ and $S_v(n)$. The idea is that two stems with similar *neighborhoods* have some synonymity relationship. In this case, we say that the relationship is indirect or induced by the neighborhood. One way to calculate such neighborhood relationships is to arrange all correlation values $s_{u,i}$ in a vector $\vec{s}_u$, to arrange all correlation values $s_{v,i}$ in another vector $\vec{s}_v$, and to compare these vectors through a scalar measure. For instance, the cosine of the angle between the two vectors is a popular scalar similarity measure.

Definition 7 *Let $\vec{s_u} = (s_{u,1}, s_{u,2}, ..., s_{u,n})$ and $\vec{s_v} = (s_{v,1}, s_{v,2}, ..., s_{v,n})$ be two vectors of correlation values for the stems s_u and s_v. Further, let $\vec{s} = (s_{u,v})$ be a scalar association matrix. Then, each $s_{u,v}$ can be defined as*

$$s_{u,v} = \frac{\vec{s_u} \cdot \vec{s_v}}{|\vec{s_u}| \times |\vec{s_v}|} \qquad (2.23)$$

The correlation matrix $\vec{s}$ is said to be induced by the neighborhood. Using it, a scalar cluster is defined as follows.

Definition 8 *Let $S_u(n)$ be a function that returns the set of n largest values $s_{u,v}$, $v \neq u$, defined according to equation 2.23. Then, $S_u(n)$ defines a scalar cluster around the stem s_u.*

A stem s_u that belongs to a cluster (of size n) associated to another stem s_v (i.e., $s_u \in S_v(n)$) is said to be a *neighbor* of s_v. While neighbor stems are said to have a synonymity relationship, they are not necessary synonyms in the grammatical sense. Often, neighbor stems represent distinct keywords that are correlated by the current query context [8]. The local aspect of this correlation is reflected in the fact that the documents and stems considered in the correlation matrix are all local (i.e., $d_j \in D_l, s_u \in V_l$.

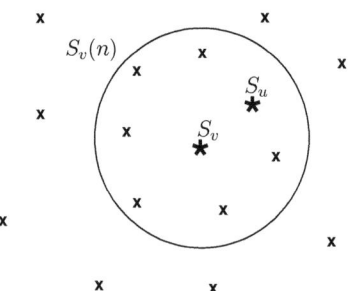

Figure 2.16: Stem s_u as neighbor of stem s_v.

Figure 2.16 illustrates a stem (or term) s_u that is located within a neighborhood $S_v(n)$ associated with the stem (or term) s_v. In general, neighbor stems are an important product of the local clustering process since they can be used for extending a search formulation in a promising unexpected direction, rather than merely complementing it with missing synonyms [8].

The qualitative interpretation of normalized and unnormalized clusters is that unnormalized clusters tend to group stems whose ties are due to their large frequencies, while normalized clusters tend to group stems which are more rare. Thus, the union of these two clusters provides a better representation of the possible correlations.

2.9 Retrieval Utilities

Experimental results reported in the literature usually support the hypothesis of the usefulness of local clustering methods. Furthermore, metric clusters seem to perform better than pure association clusters. This strengthens the hypothesis that there is a correlation between the association of two terms and the distance between them [8].

Local Context Analysis. As discussed above, clustering techniques are based on set of documents retrieved for the original query and use the top ranked documents for clustering neighbor terms using the term co-occurrence criterion inside the documents boundary. Terms that are the best query term neighbors are then used to expand the original query. A distinct approach is to search for term correlations in the whole collection (global analysis) which usually involves the building of a thesaurus that identifies term relationships in the whole collection. The local context analysis approach [164] combines global and local analysis, and is based on the use of noun groups (i.e., single noun, two adjacent nouns, or three adjacent nouns in the text), instead of simple keywords, as document concepts. For query expansion, concepts are selected from the top ranked documents (as in local analysis) based on their co-occurrence with the query terms (no stemming). However, this approach uses *passages* (text windows of fixed size) instead documents (as in global analysis). More specifically, local context analysis is divided into three steps.

- First, retrieve the top n ranked passages using the original query. This is accomplished by breaking up the documents initially retrieved by the query in fixed length passages (for example, of size 300 words) and ranking these passages as if they were documents.

- Second, for each concept c in the top ranked passages, the similarity $sim(q, c)$ between the whole query q (not individual query terms) and the concept c is calculated using a variant of tf-idf ranking.

- Third, the top m ranked concepts (according to $sim(q, c)$) are added to the original query q. To each added concept a weight is assigned given by $1 - 0.9 \times i/m$ where i is the position of the concept in the final concept ranking. The terms in the original query q might be stressed by assigning a weight of 2 to each term.

The similarity $sim(q, c)$ between each related concept c and the original query (step 3) is computed as follows.

$$sim(q, c) = \prod_{k_i \in q} \left(\delta + \frac{log(f(c, k_i) \times idf_c)}{log\ n} \right)^{idf_i} \tag{2.24}$$

where n is the number of top ranked passages considered. The function $f(c, k_i)$ quantifies the correlation between the concept c and the query term k_i and id given by $f(c, k_i) = \sum_{j=1}^{n} pf_{i,j} \times pf_{c,j}$, where $pf_{i,j}$ is the frequency of term k_i in the jth passage and $pf_{c,j}$ is the frequency of the concept c in the jth passage. Notice that this is the standard correlation measure defined for association clusters (by Equation 2.21) but adapted for passages. The inverse document frequency factors are computed as follows.

$$idf_i = max(1, \frac{log_{10} \ N/np_i}{5}) \qquad (2.25)$$

$$idf_c = max(1, \frac{log_{10} \ N/np_c}{5}) \qquad (2.26)$$

where N is the number of passages in the collection, np_i is the number of passages containing the term k_i, and np_c is the number of passages containing the concept c. The factor δ is a constant parameter that avoids a value equal to zero for $sim(q, c)$. Usually, δ is a small factor with values close to 0.1 (10% of the maximum of 1). Finally, the idf_i factor in the exponent is introduced to emphasize infrequent query terms.

The procedure to calculate $sim(q, c)$ is a non-trivial variant of $tf - idf$ ranking. Furthermore, it has been adjusted for operations with TREC data and did not work so well with different collections. Thus, it is important to have in mind that for operations with different collections, tuning might be required.

Automatic Global Analysis

In a global strategy, all documents in the collection are used to determine a global-like thesaurus structure that defines term relationships. We discuss two variants of these strategies, one based on a similarity thesaurus and a second one based on a statistical thesaurus.

Automatic Global Analysis based on a Similarity Thesaurus. The similarity thesaurus [114] proposes a term to term relationship, considering that terms are concepts in a concept space. In this concept space, each term is indexed by the documents in which it appears. Thus, terms assume the original role of documents while documents are interpreted as indexing elements. The following definitions establish the proper framework.

Definition 9 *Let t be a number of terms in the collection, N the number of document in the collections, $f_{i,j}$ be the frequency of occurrence of the term k_i in the document d_j. Further, let t_j be the number of distinct index terms in the document d_j and itf_j be the inverse term frequency for the document d_j. Then, $itf_j = log \frac{t}{t_j}$, analogously to the definition of inverse document frequency.*

Within this framework, to each term k_i a vector $\vec{k}_i$ given by $\vec{k}_i = (w_{i,1}, w_{i,2}, \ldots, w_{i,N})$ is associated where $w_{i,j}$ is a weight associated to the index-document pair $[k_i, d_j]$. These weights are computed as follows.

$$w_{i,j} = \frac{(0.5 + 0.5 \frac{f_{i,j}}{max_j(f_{i,j})}) \ itf_j}{\sqrt{\sum_{l=1}^{N}(0.5 + 0.5 \frac{f_{i,l}}{max_l(f_{i,l})})^2 \ itf_j^2}} \qquad (2.27)$$

where $max_j(f_{i,j})$ computes the maximum of all factors $f_{i,j}$ for the ith term (i.e., over all documents in the collection). We notice that the expression above is a variant of $tf - idf$ weights but one that considers inverse term frequencies instead.

2.9 Retrieval Utilities

The relationship between two terms k_u and k_v is computed as a correlation factor $c_{u,v}$ given by

$$c_{u,v} = \vec{k}_u \cdot \vec{k}_v = \sum_{\forall d_j} w_{u,j} \times w_{v,j} \tag{2.28}$$

This equation is a variation of the correlation measure used for calculating scalar association matrices. The main difference is that the weights are based on interpreting documents as index elements instead of repositories for term occurrence.

The global similarity thesaurus is built through the computation of the correlation factor $c_{u,v}$ for each pair of indexing terms $[k_u, k_v]$ in the collection. Of course, this is computationally expensive. However, this global similarity thesaurus has to be calculated only once and can be updated incrementally.

Given a global similarity thesaurus, query expansion is done in three steps:

- First, represent the query in the concept space used for representation of index terms.

- Second, based on the global similarity thesaurus, compute a similarity $sim(q, k_v)$ between each term k_v correlated with the query terms and the whole query q.

- Third, expand the query with the top r ranked terms according to $sim(q, k_v)$.

For the first step, the query is represented in the concept space of index term vectors as follows.

Definition 10 *To the query q is a vector $\vec{q}$ in the term-concept space associated given by*

$$\vec{q} = \sum_{k_i \in q} w_{i,q} \vec{k}_i \tag{2.29}$$

where $w_{i,q}$ is a weight associated to the index-query pair $[k_i, q]$.

For the second step, a similarity $sim(q, k_v)$ between each term k_v (correlated to the query terms) and the user query q is computed as

$$sim(q, k_v) = \vec{q} \cdot \vec{k}_v = \sum_{k_u \in Q} w_{u,q} \times c_{u,v} \tag{2.30}$$

where $c_{u,v}$ is the correlation factor given in the equation (2.28).

For the third step, the top r ranked terms according to $sim(q, k_v)$ are added to the original query q to form the expanded query q'. To each expansion term k_v in the query q', a weight $w_{v,q'}$ is assigned.

$$w_{v,q'} = \frac{sim(q, k_v)}{\sum_{k_u \in q} w_{u,q}} \tag{2.31}$$

The expanded query q' is used to retrieve new documents for the user.

Automatic Global Analysis based on a Statistical Thesaurus. In this section, we discuss a quite different global analysis technique proposed by Crouch and Yang [37] based on a statistical thesaurus.

The global thesaurus is composed of classes that group correlated terms in the context of the whole collection. Such correlated terms can then be used to expand the original query. To be effective, the terms selected for expansion must have high term discrimination values [139] which implies that they must be low frequency terms. However, it is difficult to cluster low frequency terms effectively due to the small amount of information about them (they occur in few documents). To avoid this problem, documents will be clustered in classes instead and low frequently terms in these document are used to define the thesaurus classes. In this situation, the document clustering algorithm must produce small and tight clusters.

A document clustering algorithm that produces such type of clusters is the *complete link algorithm* that works as follows (naive formulation).

1. Initially, place each document in a distinct cluster.
2. Compute the similarity between all pairs of clusters.
3. Determine the pair of clusters $[C_u, C_v]$ with the highest inter-cluster similarity.
4. Merge the clusters C_u and C_v.
5. Test a stop criterion. If this criterion is not met, then go back to step 2.
6. Return a hierarchy of clusters.

The similarity between two clusters is defined as the minimum of the similarities between all pairs of inter-clusters documents (i.e., two documents not in the same cluster). To compute the similarity between documents in a pair, the cosine formula of the vector model is used. As a result of this minimality criterion, the resulting clusters tend to be small and tight.

Given the document cluster hierarchy for the whole collection, the terms that compose each class of the global thesaurus are selected as follows.

- Obtain from the user three parameters: threshold class (TC), number of documents in the class (NDC), and minimum inverse document frequency (MIDF).

- Use the parameter TC as a threshold value for determining the document clusters that will be used to generate thesaurus classes. The threshold has to be surpassed by $sim(C_u, C_v)$ if the documents in the cluster C_u and C_v are to be selected as sources of terms for a thesaurus class.

- Use the parameter NDC as a limit on the size of clusters (number of documents) to be considered.

- Consider the set of documents in each document cluster preselected above (through the parameters TC and NDC). Only the lower frequency documents are used as

2.9 Retrieval Utilities

sources of terms for the thesaurus classes. The parameter MIDF defines the minimum value of inverse document frequency for any term which is selected to participate in the thesaurus class. By doing so, it is possible to ensure that only *low frequency* terms participate in the thesaurus class generated (terms too generic are not good synonyms).

Given that the thesaurus classes have been built, they can be used for query expansion. For this, an average term weight wt_C for each thesaurus class C is computed as follows.

$$wt_C = \frac{\sum_{i=1}^{|C|} w_{i,C}}{|C|} \qquad (2.32)$$

where $|C|$ is the number of terms in the thesaurus class C and $x_{i,C}$ is a pre-computed weight associated with the term-class pair $[k_i, C]$. This average term weight can then be used to compute a thesaurus class weight w_C as

$$w_C = \frac{wt_C}{|C|} \times 0.5 \qquad (2.33)$$

Experiments with well known document collections (ADI, Medlars[3], CACM[4] and ISI[5]) indicate that global analysis using a thesaurus built by the complete link algorithm might yield consistent improvement in retrieval performance [8].

The main problem with this approach is the initialization of the parameters TC, NDC, and MIDF. The threshold value TC depends on the collection and can be difficult to set properly. Inspection of the cluster hierarchy is almost always necessary for assisting with the setting of TC. Care must be exercised because a high value of TC might yield classes with too few terms while a low TC value might yield too few classes. The selection of the parameter NDC can be decided more easily once TC has been set. However, the setting of the parameter MIDF might be difficult and also requires careful consideration.

2.9.5 Passage-based Retrieval

Passage-based Retrieval [24] is based on the assumption that only a small portion of each relevant document (i.e. the relevant passage within the document) contains the information that is relevant to the query. By computing metrics that compare the entire document to the query, the noisy parts of the document (the sections that are not relevant) potentially mask the relevant segments of the document in question [64].

For example, we consider the query "passage retrieval" and a book about information retrieval containing a single section (S_1) with relevant information for the query. If the entire book was viewed as a single document, section S_1 may contribute very little to the overall similarity coefficients between the book and the passage.

Since the documents often are naturally segmented into chapters, sections, and subsections, it is reasonable to use each of these boundaries and simply rank the passages to the

---
[3] Medical Literature Analysis and Retrieval System
[4] Communications of the ACM
[5] Institute of Scientific Information

original query. A similarity coefficient must then merge the passage-based results to obtain a final coefficient.

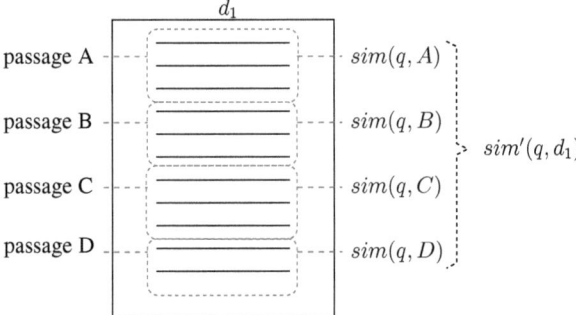

Figure 2.17: Similarity coefficients for different passages in the document d_1.

Consider a document d_1 from Figure 2.17 with sections A, B, C, and D. Further assume section C is the only section that mentions anything about a query q. A similarity coefficient $sim(q, d_1)$ could result in a coefficient that is heavily biased towards non-relevance, because sections A, B, and D have many terms that do not match with terms in the query. The similarity coefficient reflects this and given the length of the document and the relatively small proportion of matching terms, or even terms that are semantically related, the document would have a low similarity coefficient.

With passage-based retrieval, four separate coefficients are computed: $sim(q, A)$, $sim(q, B)$, $sim(q, C)$, and $sim(q, D)$ and several techniques are proposed to merge the four different similarity coefficients.

Passage-based research focuses on determining how to delimit a passage and combine each passage into a single similarity coefficient $sim'(q, d_1)$.

Discourse Passages

Documents usually have structural or logical divisions such as sentences, paragraphs, and sections, marked up in standards such as XML. The discourse (or logical) components of documents can be regarded as passages [71, 131, 159, 171]. This definition of passage is intuitive, since sentences should convey a single idea; paragraphs should be about one topic; and sections should be about one issue.

A problem with discourse passages is that they require a high degree of consistency between authors. Callan [24] observed that the structure of a document might be unrelated to its content, because documents can be structured in a particular way simply for presentation. Also, even though most documents are supplied with their structure, manual processing is required for those without it, thus making discourse passages impractical, as can be the case when a document is the output of a speech recognition system [112]. Another problem with

2.9 Retrieval Utilities

discourse passages is that their length can vary, from very long to very short. In addition long passages are likely to include more than one topic; retrieving long passages contradicts one of the main aims of passage retrieval [80].

Semantic Passages

An alternative approach is to segment documents into *semantic* passages, corresponding to the topical structure of documents [10, 70, 112, 120, 132, 137]. The main idea is to partition documents into segments, each corresponding to a topic or to a subtopic. It is therefore attractive to develop algorithms that derive segments based on topics or semantic properties. Several such algorithms have been developed. Reynar [120] proposed an algorithm that locates semantic boundaries based on detection of repetition of lexical items such as words or phrases. Beeferman et al. [10] used short- and long-term statistical models that keep track of word occurrence patterns, near and far from the current position in text, to locate topic changes, and also use lexical hints such as sentence and paragraph boundaries. Yaari [167] applied a hierarchical agglomerative clustering algorithm to partition full-text documents. The algorithm joins adjacent paragraphs on the basis of their similarity. Salton et al. [132, 137] derived text segments that helped with summarising documents by computing similarities between text paragraphs. Ponte and Croft [112] developed an algorithm that segments text into short topics, assumed to be about three sentences long.

An algorithm that is well-suited to passage retrieval from large collections such as TREC data is that of Hearst [71], known as TextTiling. This algorithm partitions full-text documents into coherent multi-paragraph units, creating a subtopic structure for documents. The model relies on word frequency and assumes that a set of words is in use during the course of a given subtopic discussion, and when that subtopic changes, a significant proportion of the vocabulary changes as well. Richmond et al. [122] extended the TextTile algorithm by introducing a new measure of word significance, which uses the relative occurrence of words in documents to compute the scores between adjacent blocks. Experimental results suggest that the extended algorithm is slightly more reliable than the original TextTile algorithm.

Regardless of the segmentation technique, an advantage of semantic passages is that they can be applied where the logical structure of document is not explicit, for example by documents created using OCR or speech recognition technology. Discovering semantic passages is computationally expensive, but this cost is only incurred once. However, the accuracy of segmentation as compared with human segmentation is not yet perfect [122, 70].

Window-based Passages

Structural properties of documents are not always explicit, retrieval requirements vary depending on the user need, and semantic segmentation can be inaccurate. An alternative to discourse and semantic passages is break to break documents into passages of fixed length, often referred to as non-overlapping windows. If paragraph boundaries are known, they can be considered, but if the are not available, then passages can simply be defined as sequences of words.

The passage should be in a fixed range of sizes based on number of words, not too long or too short. Callan [24] use a word-based approach, by defining a passage, or a window, as a fixed-length sequence of words. Zobel et al. [171] and Callan [24] considered paragraphs instead of words as the basic unit, and use heuristics to bound their lengths. For instance, short paragraphs are merged with subsequent paragraphs, and paragraphs longer than some minimum length are kept intact. Zobel et al. [171] referred to such passages as *pages*, since they approximate a physical page of text (around 2 kilobytes). Stanfill and Waltz [144] define a passage as a block of 30 words, and segment document into sequential blocks. Consecutive blocks can be joined into a larger text segment, to address the problems of retrieving blocks of text that are too short.

The main advantage of window-based passages is that they are easy to construct, irrespective of the text. However, there are disadvantages. If window-based passages are retrieved and presented to the user, they are likely to be confusing unless additional information is presented, describing the context from which the passage has been selected; and window-based passages are static, since, once the are defined, they are also indexed.

Dynamic Passages Partitioning

Different approaches have been used to automatically find good partitions. These approaches attempt to partition documents differently based on the particular query [24, 80]. One means of doing this is to find a term matches the query and then build a passage around this match. If a term matches at position n, passage A will begin at position n and continue until position $n + p$ where p is a variable passage size. The next passage B, will overlap with A and start at position $n + \frac{p}{2}$. For example, considering a term that matches at position ten, a small passage length of fifty terms results in passages around terms [10,60], [35,85], [60,110], etc. where $[i, j]$ indicates the passage starts at position i and continues to j. Overlapping passages are intended to avoid splitting sections of relevant text.

Merging Passage-based Similarity Measures

Passages contribute to the similarity coefficient in a number of different ways. Wilkinson [159] tested twenty different methods of merging passage-based contributions. These methods ranged from simply taking the highest ranked passage as the similarity coefficient to combining document level contributions with passage level contributions. Callan [24] also used a combination score with the document and the passage level evidence to obtain the best results.

2.10 Information Retrieval Evaluation

2.10.1 Recall and Precision

Consider an example information request I (of a test reference collection) and its set R of relevant documents. Let $|R|$ be the number of documents in this set. Assume that a given retrieval strategy (which is being evaluated) process the information request I and generate

2.10 Information Retrieval Evaluation

a document answer set A. Let $|A|$ be the number of documents in this set. Further, let $|R_a|$ be the number of documents in the intersection of the set R and A. Figure 2.18 illustrates these sets.

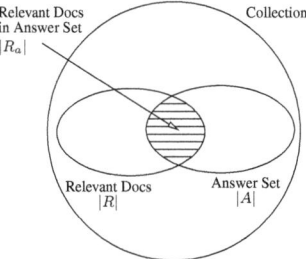

Figure 2.18: Precision and recall for a given example information request.

The recall and precision measures are defined as follows.

Definition 11 *Recall is the fraction of the relevant documents (the set R) which has been retrieved i.e.,*

$$Recall = \frac{|R_a|}{|R|} \tag{2.34}$$

Definition 12 *Precision is the fraction f the retrieval documents (the set A) which is relevant i.e.,*

$$Precision = \frac{|R_a|}{|A|} \tag{2.35}$$

Recall and precision, as defined above, assume that all the documents in the answer set A have been examined (or seen). However, the user is not usually presented with all the documents in the answer set A at once. Instead, the documents in A are first sorted according to a degree of relevance (i.e., a ranking is generated) The user then examines this ranked list starting from the top document. In this situation, the recall and precision measures vary as the user proceeds with the examination of the answer set A. Thus, proper evaluation requires plotting a precision and recall curve as follows.

As before, consider a reference collection and its set of example information request. Let us focus on a given example information request for which a query q is formulated. Assume that the set R_q containing the relevant documents for q has been defined. Without loss of generality, assume further that the set R_q is composed of the following documents.

$$R_q = \{d_3, d_5, d_9, d_{25}, d_{39}, d_{44}, d_{56}, d_{71}, d_{89}, d_{123}\} \tag{2.36}$$

Thus, according to a group of specialists, there are ten documents which are relevant to the query q.

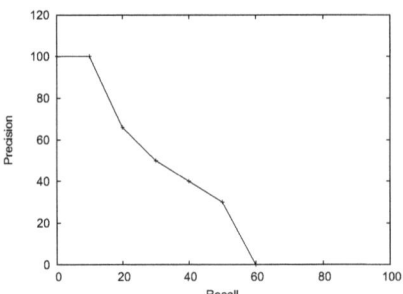

Figure 2.19: Precision at 11 standard recall levels.

Consider now a new retrieval algorithm which has just been designed. Assume that this algorithm returns, for a query q, a ranking of documents in the answer set as follows.

Ranking for query q:

1. d_{123} •   6. d_9 •   11. d_{38}
2. d_{84} 7. d_{511} 12. d_{48}
3. d_{56} •   8. d_{129} 13. d_{250}
4. d_6 9. d_{187} 14. d_{113}
5. d_8 10. d_{25} • 15. d_3 •

The documents that are relevant to the query q are marked with the bullet after the document number. If we examine this ranking, starting from the top document, we observe the following points. First, the document d_{123} which is ranked as number 1 is relevant. Further, this documents corresponds to 10% of all relevant documents in the set R_q. Thus we say that we have a precision of 100% at 10% recall. Second, the document d_{56} which is ranked as number 3 is the next relevant document. At this point, we say that we have a precision of roughly 66% at 20% recall. Third, if we proceed with our examination of the ranking generated we can plot the curve of precision versus recall as illustrated in Figure 2.19. This precision vs recall curve is usually based on 11 (instead of ten) *standard* recall levels which are 0%, 10%, 20%,...,100%. For the recall level 0%, the precision is obtained through an interpolation procedure as detailed below.

In the above example, the precision and recall figures are for a single query. Usually, however, retrieval algorithms are evaluated by running them for several distinct queries. In this case, for each query a distinct precision versus recall curve is generated. To evaluate the retrieval performance of an algorithm over all test queries, we average the precision figures at each recall level as follows.

$$\overline{P}(r) = \sum_{i=1}^{N_q} \frac{P_i(r)}{N_q} \qquad (2.37)$$

where $\overline{P}(r)$ is the average precision at the recall level r, N_q is the number of queries used,

2.10 Information Retrieval Evaluation

and $P_i(r)$ is the precision at recall level r for the i-th query.

Since the recall levels for each query might be distinct from the 11 standard recall levels, utilization of an interpolation procedure is often necessary. For instance, consider again the set of 50 ranked documents presented above. Assume that the set of relevant document for the query q has changed and is now given by

$$R_q = \{d_3, d_{56}, d_{129}\} \quad (2.38)$$

In this case, the fist relevant document in the ranking for query q is d_{56} which provides a recall level of 33.3% (with precision also equal to 33.3%) because, at this point, one-third of all relevant documents have already been seen. The second relevant document is d_{129} which provides a recall level of 66.6% (with precision equal to 25%). The third relevant document is d_3 which provides a recall level of 100% (with precision equal to 20%). The precision figures at the 11 standard recall levels are interpolated as follows.

Let $r_j, j \in \{0, 1, 2, \ldots, 10\}$, be a reference to the j-th standard recall level (i.e., r_5 is a reference to the recall level 50%). Then,

$$P(r_j) = max_{r_j \leq r \leq r_{j+1}} P_r \quad (2.39)$$

which states that the interpolated precision at the j-th standard recall level is the maximum known precision at any recall level between the j-th recall level and the $(j+1)$-th recall level.

The curve of precision versus recall which results from averaging the results for various queries is usually referred to as precision versus recall figures. Such averages figures are normally used to compare the retrieval performance of distinct retrieval algorithms.

In recent years, other measures have become more common. Most standard among the TREC community is Mean Average Precision (MAP), which provides a single-figure measure of quality across recall levels. Among evaluation measures, MAP has been shown to have especially good discrimination and stability. For a single information need, Average Precision is the average of the precision value obtained for the set of top k documents existing after each relevant document is retrieved, and this value is then averaged over information needs. That is, if the set of relevant documents for an information need $q_j \in Q$ is $\{d_1, \ldots d_{m_j}\}$ and R_{jk} is the set of ranked retrieval results from the top result until you get to document d_k, then

$$\text{MAP}(Q) = \frac{1}{|Q|} \sum_{j=1}^{|Q|} \frac{1}{m_j} \sum_{k=1}^{m_j} \text{Precision}(R_{jk}) \quad (2.40)$$

When a relevant document is not retrieved at all,[6] the precision value in the above equation is taken to be 0. For a single information need, the average precision approximates the area under the interpolated precision-recall curve, and so the MAP is roughly the average area under the precision-recall curve for a set of queries.

Using MAP, fixed recall levels are not chosen, and there is no interpolation. The MAP value for a test collection is the arithmetic mean of average precision values for individual

---

[6]A system may not fully order all documents in the collection in response to a query or at any rate an evaluation exercise may be based on submitting only the top k results for each information need.

information needs. (This has the effect of weighting each information need equally in the final reported number, even if many documents are relevant to some queries whereas very few are relevant to other queries.) Calculated MAP scores normally vary widely across information needs when measured within a single system, for instance, between 0.1 and 0.7. Indeed, there is normally more agreement in MAP for an individual information need across systems than for MAP scores for different information needs for the same system. This means that a set of test information needs must be large and diverse enough to be representative of system effectiveness across different queries.

The above measures factor in precision at all recall levels. For many prominent applications, particularly web search, this may not be germane to users. What matters is rather how many good results there are on the first page or the first three pages. This leads to measuring precision at fixed low levels of retrieved results, such as 10 or 30 documents. This is referred to as "Precision at k", for example "Precision at 10". It has the advantage of not requiring any estimate of the size of the set of relevant documents but the disadvantages that it is the least stable of the commonly used evaluation measures and that it does not average well, since the total number of relevant documents for a query has a strong influence on precision at k.

An alternative that alleviates this problem is R-precision. It requires having a set of known relevant documents Rel, from which we calculate the precision of the top Rel documents returned. (The set Rel may be incomplete, such as when Rel is formed by creating relevance judgments for the pooled top k results of particular systems in a set of experiments.) R-precision adjusts for the size of the set of relevant documents: A perfect system could score 1 on this metric for each query, whereas, even a perfect system could only achieve a precision at 20 of 0.4 if there were only 8 documents in the collection relevant to an information need. Averaging this measure across queries thus makes more sense. This measure is harder to explain to naive users than Precision at k but easier to explain than MAP. If there are $|Rel|$ relevant documents for a query, we examine the top $|Rel|$ results of a system, and find that r are relevant, then by definition, not only is the precision (and hence R-precision) $r/|Rel|$, but the recall of this result set is also $r/|Rel|$. Thus, R-precision turns out to be identical to the break-even point , another measure which is sometimes used, defined in terms of this equality relationship holding. Like Precision at k, R-precision describes only one point on the precision-recall curve, rather than attempting to summarize effectiveness across the curve, and it is somewhat unclear why you should be interested in the break-even point rather than either the best point on the curve (the point with maximal F-measure) or a retrieval level of interest to a particular application (Precision at k). Nevertheless, R-precision turns out to be highly correlated with MAP empirically, despite measuring only a single point on the curve.

2.10.2 Document Collections

One of the first collections for Information Retrieval purposes was the Cranfield collection [29], created in the 1960s and widely used by researchers. It contained approximately 1.400

2.10 Information Retrieval Evaluation

abstracts and 225 requests. Later, other collections have been created, such as the CACM[7] Collection [50] and the NPL[8] Collection [155]. They were major computing challenges when first used, but they are small for the today standards. As hardware and information retrieval matured, it was necessary to use more realistically sized collections, because small collections often do not reflect the performance of systems in large full-text searching, and certainly does not demonstrate any proven abilities of these systems to operate in real-world information retrieval environments [156].

In the 1970s, Karen Sparck Jones and Keith van Rijsbergen [77] proposed the creation of a large test collection, which was to be not only superior to the current test collections in size, but was to be carefully designed to allow controlled experimentation. They considered many factors in selecting the documents, the test requests, and creating the relevance judgements. They pointed out the need of an heterogeneous collection: different text characteristics (various writing styles), different document types (for example, general newspapers versus scientific articles), different request types (for instance, precise versus non-precise requests), etc. They obtained a controlled retrieval environment to be correlated with the various parameters used in retrieval systems.

Unfortunately, this ideal test collection was not built due to a lack of funding, forcing researcher to continue to use small test collections. The main disadvantages were their specific design characteristics to support the particular experimental purposes. For example, the Cranfield collection was built to test hypotheses about the manual indexing of documents, with careful attention paid to the location of all relevant documents and the creation of multiple types of manual indexes [156]. The CACM collection was built to study the interaction between textual and bibliographic data, with an emphasis on providing full bibliographic information, including citation links and manual categories, from a complete set of journals articles (CACM from years 1958-1979).

Furthermore, some collections did not built natural user requests but created specially constructed request sets around the documents in the collection. For example, the Cranfield requests and documents were specially constructed to obtain always a sufficient number of relevant documents. On the other side, the CACM collection created 64 independent requests, and had an independent collection (assorted abstracts, titles, and bibliographic information for 3.204 articles), but almost 50% of the articles had only a title, and there was a highly variable number of relevant documents per request, including twelve with no relevant document at all.

The peculiarity of these collections could influence the outcomes of third-party experiments based on these documents, specially when the researchers are not awarded of these particular design criteria. The reuse of these collections without recognizing the interaction of the design could cause some experimental problems.

The design of a new test collection such as the one laid out in the 1970s' ideal collection work presents many challenges. The first is to build a collection that is realistic in that it mirrors some operational situation, but also is multifaceted enough that it can be reused in many different controlled experiments. The second challenge is to sufficiently document the

---

[7]Communications of the Association of Computing Machinery
[8]National Physical Laboratory

motivation, design, and creation of this test collection such that the researchers are aware of its limitations [156].

2.10.3 The DARPA TIPSTER Project

The TIPSTER test design was based on traditional information retrieval testing models, involving a test collection of documents, user requests, and relevance assessments.

The Documents

The document collection needed to reflect the corpus seen by information analysts. This meant that a very large collection was needed to test the ability of the algorithms to handle huge numbers of full-text documents. The documents needed to cover many different subject areas in order to test the domain independence of the algorithms. Additionally, the documents needed to mirror the different types of documents used in the TIPSTER application; specially they had to be of variable length, writing style, level of editing, and vocabulary. As a final requirement, the documents had to cover information from different years to show the effects of document date.

The Requests

The requests for the new test collection were also designed to model some of the needs of analysts. It was assumed that the users needed the ability to do both high-precision and high-recall searches, and were willing to look at many documents and repeatedly modify queries in order to get high recall. The topics therefore were created to be quite specific, but included both broad and narrow searching needs.

The Relevance Assessments

The relevance assessments were made by retired analysts who were asked to view the task as if they were addressing a real information need. The narrative section of the topic contains a clear definition of what makes a document relevant, and the assessors used this section as the definition of the information need. Documents retrieved for each topic were judged by a single assessor so that all documents screened would reflect the same user's interpretation of the topic.

TIPSTER centered around two main tasks based on traditional information retrieval modes: an ad hoc task, and a monitoring (routing[9]) task. In the ad hoc task, it is assumed that new requests are being asked against a fixed set of data. This task is similar to how a researcher might use a library, where the collection is known, but the requests likely to be asked are unknown. In the routing task, it is assumed that the same topics are always being followed, but the new data is being searched. This task is similar to that done by news clipping services.

---

[9] Equivalent task name in the TREC collection

2.10 Information Retrieval Evaluation

Although the TIPSTER collection contained a very large set of document, the project involved only four DARPA detection contractors, the TREC initiative [156] opened the evaluation to the wider information retrieval research community, with twenty-five additional research groups taking part in 1992 and eighty-eight groups by 2007.

2.10.4 The TREC Collection

In the early 1990s, the TREC initiative started under the leadership of Donna Harman at the National Institute of Standards and Technology (NIST), in Maryland. This effort consisted of promoting a yearly conference, named TREC for Text REtrieval Conference, dedicated to experimentation with a large text collection comprising over a million of documents. For each TREC conference, a set of reference experiments is designed. The research groups which participate in the conference use these reference experiments for comparing their retrieval systems [9].

Since the collection was built under the TIPSTER project, the guidelines used in the TIPSTER were also been followed in TREC. The first eight cycles of TREC were centered on the traditional information retrieval modes too (Routing and Ad Hoc retrieval). As the most test collections, the TREC collection is composed of three parts: the documents, the information requests (topics), and the set of relevant documents for each information request. The documents came from different original sources distributed in six CD-ROM disks of roughly 1 gigabyte compressed text each. Its documents were selected not only because of their suitability to the TIPSTER task but also because of their availability. Table 2.5 illustrates the contents of each disk and some statistics regarding the collection (extracted from [156]).

The Topics

The TREC collection includes a set of information requests (topics) that can be used to measure the performance of a new ranking algorithm. Each topic tries to mimic a real user need in natural language, and was written by people who are actual users of retrieval systems. The topic writers, the topic format, and the method of construction have evolved over time. This evolution has had major effect on the results, and therefore care should be taken in selecting TREC topics sets for various experimental purposes.

The topics are usually automatically transformed into a machine version (system query) for the evaluation process. Some of these transformations include: stopword removing, stemming, construction of Boolean expressions, etc. The TREC designers create topics reflecting a user need statement rather than more traditional requests. Three main ideas were involved in this decision: (a) allow a wide range of query construction methods by keeping the topic distinct from the query, (b) the ability to increase the amount of information available about each topic, (c) the recognition that any future use of the test collection would need as much detailed information about the topics as possible to allow different types of experiments [156].

An example of an information request from TREC-8 is illustrated in Figure 2.20.

Table 2.5: TREC collection statistics. Stopwords are not removed and no stemming is performed.

Source	Size (Mb)	Nr. of docs	Median w/d[a]	Mean w/d
Disk 1				
Wall Street Journal, 1987-1989 (WSJ)	267	98.732	245	434,0
Associated Press newswire, 1989 (AP)	254	84.678	446	473,9
Computer Selects articles, Ziff-Davis (ZIFF)	242	75.180	200	473,0
Federal Register, 1989 (FR)	260	25.960	391	1.315,9
Abstracts of U.S. Department of Energy publications (DOE)	184	226.087	111	120.4
Disk 2				
Wall Street journal, 1990-1992	242	74.520	301	508,4
Associated Press newswire, 1988	237	79.919	438	468,7
Computer Selects articles, Ziff-Davis	175	56.920	182	452,9
Federal Register, 1988	209	19.860	396	1.378,1
Disk 3				
San Jose Mercury News, 1991 (SJM)	287	90.257	379	453,0
Associated Press newswire, 1990	237	78.321	451	478,4
Computer Selects articles, Ziff-Davis	345	161.021	122	295,4
U.S. patents, 1993	243	6.711	4.445	5.391,0
Disk 4				
Financial Times, 1991-1994 (FT)	564	210.158	316	412,7
Federal Register, 1994 (FR)	395	55.630	588	644,7
Congressional Record, 1993 (CR)	235	27.922	288	1.373,5
Disk 5				
Foreign Broadcast Information Service (FBIS)	470	130.471	322	543,6
Los Angeles Times, 1989-1990 (LA)	475	131.896	351	526,5
Disk 6				
Foreign Broadcast Information Service (FBIS)	490	120.653	348	581,3
Los Angeles Times, 1994 (LA)	475	131.896	351	526,5

[a] words/document

2.10 Information Retrieval Evaluation 57

```
<top>
<num> Number: 401
<title> foreign minorities, Germany
<desc> Description:
What language and cultural differences impede the integration
of foreign minorities in Germany?
<narr> Narrative:
A relevant document will focus on the causes of the lack of
integration in a significant way; that is, the mere mention of
immigration difficulties is not relevant. Documents that discuss
immigration problems unrelated to Germany are also not relevant.
</top>
```

Figure 2.20: A topic example of the TREC-8 collection.

The Relevance Judgements

One of the most critical elements in a test collection are the relevance judgements. For each topic, it is necessary to compile a list of relevant documents; this list needs to be as comprehensive as possible. In TREC, three possible methods for finding the relevant documents could have been used. The first and impracticable method could be a full relevance judgement over a million documents for each topic, resulting in over a hundred million judgments. As a second approach, a random sample of documents could have been taken, with relevance judgments done on the sample only. The problem with this approach is that a random sample that is large enough to find on the order of one hundred relevant documents per topic is a very large random sample, and is likely to result in insufficient numbers of relevant documents. The third method, known as the pooling method, makes relevance judgements based on the sample of document selected by various participating systems. The pooling method was recommended in 1975 to the British Library for building a very large test collection, and was adopted by TREC to build the collection [78].

To construct the pool, the following was done:

- For each topic within a set of results, the top x-ranked documents were selected for input to the pool.

- These results were merged across all systems and sorted by document numbers, and then duplicate documents were removed.

The merged list of results was then shown to the human assessors, with each topic being judged by a single assessor to ensure the best consistency of judgements. Each topic pool was sorted by document number so that the assessor could not tell if a document was highly ranked by some system or how many systems (or which systems) retrieved that document.

The TREC-8 Collection

In our experiments, we use the document collection of the TREC-8 conference, consisting of the Disks 4 and 5 from Table 2.5.

```
<DOC>
<DOCNO>FT911-3</DOCNO>
<PROFILE>_AN-BEOA7AAIFT</PROFILE>
<DATE>910514</DATE>
<HEADLINE>
FT  14 MAY 91 / International Company News:
Contigas plans DM900m east German project
</HEADLINE>
<BYLINE>By DAVID GOODHART</BYLINE>
<DATELINE>BONN</DATELINE>
<TEXT>
CONTIGAS, the German gas group 81 per cent owned
by the utility Bayernwerk, said yesterday that it
intends to invest DM900m (Dollars 522m) in the next
four years to build a new gas distribution system
in the east German state of Thuringia. ...
</TEXT>
<PUB>The Financial Times</PUB>
<PAGE>International Page 20</PAGE>
</DOC>
```

Figure 2.21: A document extract from the *Financial Times* (TREC-8).

Like most of the traditional retrieval collections, there are three distinct parts in TREC-8: the documents, the topics, and the relevance judgements. The documents are tagged using SGML to allow easy parsing (see Fig. 2.21). The philosophy in the formatting at NIST is to leave the data as close to the original as possible. No attempt is made to correct spelling errors, sentences fragments, strange formatting around tables, or similar faults.

The title field of the topics consists of up to three words that best describe the topic, and the description field is a one sentence description of the topic area containing all of the words of the title field. The narrative gives a concise description of what makes a document relevant.

Ad hoc topics have been constructed by the same person who performed the relevance assessments for that topic (called assessor).

2.11   Information Retrieval Software

In this section, software modules used and/or developed in the context of the thesis are described. The first module is a graphical application developed for the analysis of term distributions in virtual documents. It implements the mathematical functions for the Fourier series and the orthogonal polynomials (Legendre and Laguerre). The module was written in Java and permitted us to study the characteristics of the different term position representations and to evaluate the performance of the models.

The Lucene and the Terrier libraries are the base of our evaluation framework. We started using Lucene to evaluate the performance of our statistical model and to obtain some graphical representations of the ranking. Later, we changed to Terrier where specific

2.11 Information Retrieval Software 59

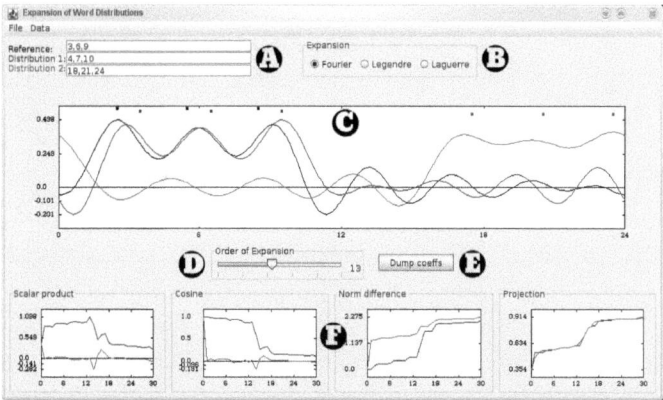

Figure 2.22: The interface of the Expansion Analyzer represents a virtual document containing three arbitrary set of terms and permits a graphical analysis of the proposed term position models.

classes for the TREC evaluation are implemented.

2.11.1 The Expansion Analyzer

With the aim of understanding the properties and behaviour of the different term positions models, the Expansion Analyzer, a Java module that emulates a "virtual document" and the position of three arbitrary group of terms was developed. This software provides a graphical view of the term position models and permits us to analyze the different mathematical operators used to compare the proposed term distribution functions.

The program interface (Figure 2.22) consists of two main groups of components: the Input Controls and the Analysis Windows:

The Input Controls

As shown in Figure 2.22, the Input Controls help the user to set the parameters of the test environment. They consist of three input fields (A), three check-boxes (B) and one slider (D). The input fields in (A) define the positions of three arbitrary term sets: the *Reference* (black), *Distribution 1* (blue), and *Distribution 2* (red). The selected check-box in (B) define the mathematical model (expansion) used to calculate the term position functions, and the slider (D) set the order of the selected expansion.

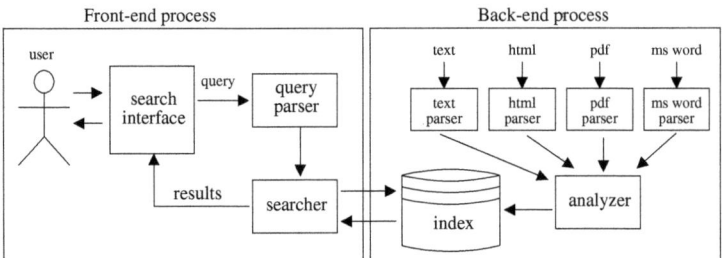

Figure 2.23: Lucene Structure.

Functions Viewers

The Functions viewers are a set of windows reproducing graphically the characteristics of the test environment defined through the Input Controls. The main viewer (C) describes the form of the term position functions in the virtual document, and the group of windows in (F) depicts four different mathematical operators applied to the input functions in the form:

- $Operator(Reference, Distribution_1)$ (blue curve), and

- $Operator(Reference, Distribution_2)$ (red curve).

The implemented operators are, from left to right: (a) the scalar product, (b) The cosine of the corresponding coefficient vectors, (c) the norm difference, and (d) the projection.

Finally, using the Button (E) one can dump the expansion coefficients of the current configuration to confirm the accuracy of the calculated coefficients.

With the help of this module it was possible to determine the most suitable configuration applied in the experimental phase.

2.11.2 Apache Lucene

Apache Lucene is a popular scalable IR library written in Java. It is a technology suitable for nearly any application that requires full-text search, especially cross-platform. Lucene is a member of the popular Apache Jakarta family of projects, licensed under the liberal Apache Software License [63].

Lucene provides a core API for indexing and search tasks that can be easily integrated in existing applications. Figure 2.23 shows the indexing architecture of Lucene. Lucene uses different parsers for different types of documents. Take HTML documents, for example – an HTML parser does some pre-processing, such as filtering the HTML tags and so on. The HTML parser outputs the text content, and then the Lucene Analyzer extracts tokens and related information, such as token frequency, from the text content. The Lucene Analyzer then writes the tokens and related information into the index files of Lucene.

2.12 Summary

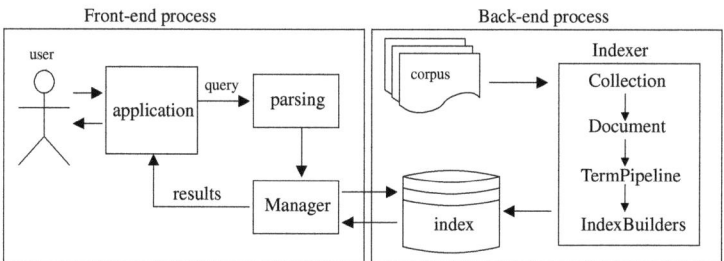

Figure 2.24: Terrier Structure.

2.11.3 Terabyte Retriever - Terrier

Terrier is a search engine that implements state-of-the-art indexing and retrieval functions providing a platform for the rapid development of large-scale retrieval applications [106].

Terrier is written in Java, and can be used for Web and Enterprise search, Desktop, Intranet and Vertical search engines, as well as developing and evaluating novel large-scale text information retrieval techniques and applications.

The open source version of Terrier provides a platform for research and experimentation in text retrieval, supporting commonly used TREC research collections (e.g. TREC CDs 1-5, WT2G, WT10G, GOV, GOV2, Blogs06).

Terrier implements two main applications: (a) Trec Terrier: an application that enables indexing and querying of TREC collections, and (b) Desktop Terrier: for the indexing and retrieval of local user content.

As shown in the Figure 2.24, Terrier has a similar indexing and retrieval structure as Lucene and also is an Open Source project (Mozilla Public Licence).

2.12 Summary

In this chapter, the basic concepts of information retrieval (IR) were examined. Starting with a brief historical review, we explored the main components of an modern information retrieval system.

Some key concepts, such as information need, document, similarity, and index were analyzed. Classical and alternative IR models were also reviewed, including a section with the most important utilities and methods to enhance retrieval, developed in the last years.

Finally, the tools used by the IR community to evaluate different algorithms and strategies were examined, they included standard document collections and some open source software platforms.

3
Related Work

3.1 Introduction

In this chapter, the most relevant work from the IR research community in relation with this thesis will be described.

Some approaches considering contextual information for improving search results will be analyzed, including a revision of the models incorporating term proximity information in the IR process.

Finally, one of the first approaches using functions to represent positional information will be analyzed in detail.

3.2 General Approaches Using Contextual Information

As mentioned in the introductory sections, the context in which information needs are determined plays a fundamental role in the development of methods to improve the information retrieval process.

Contextual information can be obtained in two ways: by the text surrounding the search terms in the document corpus, or by the context delivered by the user (i.e. *personalization*) [73]. There are approaches that utilize the query history of users [140] or the text surrounding the query [48, 118] to build augmented queries (i.e. *query expansion*) for improving the performance of interactive retrieval systems.

Relevance feedback is the most popular *query expansion* strategy [41, 18]. Here, the expanded terms are typically extracted from the retrieved documents and judged as relevant in a previous retrieval iteration. As demonstrated in several experimental studies, relevance feedback systems are quite effective [124, 19]. However, the browsing process required to determine the relevance of a document has been widely recognized as a significant limitation by the information retrieval research community.

To overcome the intervention of the user in the relevance feedback process, two basic types of strategies have been proposed: *automatic global analysis* and *automatic local analysis*. In automatic global analysis, all documents of the collection are used to determine a *thesaurus*-like structure, defining term-to-term relationships within the document corpus. In general, global analysis techniques are limited to small database applications, where doubtful improvements have been observed [6]. In automatic local analysis, the system is able to estimate the relevance of the first retrieved documents without user intervention. The main idea is to consider the *top-n* initially retrieved documents as relevant, and to use statistical heuristics to identify query related terms [43, 165]. *Noise* and *multiple topics* are two major negative factors for expansion term selection [169]. To deal with these problems, traditional clustering methods have been proposed [69]. The experiments performed by Fan et al. [45] confirm that highly-tuned ranking offers more high-quality documents at the top of the hit list.

In general, it is difficult to determine correlated terms inside a document, because these terms do not necessarily co-occur very frequently with the original query terms if the document is considered as a whole. In fact, it is common to have unrelated terms co-occurring with query terms very frequently [146]. To address this problem, page segmentation strategies have been suggested [169, 23]. They provide a better document partitioning at the semantic level and reduce the probability to carry irrelevant terms to the query expansion process. In general, an important drawback of automatic local analysis strategies is the considerable amount of computation, which represents a substantial problem for interactive systems [92].

An approach that applies term positional data in retrieval feedback is the work of Attar and Fraenkel [7]. They propose different models to generate clusters of terms related to a query (searchonyms) and use these clusters in a local feedback process. In their experiments with English and Hebrew documents, they confirm that metrical methods based on functions of the distance between terms are superior to methods based merely on weighted co-occurrences of terms.

Katz [81] has analyzed the distribution of content-bearing terms in technical documents. Important concepts supporting word occurrence models, such as *inter-/within-document* relationships, *topicality* and *burstiness* are proposed. The author concentrates on the modeling of the *inter-document* distributions of content words, while our work focuses on the *within-document* relationships applied to relevance evaluation in the information retrieval process. Another interesting approach on this subject has been proposed by Fernández et al. [47], where words appearing in a similar syntactic context are used for lexical and syntactic disambiguation in a natural language parsing process.

One of the first approaches applying Fourier analysis to term distributions in documents is Fourier Domain Scoring (FDS), proposed by Park et al. [116]. FDS performs a separate magnitude and phase analysis of term position signals to produce an optimized ranking. It creates an index based on page segmentation, storing term frequency and approximated positions in the document. FDS processes the indexed data using the *Discrete Fourier Transform* to perform the corresponding spectral analysis. The approaches proposed in this thesis, on the other hand, represent the term signal information (series coefficients) directly as an n-dimensional vector using the corresponding analytic transform, thus permitting an immediate and simple term comparison process.

In the next two sections, two aspects closely related to the basic ideas of the proposed approach are analyzed: the term proximity models and the retrieval model based on Fourier analysis.

3.3 Term Proximity

The use of term proximity in IR is not really new. Numerous retrieval applications have implemented tools to define term proximity at the query formulation level [5, 67]. However, despite their benefits confirmed by professional searchers, these tools are less effective and rarely utilized by common searchers. The reason is that proximity implementation and syntax is possibly the worse parts of many search interfaces. It is neither easy to learn nor to use. Consistency, both within one system and between systems is scarce, it requires considerable memorization and the user help is poor [83]. Some studies [82] confirm that even a two-term proximity-search offers several hundred possibilities if all options are considered. This suggests either that systems should offer only a restricted set of options, or that some means of automating the application of the options can be devised, so that proximity specifications are automatically adjusted by the system to become productive [83].

According to these challenges, many approaches have proposed different heuristics to incorporate term positional information in the retrieval process. Some of them define new ranking models based on term proximity heuristics and others use this positional information to improve the performance of existing retrieval methods. In the next section, we examine some of these approaches.

3.3.1 Shortest-Substring Model

The Shortest-Substring approach [28] is a passage retrieval technique that incorporates Boolean operators. The result of a search is a set of *extents* (passages) over a single string that represents the whole collection. As expressed in the model's name, the ranking algorithm is based on the smallest extents that satisfy the query.

Notation

For search and retrieval purpose the text is viewed as a string of symbols $C_1, \ldots, C_N$ drawn from a *text alphabet* Σ.

The short poem [149] in Figure 3.1 is used as a recurring example. Here, a reasonable choice for the text alphabet consists of the English words appearing in the text with all characters mapped to lowercase.

$\Sigma = \{$a, am, an, and, as, at, autumn, bells, can, clang, clock, cold, crowed, cry, day,... $\}$

In the example, the superscripts indicate positions in the text sequence. An index function $\mathscr{I}$ maps each symbol in the text alphabet to the set of positions in the database string where the symbol appears ($\mathscr{I} : \Sigma \to 2^{\{1...N\}}$).. In the example, we have

$$\mathscr{I}(\text{``bells''}) = \{1, 20, 50, 62, 65, 68\} \tag{3.1}$$

3 Related Work

Bells^1

At^2 *six*^{3} *o'*^{4} *clock*^{5} *of*^{6} *an*^{7} *autumn*^{8} *dusk*^{9}
With^{10} *the*^{11} *sky*^{12} *in*^{13} *the*^{14} *west*^{15} *a*^{16} *rusty*^{17} *red*,^{18}
The^{19} *bells*^{20} *of*^{21} *the*^{22} *mission*^{23} *down*^{24} *in*^{25} *the*^{26} *valley*^{27}
Cry^{28} *out*^{29} *that*^{30} *the*^{31} *day*^{32} *is*^{33} *dead*.^{34}

The^{35} *first*^{36} *star*^{37} *pricks*^{38} *as*^{39} *sharp*^{40} *as*^{41} *steel*^{42}
Why^{43} *am*^{44} *I*^{45} *suddenly*^{46} *so*^{47} *cold*?^{48}
Three^{49} *bells*,^{50} *each*^{51} *with*^{52} *a*^{53} *separate*^{54} *sound*^{55}
Clang^{56} *in*^{57} *the*^{58} *valley*,^{59} *wearily*^{60} *tolled*.^{61}

Bells^{62} *in*^{63} *Venice*,^{64} *bells*^{65} *at*^{66} *sea*,^{67}
Bells^{68} *in*^{69} *the*^{70} *valley*^{71} *heavy*^{72} *and*^{73} *slow*^{74}
There^{75} *is*^{76} *no*^{77} *place*^{78} *over*^{79} *the*^{80} *crowded*^{81} *world*^{82}
Where^{83} *I*^{84} *can*^{85} *forget*^{86} *that*^{87} *the*^{88} *days*^{89} *go*.^{90}

(*Sara*^{91} *Teasdale*^{92})

Figure 3.1: Example text. Superscripts indicate word positions.

The document boundaries are in this case ignored and multiple documents are treated as if concatenated into a single long document.

Model

The result of the search is represented as a set of ranges or *extents* over the string that forms the database. Each extent is of the form (p, q), where p is the start position of the extent, while q is the end position of the extend.

An extent (p, q) *overlaps* an extent (p', q') if either $p' \leq p \leq q'$ or $p' \leq q \leq q'$ but not both. An extent (p, q) is *nested* in an extent (p', q') if $(p, q) \neq (p', q')$ and $p' \leq p \leq q \leq q'$. If $a = (p, q)$ and $b = (p', q')$ are extents, the notation $a \sqsubset b$ indicates that a nests in b; the notation $a \sqsubseteq b$ indicates that a is *contained* in b– that either a and b are equal or that a nests in b. Extents form a partial order in $\sqsubseteq$.

A solution to a query is a set of extents. Over the database string $C_1 \ldots C_N$, the range of the index function $\mathscr{I}$ is limited to N positions. However, there are $O(N^2)$ extents over this same range–every (p, q) such $1 \leq p \leq q \leq N$. Depending on the query, any of these $O(N^2)$ extents could be a candidate for inclusion in the query's solution set. For example, given a query for a particular word (e.g., "bells") every extent that overlaps an occurrence of the word might reasonably be viewed as a potential member of the solution set, including the extent $(1, N)$ corresponding to the entire database. Similarly, if a query consists of the conjunction of two terms (e.g., "bells" AND "valley") every extent that contains both terms might be considered as a potential solution extent.

Many of these extents overlap and nest. In order to reduce the number of extents that

3.3 Term Proximity

result from the search, nested solution extents are not allowed. However solution extents are permitted to overlap. This approach of eliminating nested extents is called the *shortest-substring search model*: the resulting set is called a *generalized concordance list*.

Generalized Concordance List. A set of non-nesting extents is referred to as a *generalized concordance list*, or simply *GC-list*. In the case of a search for a single word that occurs once in the database, the corresponding generalized concordance list contains a single extent of unit length that begins and ends at the word's position. The index function $\mathscr{I}$ may be viewed as mapping symbols in the index alphabet onto GC-lists: the elements of the results are interpreted as extents that begin and end at a single position. For example,

$$\mathscr{I}(\text{``bells''}) = \{(1,1),(20,20),(50,50),(62,62),(65,65),(68,68)\}.$$

By viewing the index function as producing extents, it may be augmented to encompass phrase matching. For example,

$$\mathscr{I}(\text{``the valley''}) = \{(26,26),(58,59),(70,71)\}.$$

Similar extensions may be used to support truncation and stemming.

The reduction of a set of extents S to a generalized concordance list may be formalized as a function (S):

$$\mathscr{G}(S) = \{a | a \in S \text{ and } \nexists\, b \in S \text{ such that } b \sqsubset a\}. \qquad (3.2)$$

A set S of extents is a GC-list if and only if

$$S = \mathscr{G}(S) \qquad (3.3)$$

Boolean Operators. Given a query Q, an extent (p,q) *satisfies* Q if the substring of the database beginning at position p and ending at q would match the query if the substring was treated as a document under the standard set-based Boolean model. More precisely,

1. an extent (p,q) satisfies a query Q_1 AND Q_2 if the extent satisfies Q_1 and satisfies Q_2.

2. an extent (p,q) satisfies a query Q_1 OR Q_2 if the extent satisfies Q_1 or satisfies Q_2.

3. an extent (p,q) satisfies a term T if the term occurs in the interval of text corresponding to the extent.

To operators, "one of" ($\triangledown$), corresponding to OR, and "both of" ($\triangle$), corresponding to AND, are defined to effect this shortest-substring model of Boolean search.

$$A \triangledown B = \mathscr{G}(\{c | \exists a \in A \text{ such that } a \sqsubseteq c \text{ or } \exists b \in B \text{ such that } b \sqsubseteq c\}) \qquad (3.4)$$

$$A \triangle B = \mathscr{G}(\{c | \exists a \in A \text{ such that } a \sqsubseteq c \text{ and } \exists b \in B \text{ such that } b \sqsubseteq c\}) \qquad (3.5)$$

Under the shortest-substring model the query

"bells" AND ("sky" OR "valley")

is interpreted as

$$\mathscr{G}(\text{``bells''}) \triangle (\mathscr{G}(\text{``sky''}) \triangledown \mathscr{G}(\text{``valley''}))$$

which specifies the set of extents

$$\{(1,12),(12,20),(20,27),(27,50),(50,59),(59,62),(68,71)\}$$

over the text in Figure 3.1. The extents (35,61), (62,71), (1,90) and many others all satisfy the query, but are eliminated by the shortest-substring rule.

Solution Sets. The algorithm may be viewed as a generalization of the "index-skipping" algorithms used to optimize the evaluation of Boolean queries under the standard set-based model [152, 100].

The algorithm is based on two *access functions* defined over the database string $C_1 \ldots C_N$. The values computed by the access functions are defined as follows:

$$r(S,k) = \begin{cases} q & \text{if } \exists (p,q) \in S \text{ such that } k \leq p \\ & \text{and } \not\exists (p',q') \in S \text{ such that } q' < q \text{ and } k \leq p' \\ N+1 & \text{if } \not\exists (p,q) \in S \text{ such that } k \leq p \end{cases} \quad (3.6)$$

$$l(S,k) = \begin{cases} p & \text{if } \exists (p,q) \in S \text{ such that } k \geq p \\ & \text{and } \not\exists (p',q') \in S \text{ such that } q' > q \text{ and } k \geq p' \\ 0 & \text{if } \not\exists (p,q) \in S \text{ such that } k \geq p \end{cases} \quad (3.7)$$

where S is a GC-list, while k is a position in the database string. In these definitions, the extent $(0,0)$ and $(N+1, N+1)$ essentially act as "end of file" markers for the GC-lists.

Informally, the function $r(S,k)$ returns the end position of the first extent in S that starts at or after the position k, and $l(S,k)$ returns the start position of the last extent in S that ends at or before position k. Over the test in Figure 3.1, the solution to $\mathscr{I}(\text{``bells''})$ is the set of extents

$$S = \{(1,1),(20,20),(50,50),(62,62),(65,65),(68,68)\}.$$

Over the set, $r(S,18) = 20$, $l(S,64) = 62$, and $r(S,69) = N+1 = 93$.

These access functions are extended from CG-lists to queries in the following way: if Q is a query, and S is the solution set, then $r(Q,k) = r(S,k)$ and $l(Q,k) = l(S,k)$

For the $\triangledown$ and $\triangle$ operations, implementation of the access functions is defined by the following equations:

$$\begin{aligned} r(A \triangle B, k) &= \max(r(A,k), r(B,k)), \\ r(A \triangledown B, k) &= \min(r(A,k), r(B,k)), \\ l(A \triangle B, k) &= \min(l(A,k), l(B,k)), \text{ and} \\ l(A \triangledown B, k) &= \max(l(A,k), l(B,k)). \end{aligned} \quad (3.8)$$

3.3 Term Proximity

The two access functions r and l may be used in concert to compute the solution set for a query Q. Thus, the third access function τ is defined which indexes into a GC-list and returns a complete extent, rather than a start or end position. If S is a GC-list, the value returned by the access function over the database string $C_1 \ldots C_N$ is defined as follows:

$$\tau(S,k) = \begin{cases} (p,q) & \text{if } \exists (p,q) \in S \text{ such that } k \leq p \\ & \text{and } \not\exists (p',q') \in S \text{ such that } q' < q \text{ and } k \leq p' \\ (N+1, N+1) & \not\exists (p,q) \in S \text{ such that } k \leq p \end{cases} \quad (3.9)$$

The access function τ returns the first extent from S that ends at or after position k. Once again, the access function is extended from GC-list to queries, by defining $\tau(Q,k) = \tau(S,k)$, where S is the solution set for query Q. The relationship between the three functions is defined as follows: Let S be a GC-list. Let $v = r(S,k)$. If $v \neq N+1$; let $u = l(S,v)$; otherwise, let $u = N+1$.

$$\tau(S,k) = (u,v) \quad (3.10)$$

where S is a GC-list, $v = r(S,k)$, and

$$u = \begin{cases} l(S,v) & \text{if } v \neq N+1 \\ N+1 & \text{otherwise.} \end{cases}$$

Ranking

Under the shortest-substring search model, the result of a query is the set of shortest extents that satisfy the specified Boolean predicate. Each extent in the solution set represents an interval in the text. Each document in the database may contain one or more of the solution intervals. Ranking is based on two assumptions:

Assumption A: The shorter a solution extent, the greater the likelihood that an interval of text containing the extent is relevant.

Assumption B: The more solution extents contained within a document, the greater the likelihood that the document is relevant.

The first assumption suggests a basis for ranking individual solution extents; the second suggest a basis for ranking documents in terms of the solution extents contained within them. Both assumptions are superficially reasonable.

Consistent with Assumption B, a score for a document might be obtained by summing individual scores for the solution extents contained within it. Consistent to Assumption A, the score for an extent (p,q) might be based on the inverse of its length $q - p - 1$:

$$Score\,of\,(p,q) \propto \left(\frac{1}{q-p-1}\right)^{\alpha}, \quad (3.11)$$

with a *falloff* parameter $\alpha > 0$.

During preliminary trials of the technique it was observed that if the length of an extent was below a threshold of a dozen or so words, Assumption A no longer appeared to hold as strongly and all extends appeared to be a more or less equally good indicator of likely relevance. As a result, a *cutoff* parameter $\mathcal{K} > 0$ was added to the scoring function:

$$I(p,q) = \begin{cases} \left(\frac{\mathcal{K}}{q-p-1}\right)^\alpha & \text{if } q - p + 1 \geq \mathcal{K} \\ 1 & \text{if } q - p + 1 \leq \mathcal{K} \end{cases} \quad (3.12)$$

For any extent (p, q), $I(p, q) > 0$. If solution extents $(p_1, q_1), \ldots, (p_N, q_N)$ are contained in a document, the score for the document is

$$\sum_{i=1}^{N} I(p_i, q_i). \quad (3.13)$$

Shortest-substrings retrieval computes the set of solutions extents for a specified query. The ranking procedure then filters this set of extents against a list of extents representing document boundaries before computing the final scores and generating the ranking. Evaluation of a query proceeds in five steps:

1. Determine the set of solutions extents

2. For each solution extent, either determine the document extent that contains it, or if it overlaps document boundaries, eliminate it.

3. For each document extent containing one or more solution extents, calculate its score.

4. Sort the document extents by score.

5. For the top-ranking documents, translate the document extents into external identifiers.

Using the text of the poem from Figure 3.1 and the query:

"bells" AND ("sky" OR "valley")

we obtain the set of extents

$$\{(1, 12), (12, 20), (20, 27), (27, 50), (50, 59), (59, 62), (68, 71)\}.$$

Treating each of the three verses as a separate document eliminates $(27, 50)$ and $(59, 62)$, which overlap verses, and $(1, 12)$, which overlaps the title. Scoring each verse separately, and for the purpose of this example using a cutoff of $\mathcal{K} = 4$ and a falloff of $\alpha = 1$, gives a score for each verse as follows:

$$\begin{aligned} \text{first} &: I(12, 20) + I(20, 27) \approx 0.44 + 0.50 = 0.94 \\ \text{second} &: I(50, 59) = 0.40 \\ \text{third} &: I(68, 71) = 1.00 \end{aligned}$$

The third verse outscores the first, but contains fewer solution extends. Despite the many substrings that satisfy the query, few contribute to the scores.

3.3 Term Proximity

Evaluation

Experiments using the the TREC-4 collection demonstrated that the shortest-substring ranking slightly outperforms the Okapi ranking, but this performance difference is statistically not significant.

3.3.2 Fuzzy Proximity Model

Based on the idea that the closer the query terms are in the document, the more relevant this document is, Beigbeder et al. [11] estimated the relevance of a document to a query computing the fuzzy proximity degree of the query terms occurrences in such document. This model is able to deal with Boolean queries, but contrary to the traditional extensions of the basic Boolean model, it does not explicitly use a proximity operator. The fuzzy term proximity is controlled with an influence function. Given a query term and a document, the influence function associates to each position in the text a value dependant on the distance of the nearest occurrence of this query term. To model proximity, this function is decreasing with distance where different forms of functions with limited support can be used: triangular, Gaussian, etc. Once the fuzzy proximity for each query term are calculated, the document score is computed applying the traditional methods of fuzzy IR models.

Notation

Let T the set of terms appearing in the documents of a collection C, a document is represented (in the most basic Boolean model) as a set of terms where $d \in \{0,1\}^T$. This expression can be easily extended to the one used in the Boolean models based on the fuzzy set theory [99], where $d \in [0,1]^T$. Thus, a document d is a function $d : T \to [0,1]$ and $d(t)$ is the membership degree of the document d to the term t considered as fuzzy set. In the vector model context, $d(t)$ is usually called the weight of the term t within the document d, and usually written $w_{d,t}$. Note that in the vector model the range of the d is likely to be $\mathbb{R}^+$ (and even $\mathbb{R}$), rather than the interval $[0,1]$.

The collection model is a set of documents, so C is a collection iff: $C \subset \{0,1\}^T$ for the basic Boolean model, or $C \subset [0,1]^T$ for any fuzzy model, or $C \subset \mathbb{R}^T$ for the other extended Boolean models and the vector space model.

Given these definitions and notations, one can consider the family of functions $(\mu_t)_{t \in T}$ defined by $\mu_t(d) = d(t)$. When C is a subset of $\{0,1\}^T$, μ_t is the characteristic function of the set of documents containing at least one occurrence of the term t. When C is a subset of $[0,1]^T$, μ_t is the membership degree function of the *fuzzy* set of documents containing the term t.

Model

The proposed model represents the documents considering their term positions and it is based on a fuzzy proximity function between each position in the document text and the query. This fuzzy proximity function is assumed up over $\mathbb{Z}$ to score the document.

3 Related Work

Let $d^{-1}(t)$ be the set of the positions in the document d where the term t appears, the elements in d satisfying the following condition: $\exists\, l \in \mathbb{N},\, d^{-1}(T) = [0, l-1]$. Moreover, $d^{-1}(T)$ is the set of positions of actual terms appear.

Figure 3.2 shows an example of a collection C of four documents (d_0 to d_3) where only two different elements of T, A and B, are represented. From this example: $d_3(2) = A$, $d_3(3) = A$, and $d_3^{-1}(A) = \{2, 3\}$.

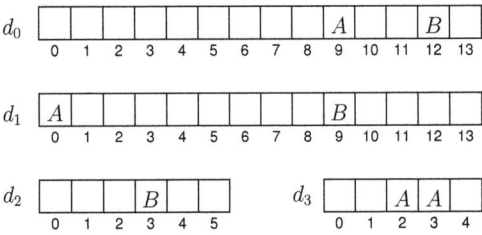

Figure 3.2: Example of a collection C containing the documents d_1, d_2, d_3 and d_4. A and B are some elements of T.

Local Term Proximity. Within the basic Boolean model, it is easy to define a NEAR operator at the leaf level. For instance, the query A NEAR 5 B is evaluated to true if there exists one occurrence of the term A and one occurrence of the term B with less than five other words between them. This is a *binary* proximity value, and this notion will be in this approach *fuzzyfied* by taking into account the number of words between the two term occurrences.

In fact, a new notion of proximity will be defined, does not consider the proximity between two terms in the text, but between a position in the text and one term. Formally, we define the proximity function $\mu_t^d : \mathbb{Z} \to [0, 1]$ with

$$\mu_t^d(x) = \max_{i \in d^{-1}(t)} (\max(\frac{k - |x - i|}{k}, 0)), \tag{3.14}$$

where k is some integral parameter which controls to which extend one term occurrence spreads its influence.

In the following examples, the value $k = 4$ is used. The function μ_t^d reaches its maximum (the value 1) where the term t appears and it decreases with a constant slope down to zero on each sides of this maximum. In other words, this function has a triangular shape at each occurrence of the term t. Figure 3.3 shows $(\mu_A^d)_{d \in C}$ and $(\mu_B^d)_{d \in C}$ for the collection C shown in Figure 3.2.

This function can be interpreted as the membership degree of any text position x in the document d to the fuzzy set (d, t).

3.3 Term Proximity

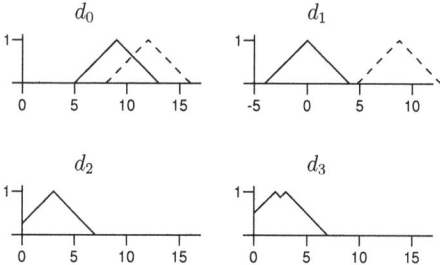

Figure 3.3: The functions $(\mu_A^d)_{d \in C}$ plotted with plain lines and $(\mu_B^d)_{d \in C}$ plotted with dashed lines for the collection C and $k = 4$.

Local Query Proximity. Now, a local proximity function between a text position and a query will be defined. The implemented query model is that of the Boolean model. The functions μ_t^d defined in the previous section are associated to the leaves of the query tree. Defining the local proximity at a given OR node as

$$\mu_{(\mathrm{OR},(q_i)_i)} = \max_i \mu_{q_i}, \qquad (3.15)$$

and likewise

$$\mu_{(\mathrm{AND},(q_i)_i)} = \min_i \mu_{q_i}, \qquad (3.16)$$

where $(q_i)_i$ is a finite subset of the query set Q. This are the same scoring formulas of the basic Boolean model, but in this case the functions are defined over $\mathbb{Z}$ [11].

The recursive application of the previous formula up to the root q leads to a local proximity function between a document and the query q. This proximity means that the closer the terms requested by the AND operators are, the higher the value of the function is. Moreover, this value is augmented by the closest of the terms requested by an OR operator. This function can be interpreted as the membership degree of any text position x in the document d to the fuzzy set (d, q).

Figure 3.4 and Figure 3.5 plot $\mu_{A\ \mathrm{OR}\ B}^d$ and $\mu_{A\ \mathrm{AND}\ B}^d$ (respectively) for the documents of the collection C of Figure 3.2. Although the the document d_1 contains both terms A and B, the function $\mu_{A\ \mathrm{AND}\ B}^{d_1}$ is uniformly zero, because the occurrences of A and B in d_1 are too distant.

Ranking

One of the first similarity measures between a document and a query was the *coordination level* [94]. It operates by counting the number of occurrences of the query terms. The idea, which was carried out further in the vector model, is to accumulate pieces of evidence for relevance. This similarity measure c defined in this model also may be interpreted as the

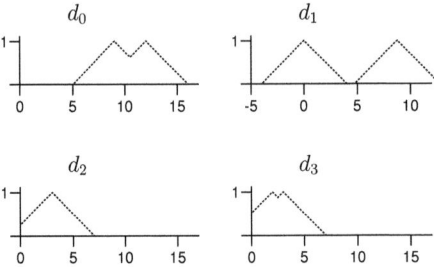

Figure 3.4: $\mu^d_{A \text{ OR } B}$ for the collection C of Figure 3.2.

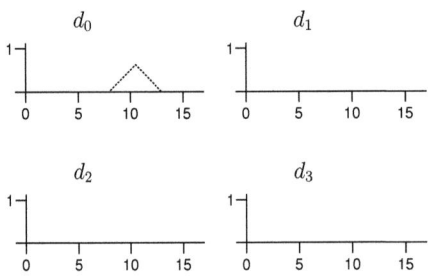

Figure 3.5: $\mu^d_{A \text{ AND } B}$ for the collection C of Figure 3.2.

number of elements of the set of positions in the text where one of the query terms appears

$$c(q,d) = |\cup_{t \in q} d^{-1}(t)|. \qquad (3.17)$$

As the sets given in the union are mutually disjoint, we have

$$c(q,d) = \sum_{t \in q} |d^{-1}(t)|, \qquad (3.18)$$

or

$$c(q,d) = \sum_{x \in \mathbb{Z}} \nu^d_q(x), \qquad (3.19)$$

with $\nu^d_q(x) = 1$ iff $d(x) \in q$ and $\nu^d_q(x) = 0$ otherwise. Note that in this case the query is a set of terms. Computing the relevance score with the coordination level method is not possible with Boolean queries. In the proposed model, the relevance score of a document d to the query q is defined by

$$s(q,d) = \sum_{x \in \mathbb{Z}} \mu^d_q(x). \qquad (3.20)$$

3.3 Term Proximity

According to the fuzzy set model, this is the fuzzy number of elements of the set of positions in the document d. Here, $x \mapsto \mu_q^d(x)$ represents the local proximity to the request for the document d while $x \mapsto \nu_q^d(x)$ represents the binary proximity to a (non fuzzy) set of terms.

The relevance score is a positive real number and the documents can be ranked according to their scores.

Evaluation

An evaluation using the TREC WT10g collection has demonstrated that the performance of the proposed method is comparable to the Okapi model [126].

Drawbacks

One problem not discussed in Beigbeder's papers is that simple queries based on the OR operator produce ranking scores that contradict the model hypothesis. For example, considering the query $q = \{A \text{ OR } B\}$ and the documents of Figure 3.2, one can observe that although the terms A and B are in the document d_0 closer than in the document d_1, the relevance score $s(q, d_0)$ is smaller than $s(q, d_1)$.

3.3.3 A Proximity Weighting Model

The work of Rasalofo and Savoy [117] suggests the use of proximity measurement in combination with the Okapi probabilistic model [126]. The authors intend to enhance the retrieval performance by applying a term-proximity scoring heuristic to the top documents returned by a keyword-based system. This approach is based on the assumption that if a document contains sentences having at least two query terms within them, the probability that this document will be relevant must be greater. Moreover, the closer are the query terms, the higher is the relevance probability.

To achieve this objective, the original query is expanded using keywords pairs extracted from the query's wording, assuming that the queries are short, the queries have more than one term, and the users will only write relevant terms.

Model

First, the set of all possible search keyword pairs is established. If the query wording consists of $q = (t_i, t_j, t_k)$, we obtain the following set S of term pairs: $\{(t_i, t_j), (t_i, t_k), (t_j, t_k)\}$, with the ordering of terms not being important. The term pair retrieval within a given document is performed by sequentially reading the query term positions, and for each instance the term pair (t_i, t_j) within a maximal distance of five (or having a maximal of four terms between the keyword pair), the term pair instance (tpi) weight is computed:

$$tpi(t_i, t_j) = \frac{1.0}{d(t_i, t_j)^2} \tag{3.21}$$

where $d/t_i, t_j)$ is the distance expressed in number of words between search term t_i and t_j.

The hypothesis is that the closer two search keywords appear together within a document, the higher is the weight attached to the occurrence of this term pair. Based on this formulation, the higher value is 1.0, corresponding to a distance of one (the terms are adjacent), and the lower value is 0.04 corresponding to a distance of 5. For example, based on the request "information retrieval", the resulting tpi of an occurrence of the same string "information retrieval" will be 1.0 while the tpi of "the retrieval of medical information" will be 0.11.

Of course, a given term pair may appear more than once in a document. Therefore, the weight attached to this given term pair (t_i, t_j) is evaluated by summing all the corresponding term pair instances tpi. In a manner similarly to the Okapi weighting scheme [126]:

$$w_d(t_i, t_j) = (k_l + 1) \cdot \frac{\sum_{occ(t_i,t_j)} tpi(t_i, t_j)}{K + \sum_{occ(t_i,t_j)} tpi(t_i, t_j)} \qquad (3.22)$$

where

$$K = k\left[(1-b) + b\frac{l}{avdl}\right]$$

l : is the document length,
$avdl$: is the average of the document length (set to 750)
b : is a constant (set to 0.9)
k : is a constant (set to 2)
k_l : is a constant (set to 1.2)

Ranking

Based on the *Retrieval Status Value (RSV)* proposed by Okapi, the contribution of all occurring query term pairs in a document ($TPRSV$) will be calculated. Given the request q and the document d, the $TPRSV$ value is defined as:

$$TPRSV(d,q) = \sum_{(t_i,t_j) \in S} w_d(t_i, t_j) \cdot \min(qw_i, qw_j) \qquad (3.23)$$

where S is the set of all query term pairs in q, qw_i and qw_j are the weights of the query terms t_i and t_j calculated according to

$$qw_i = \frac{qtf_i}{k_3 + qtf_i} \cdot \log\left(\frac{n - df_i}{df_i}\right) \qquad (3.24)$$

where

qtf_i : is the frequency of term t_i in the query,
df_i : is the number of documents in the collection containing the term t_i,
n : is the number of document included in the collection,
k_3 : is a constant (set to 1000)

Due to efficiency needs, the $TPRSV$ value is only calculated for the top 100 documents returned by the Okapi search model. The final retrieval status (ranking) for a given document d, denoted

$$RSV_{New}(d,q) = RSV_{Okapi}(d,q) + TPRSV(d,q) \qquad (3.25)$$

3.3 Term Proximity

This formulation accounts for both the original Okapi score (RSV_{Okapi}) and the proposed proximity scoring function ($TPRSV$). During this process no new document is retrieved, as it is performed on the top 100 documents retrieved by Okapi. Instead, the scores and therefore the ranks of documents containing at least one query term pair are improved based on the following assumption: The presence of query terms within a document would not always imply a match related to the true meaning of the request, whereas account for search keywords pairs using some distance constraint may reduce this error. Using this idea and for example in response to the request "operating system", a document containing the two terms close each other will be presented to the user before any other document having these two terms within two different paragraphs.

Evaluation

Experiments conducted on the TREC-8, TREC-9 and TREC-10 collections reveal that precision improvements obtained by the proximity measure are more noticeable after retrieving 5 documents, and in this case the overall performance is around $8, 2\%$. Such results would prove useful for those users looking at the top 5 or 10 documents returned.

3.3.4 Arbitrary Passage Retrieval

The term similarity concept is also related to passage retrieval [24, 80, 93, 131, 150], where documents are often pre-segmented into small passages, which are then taken as units for retrieval. Since matching a passage implies imposing a proximity constraint on the matched query terms, passage retrieval can also capture proximity at a coarse granularity level, though it is clear that proximity can only be captured in a limited way with this approach [147].

The passage retrieval methods discussed in Section 2.9.5 are defined before or during the indexing, which has several consequences. First, documents are partitioned into passages without consideration of individual queries. Second, when discourse passages such as paragraphs are used, long sections may be split into passages that are individually less informative, which is undesirable if the entire section is relevant to a given query. Third, the definition of a passage is subjective, and depends on document structure.

The effectiveness of the passages types mentioned before, varied and did not identify a clear winner.

Model

Kaszkiel and Zobel [80] proposed an alternative passage model. They define an *arbitrary passage* as any sequence of words of any length starting at any word in the document. The location and dimensions of the passages are delayed until the query is evaluated, so that the similarity of the highest-ranked sequence of words, from anywhere in the document, defines the passage to be retrieved; or in the case of document retrieval, determines the document's similarity. Two subclasses are defined,

- *Fixed-length passages*, where the length of the passage is set before query evaluation, and

- *Variable-length passages*, where passage can be of any length.

Fixed-length arbitrary passages do have one serious drawback: the cost of ranking passages is high and impractical. Experiments based on TREC collections demonstrate that retrieval based on fixed-length arbitrary passages was significantly better than document ranking, for both short and long queries. However, comparing document retrieval based on fixed-length passages and predefined passages, no significant differences were found.

The experiments of Kaszkiel and Zobel [80] have shown that, on the average, document retrieval using fixed-length passages is at least as effective as with predefined passages. However, they discovered that no particular length was superior. That is, for queries of the same type, one passage length worked best for some queries but not for others. A solution to the limitation of fixed-length arbitrary passages is to select a passage length most likely to suit the query. The best passage length can also depend on the document ranked. For instance, given a query, one could find two long documents, where in one the start of document or the abstract is relevant, and in the other a 400-word section is relevant. Adjusting the passage length to the type of text should result in improvement retrieval.

Therefore, a more flexible approach would be to extract passages of different lengths, and select the best one to represent each document. A variable-length passage is of any length that is determined by the best passage in a document, when the query is evaluated.

Ranking

Since documents are represented by passages of different lengths, variable-length passage ranking has to deal with two basic problems: first, how to discriminate between passages of different length in the same document; second, how to discriminate between passages of different length drawn from different documents.

In the absence of length normalization in the similarity measure, the longest passage for each document determines the rank of the document. This is undesirable because, as observed by fixed-length passages [80], effectiveness degrades with passages in excess of 450 words. To select a passage to represent a document, pivoted-cosine normalization can be used, which is restated here for variable-length passages:

$$W_p = (1 - slope) + slope \cdot \frac{p_{len}}{\Delta_{len}} \tag{3.26}$$

where $slope$ is set to 0.2 (which has shown to be effective in the context of predefined passage ranking), p_{len} is the length of fragment p in bytes, and $Delta_{len}$ is the average length of all fragments in the collection. This formula has been shown to be effective for predefined passage types and minimizes the fragility of ranking fragments of varying length. The overall similarity of passage p to a query q is:

$$\frac{sim(q,p)}{W_p} \tag{3.27}$$

3.3 Term Proximity 79

Formally, this is not applicable to variable-length passage ranking since it requires averages over all passages lengths in the collection, which is not meaningful in the context of variable-length passages. Singhal et al. [141] have argued that this length formulation is reasonably robust if Δ_{len} is set to an overall average, which in this case is the average passage length used (about 300 words). This approach is referred to as *Variable*. The similarity score for a document d to a query q is based on the best-scoring passage among twelve different lengths in the range of 50 to 600 words.

$$sim(q,d) = \max \left(\frac{sim(q,d,p_{50})}{W_{p,50}}, \frac{sim(q,d,p_{100})}{W_{p,100}}, \ldots, \frac{sim(q,d,p_{600})}{W_{p,600}} \right) \quad (3.28)$$

where $sim(q,d,p_{len})$ is the similarity of passage p of length len in document d to query q, based on the cosine measure. The value of $W_{p,len}$ is the pivoted-cosine normalisation component for passage p of length len.

Evaluation

The experiments executed by Kaszkiel et al.[80] show that the effectiveness improvements achieved by the use of passage are significant for databases for which the variability of document length is large, but for databases with uniform document length the improvement is smaller. The improvement obtained by passage ranking compared with whole-document ranking varied depending on the passage type, collection and query set, with the greatest improvement in average precision for passage ranking from 20% to 50%. For a text collection with uniform document lengths, the improvements did not exceed 7%.

Compared with the best predefined passage ranking, the effectiveness of variable-length arbitrary passage ranking is consistently improved.

Despite of the general improvements in effectiveness of passage-based ranking, no single passage type showed superior retrieval effectiveness across five different text collections and two query sets.

A Similar Approach

Variable-length arbitrary passage is similar to locality-based retrieval proposed by de Kretser and Moffat [38], where document boundaries are ignored and text is treated as a continuous sequence of words. The similarity scores for passages are according to how many query term occurrences appear near to each other. Shape, height, and spread of a function is used to calculate the contribution of query terms to text regions. High-scoring regions are identified and passages that contain them retrieved. In this approach, the length of the passage depends on a scoring function and the corresponding parameters are used to identify text regions. The parameters used in the function need to be adjusted for different collections and query sets, and no consistent results for any functions were reported [38].

Passage Retrieval in Relevance Feedback

The effectiveness of automatic query expansion is degraded when long documents are used [3]; instead, only the part of the document that is most similar to the query should be used for feedback. Allan [3] and Xu and Croft [166] showed that using passage instead of full-text documents in automatic query expansion can improve the retrieval effectiveness of queries. Passages have also been used in other works of relevance feedback [34, 107]

3.3.5 Proximity and Relevance Feedback

One of the first approaches applying term positional data in retrieval feedback is the work of Attar and Fraenkel [7]. They propose different models to generate clusters of terms related to a query (searchonyms) and use this clusters in a local feedback process. The proposed clustering methods are divided in three categories:

- Local Relative Frequencies,
- Local Association Matrix,
- Metric Correlations.

The first two methods are based on term frequency data; for this reason, they will be not considered in our analysis. The latter methodology uses term position information to build the proposed clusters.

Based on some experiments with English and Hebrew documents the authors confirm that metrical correlations, i.e. methods based on functions inversely proportional to the distance between terms, are superior than methods based merely on weighted co-occurrence of terms.

Metric Correlation Methods

Attar and Fraenkel [7] proposed basically two metric correlations: the *reference vectors and eigenvectors* and the *scalar product clusters*. To analyze these methods, the following are notations introduced: a *form* is an ordered strings of letters, preceded an followed by a space. A *word* is an occurrence of a form in the text counting multiplicities. A *coordinate* of a word is an ordered six-tuple consisting of the author code, volume, document number, paragraph number, sentence number, and word number within the sentence. Let $G(s)$ be a nonempty subset of forms which are grammatical variants of each other. A canonical form s of them is called *stem*.

Reference Vectors and Eigenvectors. For a given text D_g, F_g, C_g, and S_g are set of all its documents, forms, coordinates, and stems, respectively. They are also called (global) database of documents, forms, coordinates, and stems, respectively. Similarly, D_l, F_l, C_l, and S_l are the set of all documents, forms (words) coordinates, and stems, respectively, of a subset of the database, such as the (local) set of all documents returned from a given search formulation. Also W_g and W_l are the sequence of all words in the global and local text respectively.

3.3 Term Proximity

Now, for any stem $s \in S_l$, let $w_s(i) \in C_g$ be the coordinate of the ith occurrence of any variant of s. If $x \in S_l$, we define the function

$$b(s,x) = \sum_i \sum_j F(w_s(i), w_x(j)), \qquad (3.29)$$

where the summation is over all i,j such that $w_s(i), w_x(j) \in C_l$, and F is a suitable function of distance $d = |w_s(i) - w_x(j)|$ in words between $w_s(i)$ and $w_x(j)$ in the text. After some experimental tests, the following distance function was selected:

$$F(w_s(i), w_x(j)) = \begin{cases} 1/d & \text{if } w_s(i), w_x(j) \text{ are in the same sentence and } d \leq 20, \\ 0 & \text{otherwise} \end{cases} \qquad (3.30)$$

For a fixed $s \in S_l$, let x_i run over S_l and generate a linear list of the $b(s,x_i)$ ranked on non increasing size and a linear list of the corresponding x_i. Selecting the first n terms in each of these lists gives the eigenvector

$$E_n(s) = E_n^u(s) = (b_1(s), b_2(s), \ldots, b_n(s)), \ b_1(s) \geq b_2(s), \ldots, b_n(s) \qquad (3.31)$$

and the induced reference vector

$$R_n(s) = R_n^u(s) = (x_1, x_2, \ldots, x_n). \qquad (3.32)$$

An examination of the reference vectors $R_n(s)$ reveals that the relation between s and the stems $x_i \in R_n(s)$ is of two kinds:

- A *synonymity* relation, either global, pertaining to the entire language, or local, relating to the search at hand.

- A *neighborhood* relation, reflecting the neighborhood of s, overwhelmingly the dominant relation.

The second relation (neighborhood) induces a relation on the components of $R_n(s)$. Let $x \in R_n(s)$. If y is a synonym of x which occurs in the database, it is likely to appear also in $R_n(s)$, since it may replace x in some of the neighborhoods of s. This "indirect" synonymity relation is more frequent than the "direct" synonymity relation between s and x.

Scalar Product Clusters. Based on the *neighborhood* relation defined above, it may be assumed that two stems with "similar" neighborhoods have some synonymity relation that can be measured using the *scalar product*. Arranging the components in the eigenvectors E and reference vectors R introduced before and aligning terms:

$$\begin{aligned} E_k(s_1) &= (b_1(s_1), b_2(s_1), \ldots, b_k(s_1)), \\ E_k(s_2) &= (b_1(s_2), b_2(s_2), \ldots, b_k(s_2)), \end{aligned}$$

with common reference vector $(x_1, x_2, \ldots, x_k)$; i.e. $b_1(s_1)$ and $b_1(s_2)$ are coefficients of the same term x_1, $(1 \leq i \leq k \leq 2n)$. Then,

$$cos_k(s_1, s_2) = \frac{E_k(s_1), E_k(s_2)}{(E_k(s_1), E_k(s_1))^{1/2}(E_k(s_2), E_k(s_2))^{1/2}} \qquad (3.33)$$

is the scalar product of the vectors $E_k(s1)$, $E_k(s_2)$. The function $cos_k(s, x)$ is computed for all stems x in the set $U = \{y : y \in \cup R_{20}(s)\}$, where the union is over all stems $s \in T$. For each $x \in U$, $E_k(x)$ was computed and then $cos_k(s, x)$. The scalar product cluster is defined by

$$P_n(s) = (x_1, x_2, \ldots, x_n), \qquad (3.34)$$

induced by

$$(cos_k(s, x_1), cos_k(s, x_2), \ldots, cos_k(s, x_n)), \qquad (3.35)$$

where $cos_k(s, x_1) \geq cos_k(s, x_2) \geq \cdots \geq cos_k(s, x_n)$, $x_i \in U$. Experimental results demonstrate that Scalar Product Clusters are useful to produce synonyms with little noise, however their retrieval capability is generally inferior to that of eigenvectors.

The additional terms generated through the clusters $R_n(s)$ or $P_n(s)$ are used to augment the initial query (s) in next retrieval iterations, obtaining $R_n(s)$ as the best performance in the experimental phase.

3.4 Fourier Domain Scoring

Fourier Domain Scoring (FDS) processes the document spatial information of the document and uses it to rank documents. The main difference between FDS and other vector space similarity measures is that, rather than storing only the count of a frequency term per document, FDS stores a term signal. The term signal shows how the term is spread throughout the document [110]. Comparing the spectrum of query term signals in documents, FDS permit to observe the following features:

- which documents have a high occurrence of the query terms.

- which documents have the query terms appearing together.

This information is obtained by comparing the *magnitude* and the *phase* of the spectrum across different term signals.

Documents that contain query terms that all follow a similar positional pattern are considered more relevant than documents whose query terms do not follow similar patterns.

3.4.1 FDS Methodology

To make use of the spatial information of the document, the vectors used in the FDS model represent the position of query terms throughout the document. Documents that have keywords appearing periodically and that contain the keywords together are given a higher relevance than the documents that have the keywords apart [109].

3.4 Fourier Domain Scoring

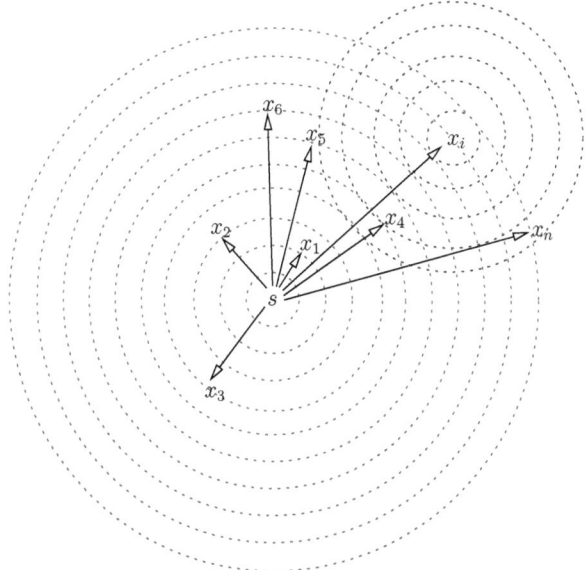

Figure 3.6: A graphical representation of the Reference Vector R_n considered in the first metric correlation proposed by Attar and Fraenkel. Note that in the second metric (Scalar Product Clusters), for each element x_i in R_n, the vector $E(x_i)$ will be calculated to obtain the vector $P_n(s)$.

To analyze the relative positions, the vectors are mapped into the frequency domain. The word position is treated as the position in time. Performing the Discrete Fourier Transform (DFT) allow us to observe the *word spectrum* in relation to a certain document. By splitting the *word spectrum* into the *magnitude* and *phase*, one can determine the *power* and *delay* of the word at certain frequencies.

To estimate the document relevance, FDS examines the positions of the query terms in the document by comparing their *phase* (per frequency component) and adjust it according to the appearance of the term by observing the *magnitude*.

3.4.2 Words Position Representation

By treating the word as a discrete time interval, one gets a string of ones and zeros. To be more efficient, sequences of words can be clustered into *bins* (e.g. the first fifty words in the bin_0, the second fifty words in the bin_1, etc). This reduces the size of the input to the DFT and also gives larger counts than one in each bin [109].

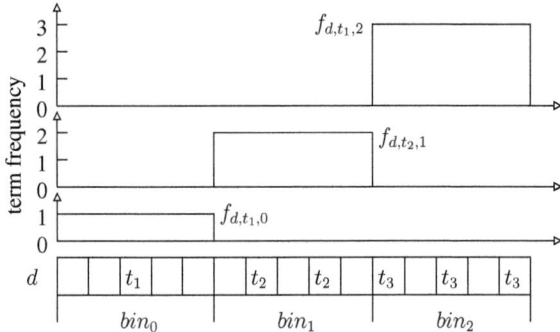

Figure 3.7: Word positions representation in FDS for the terms t_1, t_2, t_3 in the document d, using a bin of five words.

For example, Figure 3.7 gives the positions of the terms t_1, t_2, and t_3 through out a document d. By choosing a bin of five words, we obtain the term signals [1 0 0], [0 2 0] and [0 0 3], respectively.

Applying this scheme, a set of *Term Signals* for each document in the collection is calculated as a sequence of values that show the occurrence of a particular term in a particular bin of the document. The Term Signal for the term t in the document d is represented by:

$$\tilde{f}_{d,t} = [f_{d,t,0}, f_{d,t,1}, \ldots, f_{d,t,B-1}], \qquad (3.36)$$

where $f_{d,t,b}$ is the value of the signal component.

Having B signal components and D terms in the document, the value of the bth component is computed by counting the occurrences of term t between the $(\frac{bD}{B})^{th}$ word in the document and the $(\frac{(b+1)D}{(B-1)})^{th}$ word in the document. Therefore, if $B = 8$, $f_{d,t,0}$ would contain the number of times the term t occurred in the first eighth of document d. If $B = 1$, $f_{d,t,0}$ would contain the count of therm t throughout the whole document.

3.4.3 Weighting Bins

Before the Fourier Transform will be applied, the calculated bin components are weighted using a BD-ACI-BCA weighting scheme [170], obtaining the following values:

$$\omega_{d,t,b} = \Omega_d(f_{d,t,b}) = \frac{1 + \log_e f_{d,t,b}}{(1-s) + s \cdot W_d/av_{d \in D} W_d}, \qquad (3.37)$$

where $f_{d,t,b}$ is the count of term t in bin b of document d, s is the slope factor (set to 0.7), $W_d, av_{d \in D} W_d$ are the document vector norm and the average document vector norm, respectively.

3.4 Fourier Domain Scoring

The BD-ACI-BCA weighting scheme uses a pivoted document normalization, which reduces the effect of repetition of a word in a document and negate any effect of the document size has on a query.

Through the weighting process the term signal will be mapped to the *Weighted Term Signal* vector:

$$\tilde{w}_{d,t} = [w_{d,t,0}, w_{d,t,1}, \ldots, w_{d,t,B-1}] \tag{3.38}$$

3.4.4 Applying the Discrete Fourier Transform

As described in [108], FDS applies the Discrete Fourier Transform to the Weighted Term Signal $w_{d,t,b}$, the original function will be decomposed into a superposition of linearly independent sinusoidal terms given by:

$$\zeta_{d,t,\beta} = \sum_{b=0}^{B-1} w_{d,t,b}\, e^{\frac{-i2\pi\beta b}{B}} \tag{3.39}$$

Since each $\zeta_{d,t,\beta}$ (component of the series) is the projection of the word signal $\tilde{w}_{d,t}$ onto a sinusoidal wave of frequency β, the signal $\tilde{\zeta}_{d,t}$ is the spectrum of the given term signal given by:

$$\tilde{\zeta}_{d,t} = [\zeta_{d,t,0}, \zeta_{d,t,1}, \ldots, \zeta_{d,t,B-1}], \tag{3.40}$$

where $\zeta_{d,t,b} = H_{d,t,b} e^{i\theta_{d,t,b}}$ is the bth spectral component with magnitude $H_{d,t,b}$ and phase $\theta_{d,t,b}$.

The word spectrum shows the frequency components the word signal is made up of. Each frequency component is a complex number of the form:

$$H_f\, e^{-i\phi_f}, \tag{3.41}$$

where $H_f \in \mathbb{R}$ represents the power of the frequency component f, and $\phi_f \in \mathbb{R}$ is the phase shift of f. Each frequency component contains magnitude and phase information which can be interpreted as the effect and shift of the component respectively. The effect gives us an idea of the shape of the word signal.

Applying the Nyquist-Shannon Sampling Theorem [76], the frequency components will be limited to $\frac{B}{2}$, obtaining the vector:

$$\tilde{\zeta}_{d,t} = [\zeta_{d,t,0}, \zeta_{d,t,1}, \ldots, \zeta_{d,t,\frac{B}{2}}] \tag{3.42}$$

Discussion

We want to remark that the number of coefficients calculated in the Fourier expansion and the use of the sampling theorem play a critical role in the FDS procedure, because it determines the amount of positional data stored finally in the index. On this account, we made a detailed analysis of the expression (3.39) and detected that the reduction of the number of frequency components does not concern with the use of the Sampling Theorem, but with two properties of the proposed Fourier Transform:

(a) the Discrete Fourier Transform from (3.39) is periodic in β, that is:

$$\zeta_{d,t,\beta+B} = \zeta_{d,t,\beta} \qquad (3.43)$$

(b) the Weighted Term Signal ($w_{d,t,b}$) is not complex, therefore all negative values of β have the same value of its complex conjugate:

$$\zeta_{d,t,-\beta} = \zeta^*_{d,t,\beta} \qquad (3.44)$$

As depicted in Figure 3.8, using the Term Signal $\tilde{f}_{d,t} = [1\ 0\ 0\ 2\ 0\ 2\ 0\ 0]$ from a document with eight bins, we can observe the properties of periodicity derived from the expressions (3.43) and (3.44), and conclude that the whole spectrum information of the function $\zeta_{d,t,\beta}$ is contained in the coefficients from 0 to $\frac{B}{2}$, which has nothing to do with the use of the Sampling Theorem.

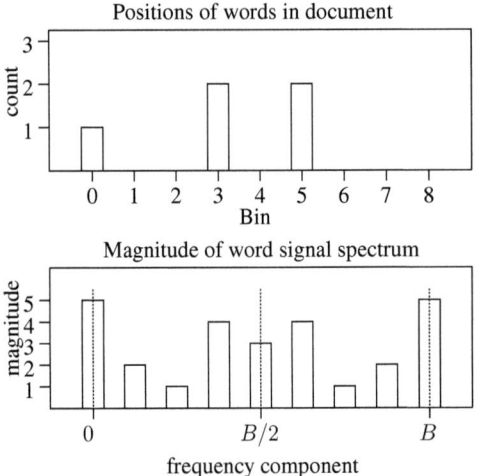

Figure 3.8: Analysis of the Discrete Fourier Transform periodicity.

3.4.5 The Score Calculation

The basic idea in the FDS approach is that relevant documents should have large magnitudes and the corresponding phase of each query term should be similar (in phase). To analyze these properties, FDS deals with the magnitude and phase separately, obtaining from the calculated spectral components the magnitude $H_{d,b}$ and phase precision $\Phi_{d,b}$. These values will be combined in the ranking process to obtain the final document score.

3.4 Fourier Domain Scoring

The first concepts involved in the score calculation are: (a) the *Unit Phase* Φ and (b) the *Zero Phase Precision* $\bar{\Phi}$ (corresponding to the averaged value of Φ over all query terms).

$$\Phi_{d,t,b} = \frac{\zeta_{d,t,b}}{H_{d,t,b}} = e^{i\theta_{d,t,b}}, \ 0 < \theta < 2\pi \tag{3.45}$$

$$\bar{\Phi}_{d,b} = \frac{1}{\#Q} \left| \sum_{t \in Q, \ H_{d,t,b} \neq 0} \Phi_{d,t,b} \right| \tag{3.46}$$

The basic idea is to obtain the mean (average over the terms t of the query Q) of the unit phases $\Phi_{d,t,b}$ for a document d and frequency b.

In the next step, the weighted sum of the magnitudes $H_{d,t,b}$ will be calculated:

$$\bar{H}_{d,b} = \sum_{t \in Q} \omega_{Q,t} H_{d,t,b} \tag{3.47}$$

where $\omega_{Q,t}$ is the applied weighting scheme for a query term t in Q.

Hence, the corresponding components of the score vector will be calculated as follows:

$$\tilde{s}_d = [s_{d,0}, s_{d,1}, \ldots, s_{d,B-1}], \tag{3.48}$$

$$s_{d,b} = \bar{\Phi}_{d,b} \bar{H}_{d,b} \tag{3.49}$$

Finally, the document score S_d is represented as the l_p norm of $\tilde{s}_d$:

$$\|\tilde{s}_d\|_p = \sqrt[p]{\sum_{b=0}^{B-1} |s_{d,b}|^p}, \tag{3.50}$$

where a value of $p = 2$ corresponds to the usual Euclidean norm.

Figure 3.9 represents the geometrical view of the components involved in the FDS ranking. Here, the first spectral components ($\tilde{\zeta}_{d,t_1,0}$ and $\tilde{\zeta}_{d,t_2,0}$) of two arbitrary terms t_1 and t_2 in the document d are operated to obtain their corresponding similarity value $S_{d,0}$.

Additional Ranking Methods

Optional methods to the FDS ranking calculation are:
(a) the sum of all components:

$$S_d = \sum_{b=1}^{B/2+1} S_{d,b} \tag{3.51}$$

(b) the sum of the largest score vector elements:

$$\begin{aligned} S_d &= S_{d,b_1} + S_{d,b_2}, \\ S_{d,b_1}, S_{d,b_2} &\geq \max_{\forall \ b \neq b_1, b_2} (s_{d,b}) \end{aligned} \tag{3.52}$$

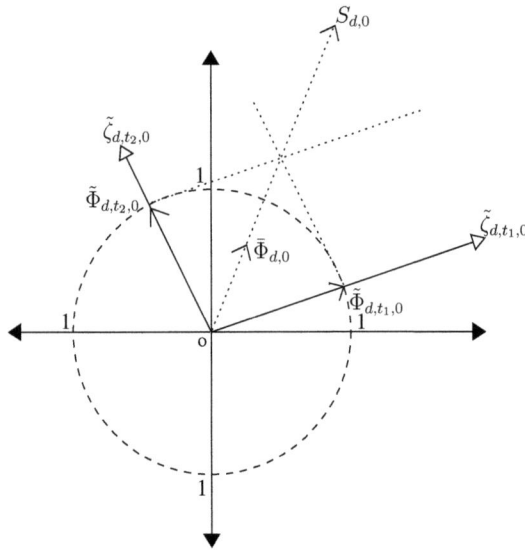

Figure 3.9: A geometrical representation of the ranking model used in the FDS considering the first spectral components $\tilde{\zeta}_{d,t_1,0}$ and $\tilde{\zeta}_{d,t_2,0}$ of the terms t_1 and t_2.

(c) the sum of the largest phase precision components:

$$\Phi^*_{d,b_1}, \Phi^*_{d,b_2} \geq \max_{\forall\, b \neq b_1, b_2} (\Phi^*_{d,b}) \qquad (3.53)$$

(d) the sum of the largest magnitude components:

$$H^*_{d,b_1}, H^*_{d,b_2} \geq \max_{\forall\, b \neq b_1, b_2} (H_{d,b}) \qquad (3.54)$$

(e) and the sum of the largest phase precision components:

$$S_d = \sum_{b\, \in\, \{c | \Phi^*_{d,c} > P\}} S_{d,b} \qquad (3.55)$$

Discussion

When the query terms appear in a document with a similar pattern, we would expect that the standard deviation of a phase angle of their spectral components for a given frequency b is small.

$$\Delta_{d,b} = \sqrt{\frac{1}{\#Q}\sum_{t\in Q}(\theta_{d,t,b} - \text{mean}(\theta_{d,b}))^2} \qquad (3.56)$$

$$\text{mean}(\theta_{d,b}) = \frac{1}{\#Q}\sum_{t\in Q}\theta_{d,t,b} \qquad (3.57)$$

where $\text{mean}(\theta_{d,b})$ is the *average phase angle*. If all phase angles would be considered modulo 2π, this calculation will be correct. Alternatively, we can use the unit phase $\Phi_{d,t,b} = \exp(i\theta_{d,t,b})$:

$$\Delta'_{d,b} = \sqrt{\frac{1}{\#Q}\sum_{t\in Q}(\Phi_{d,t,b} - \text{mean}(\Phi_{d,b}))^2} \qquad (3.58)$$

But instead of this value the model applies the expression (3.46).

3.4.6 Further Assumptions

- About magnitude
  - If a lower frequency component magnitude is large with respect to the other components, then the word should appear clustered in a few places in the document.
  - Is a higher frequency component magnitude is large with respect to the other components, then the word clusters would be scattered throughout the document.

- About phase
  - If two signals have the same phase (are in phase), then they appear together throughout the document.
  - If two signals have the opposite phase (out of phase), then they not appear most of the time together in the document.

Terms made from several words are normally the topic of the document when the words appear close together and periodically. Therefore, a document in which the frequency f has a large magnitude (H_f) for all the words of the topic set T, and the phase of each word of T is similar, then it is most likely that T is a subset of the topic.

3.5 Summary

In this chapter, the most relevant work from the IR research community related with the matter of this thesis were considered.

We began describing some approaches considering contextual information for improving search results, and revised the main models incorporating term proximity information in the IR process.

Finally, one of the first approaches using functions to represent positional information was analyzed in detail.

4
The Gauss Model

4.1 Introduction

In this chapter, the Gauss model, a novel methodology to improve document relevance evaluation is proposed. The Gauss model is based on a compressed statistical description of the word positions in a document collection, represented through their measures of *center* and *spread*.

As a complement to the term frequency/inverse document frequency (*tfidf*) metric, the *term density distribution* measure to estimate a document's relevance is introduced. Furthermore, a new query expansion algorithm is proposed. It is based on overlapping the distributions of query terms in the top-ranked documents.

Experimental results obtained for the TREC-8 document collection demonstrate that the Gauss model is superior to the *tfidf* weighting scheme without applying query reformulation or relevance feedback techniques. Furthermore, a query expansion methodology to support the user in the query refinement process is developed.

Part of the material presented in this chapter has been published in [57].

4.2 Term Distribution Analysis

The previous studies corroborate that, independent of the applied technology, the analysis of relationships between words in a document collection is a significant way to improve relevance estimation in information retrieval systems. On the other hand, the analysis of word distributions in a text reveals that content-bearing words are likely to repeat in close proximity to each other [15].

In this section, a novel approach is proposed in order to obtain a *compressed representation* of the relationships between words using simple methods of descriptive statistics applied to the word positions in documents. One naive method is to calculate the distance

Table 4.1: Positions of words a and b in a linear representation of document d.

1	2	3	4	5	6	7	8	9	10	11	12	13	14	15	16	17	18
a			a					a						a			
					b		b		b		b		b				

Table 4.2: Interquartile range for the position of a and b in the document d.

Word	Positions	1^{st}quartile(Q_{25})	median (Q_{50})	3^{rd}quartile (Q_{75})
a	1 | 4 | 9 | 15	1.75	6.5	13.5
b	6 | 8 | 10 | 12 | 14	7	10	13

between all word pairs. Applying this procedure, one can expect that, if two words are near to each other in a set of documents, some semantic relationship is likely to exist between these two words. Unfortunately, such a method is computationally costly due to (a) the excessive increase of the dimensions of the index matrix that contains information about each word position in the document collection, and (b) the distance computations between the query and the document terms.

Our proposed method permits us to obtain semantic information about the relationships between words based on only two statistical parameters describing the positions of words in the corresponding document: the statistical measures of *center* and *spread*. The most common measures of center and spread are the mean (μ) and the standard deviation (σ). Because the mean and standard deviation suffer from the influence of extreme observations, resistant measures of center and spread, such as the *median* and *percentiles*, will be used to better deal with outliers and common irregularities in the data. As shown in the next subsection, these statistical values can be easily incorporated in standard index structures (i.e. an inverted index), extending the capabilities to recognize relevant documents in a set of retrieved documents.

4.2.1 Descriptive Statistics and Document Semantics

In Table 4.1, we see a linear representation of a document d, where several instances of the words "a" and "b" are located in their respective positions along the document body. The idea is to analyze how these words are distributed within the document and to find a reduced representation that permits to compare their context.

Table 4.2 shows the interquartile range [151] for the positions of a and b in document d.

Using the calculated parameters, their interquartile ranges are shown in Fig. 4.1. It can be observed that the instances of word a are mainly situated in the first half of the document with $Q_{25} = 1.75$ and $Q_{75} = 13.5$, while the instances of word b are distributed approximately in the middle of the document with $Q_{25} = 7$ and $Q_{75} = 13$.

This statistical representation of the word positions gives a concrete picture of their dispersion within the document, such that the distributions of two or more words can be compared.

The interquartile range allows us to reach some conclusions about specific scores in our

4.2 Term Distribution Analysis

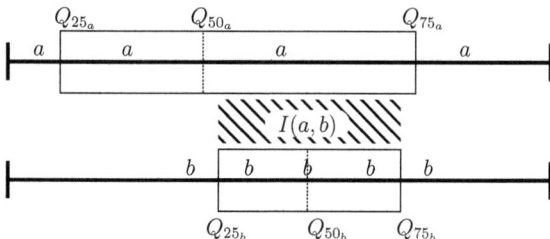

Figure 4.1: Interquartile range for the positions distribution of a and b

distribution. Approximately 50% of the instances of word a are located in its corresponding interquartile range $r_a = [Q_{25_a}, Q_{75_a}]$, and about 50% of the instances of word b are located in the range $r_b = [Q_{25_b}, Q_{75_b}]$. Using the document length $|L|$, the equations can be normalized: $0 \leq R_a \leq 1$ and $0 \leq R_b \leq 1$, where $R_a = \frac{r_a}{|L|}$ and $R_b = \frac{r_b}{|L|}$. Thus, if the range of a word in the document is near to 1, the instances of this word are widely distributed within the document body. Similarly, if the *intersection range* (I) of two words is determined, we can expect that the word instances situated in this common document region are close to each other: $I(a,b) = R_a \cap R_b$. Based on this information, two approximations are proposed in the following subsection.

4.2.2 The Document Relevance Estimator

Let R_{a_d} be the distribution range of word a in document d, and ρ_{a_d} the word density (number of occurrences) of word a in document d. Then, the *Term Density Distribution (TDD)* is defined as an estimator for the relevance of word a in document d:

$$TDD(a)_d = R_{a_d} \cdot (1 + log\{\rho_{a_d}\}) \tag{4.1}$$

A wide range and a high frequency of word a imply that word a is regularly distributed within the document body, and it could be considered as a relevant key to describe the document content. For example, considering the documents of Fig. 4.2 and the query $q = \{a\}$, then the document d_1 will be more relevant than the document d_2, because $TDD(a)_{d_1} > TDD(a)_{d_2}$.

4.2.3 The Semantic Distance Estimator

By calculating the *intersection range* between two words $I(a,b)$ and their *word densities* in document d, one can estimate their *semantic statistical distance* ($\delta_{a,b}$) in the document:

$$\delta_{a,b} = \frac{n}{\sum_{d=1}^{n} I(a,b)_d \cdot (1 + log\{\rho_{(a,b)_d}\})} \tag{4.2}$$

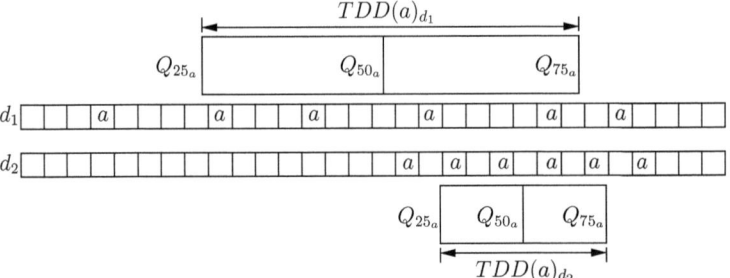

Figure 4.2: Dispersion of the word a in two arbitrary documents.

where $I(a,b)_d$ is the *intersection range* between the words in document d, $\rho_{(a,b)_d}$ is the *word density* of *(a+b)* in document d, and n is the number of documents in the collection containing word a and word b.

The higher the *intersection range* between two words and the higher the *word density* in the same range, the closer their position is in the document, implying some *semantic connection* between them.

4.3 Implementation Issues

4.3.1 Index, Search and Ranking

In the implementation of the proposed approach, the statistical computations are performed simultaneously with the indexing process. To achieve this task, the open source information retrieval software library *Lucene*[1] is used. Some of the main components of *Lucene* have to be extended in order to calculate, store, and apply the word distribution information along the retrieval process.

Using the statistical information contained in the extended index structure, a new search algorithm is proposed. First, an initial approximation of relevant documents based on the *tfidf* criterion and the query q is retrieved. Then, a procedure consisting of the following two simultaneous tasks is started.

Ranking Optimization.

Selecting the first k documents from the initial *tfidf* ranking and applying the *TDD* estimator of equation (4.1), we calculate $D = \{d_1, d_2, d_3, \ldots, d_k\}$, an optimized document list based on the dispersion of the query q in the top-ranked documents.

The *TDD* value for each document d_i is obtained by applying equation (4.3), and the final ranking value is computed using a weighted combination of *TDD* and *tfidf* as shown in

---

[1] http://lucene.apache.org

4.4 Experimental Results

formula (4.4). An optimal value for the weighting coefficient *w* is estimated experimentally.

$$TDD(q)_{d_i} = R_{q_{d_i}} \cdot (1 + log(\rho_{q_{d_i}})) \tag{4.3}$$

$$FinalRanking = w \cdot TDD + (1-w) \cdot tfidf \tag{4.4}$$

Query Expansion.
Using the term frequency values provided by the *Lucene* index, we first calculate $T = \{t_1, t_2, t_3, \ldots, t_m\}$, the *m*-most frequently occurring terms in D. Then, our δ estimator in equation (4.5) is applied to compute the *semantic distance* between the query q and the words in T. Finally, the semantic distance threshold ϵ is used to build the term list Q_e representing both the *semantic neighborhood* of the query in the retrieved documents and the candidate terms to expand the query (equation (4.6)).

$$\delta_{t_i,q} = \frac{d}{\sum_{j=1}^{d} I(t_i,q)_j \cdot (1 + log\left(\rho_{(t_i,q)_j}\right))}, \quad i = 1 \ldots t \tag{4.5}$$

$$Q_e = \{t_1, t_2, t_3, \ldots, t_k\} \tag{4.6}$$

where $t_j \in Q_e \iff \delta_{t_j,q} \leq \epsilon$, and ϵ is a semantic distance threshold.

From the initial results, the necessary information to accomplish two tasks is obtained: (a) estimating the query terms distribution for immediate ranking optimization and (b) calculating the query neighborhood, giving the possibility to incorporate these new terms in a query refinement process.

4.4 Experimental Results

The TREC-8 document collection has been used to compare the performance of our approach with the *tfidf* weighting scheme. The goal of this evaluation is to determine how well our approach is able to identify relevant documents in the collection.

The evaluation framework consists of the following components: (a) *The Ad Hoc Test Collection* containing 556,077 documents (2.09 Gigabytes) corresponding to the Tipster disks (3 and 4), (b) *The Topics and Relevance Judgments* (qrels), (c) *Our algorithm* consisting of 4 java modules for indexing, search, graphical evaluation and tuning tasks, and (d) *The results analysis* where the effectiveness of our approach will be estimated.

To evaluate the performance of the word distribution and semantic distance concepts, two groups of experiments, consisting of 28 and 14 runs are executed.

4.4.1 The Dispersion Runs

In the first group of experiments, the effectiveness of our word dispersion indicator is measured. Based on a short query (*qrel* title) and running the *tfidf* algorithm, we obtain a preliminary group of relevant documents (*tfidf* results). Subsequently, applying the word dispersion criterion, we estimate how the query terms are distributed in the retrieved documents and use this information to optimize the ranking (dispersion results).

Equation (4.7) represents the dispersion considering a query q having one or more terms and an arbitrary document d from the *tfidf*-ranking. The performed runs have been divided into four groups delimited by the dispersion models executed in the initial ranking:

OTD model : $disp(i)_d = iqr(i)_d/length_d$
LIN model : $disp(i)_d = tf(i)_d \cdot iqr(i)_d/length_d$
SQR model : $disp(i)_d = \sqrt{tf(i)_d} \cdot iqr(i)_d/length_d$
LOG model : $disp(i)_d = log(tf(i)_d) \cdot iqr(i)_d/length_d$

Applying equation (4.8), each model is tested with six different dispersion weighting schemes: $w = \{0.2, 0.3, 0.4, 0.5, 0.6, 0.7\}$.

$$Disp(q)_d = \sum_{i \in q} disp(i)_d \qquad (4.7)$$

$$DRank(d)_w = w \cdot Disp(q)_d + (1-w) \cdot tfidf(q)_d \qquad (4.8)$$

where q are the query terms, $iqr(i)_d$ is the interquartile range of term i in document d, $length_d$ is the length of document d, $tf(i)_d$ is the frequency of term i in document d, $disp(i)_d$ is the dispersion of term i in document d, $Disp(q)_d$ is the dispersion of query terms q in document d, $tfidf(q)_d$ is the tfidf of document d by query q, $DRank(d)_w$ is the dispersion ranking of document d using a weighting scheme w.

Based on this scenario, a total of 28 runs using the previously generated *index* and the *title-tag* of the TREC-topics as a query were performed. For each run, the corresponding *results_file* using the *trec_eval* program was generated, obtaining the *map* and *R-Precision* values (see Section 2.10) for *tfidf* and the different weighting schemes of the dispersion ranking. From Fig. 4.3, the performance gain (*map* and *R-Precision*) of the dispersion ranking over *tfidf* is evident practically for all models, obtaining the OTD, LOG and SQR models as the best results.

By comparing the *map* values of *tfidf* and the dispersion ranking for all queries derived from the TREC-8 qrels, our approach outperforms the *tfidf* ranking by 6.6%.

Factors Influencing the Relevance Increase in the Dispersion Runs.

In the following figures, the query-words distribution for the top ranked documents is presented, based on topic 430 for the *tfidf* and *dispersion* algorithms as an example. From Fig. 4.4, a clear difference in the document ranking positions and how the query terms are distributed in the document body can be observed. The document ranking positions change once the dispersion criterion is applied. For example, the document LA080389-0111 holding the first place in the dispersion ranking (right) partially presents (per term) a more distributed term position than the first ranked document in the *tfidf* ranking. Furthermore, analyzing this particular result with *trec_eval*, a *map* gain of 17.2% (*tfidf*: 0.1944, *dispersion*: 0.2278) is achieved.

4.4 Experimental Results

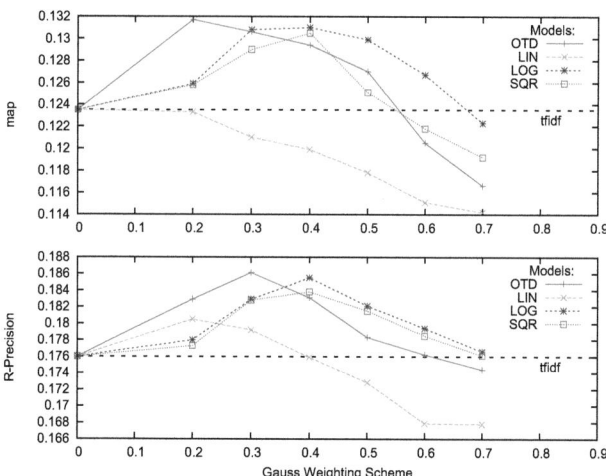

Figure 4.3: Comparing the performance of all Gauss models vs. *tfidf* using *map* and *R-Precision* values.

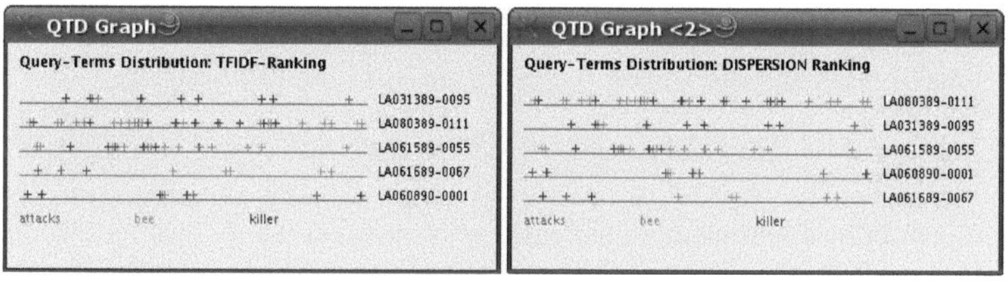

Figure 4.4: Tfidf (left) and Dispersion Ranking (right) for Topic 430.

Usually, a slight positive variation of the *map* value generates an important difference in the distribution of query terms in the "new" top-ranked documents. We observe that the document *LA080389-0111* which ascends to the first position in the dispersion ranking, presents a more extensive description of the document *LA031389-0095* which previously occupied the first position in the *tfidf* ranking. Furthermore, in *LA080389-0111* a wider distribution of all query terms along the document body than in document *LA031389-0095* can be observed. Thus, documents where all query terms are regularly distributed will be favored in the ranking obtained from applying the dispersion criterion. This avoids two unfavorable situations: (a) *query term agglutination*, i.e. high frequency terms allocated in a small document fragment, and (b) *query term predominance*, i.e. the disproportioned effect of high frequency single query terms over low frequency ones. In our example, the influence of the high frequency term "bee" (*freq*=16) compensates the low frequency of the term "attack" (*freq*=1), nevertheless this document is placed in the first position of the *tfidf*-ranking.

Comparing our results with 13 participants of the ad hoc retrieval task who utilize an analog evaluation framework (based on the topic title), we observe that the *median* improvement over the baseline achieved by these participants is about 11.3%, with lower and upper quartiles of 3.5% and 13%, respectively. The performance gain of our approach inside the inter-quartile range is evident; as already mentioned, a performance gain of about 6.6% over *tfidf* is obtained. Compared to results of the selected TREC-8 participants, this value corresponds to about 58% of the participants's performance using relevance feedback techniques. In contrast, our results are achieved by applying the dispersion model only (without query reformulation).

4.4.2 The Query Expansion Runs

Query expansion (or term expansion) is a process of supplementing the original query with additional terms, with the aim of improving retrieval performance [42, 13]. It should be emphasized that our query expansion experiments are based on the search results only. No internal/external knowledge structure was used to leverage the re-ranking procedure. In the group of runs described in the following, the proposed query expansion model based on the *Semantic Distance Estimator* δ is evaluated. For the top-n ranked documents, the *query-nearest-terms* to expand the query is computed and the ranking is recalculated.

The query reformulation and ranking procedure consists of the following stages:

1. Calculate the expanded query terms (eT) using the top-n documents from the dispersion ranking.

2. Get the top-r relevant terms from the expanded query $eT(r)$.

3. Reformulate the original query (oQ) adding the terms from $eT(r)$ using formula (4.9).

4. Execute *tfidf*-search using $eQuery$:

$$eQuery = oQ \wedge 0.5 \times (eT_1 \vee eT_2 \vee \cdots \vee eT_r) \qquad (4.9)$$

4.5 Summary

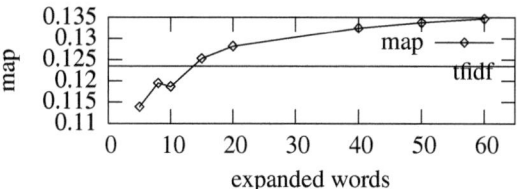

Figure 4.5: Query expansion results: the averaged *map* for each query expansion scheme.

where: $eQuery$ represent the expanded query, oQ is the original query and eT_i is the expanded term i.

For the top-5 ranked documents (n=5), 14 different query expansion schemes were applied: $r = \{1, 2, 3, 4, 5, 6, 8, 10, 15, 20, 30, 40, 50, 60\}$.

The results are depicted in Fig. 4.5, where the averaged *map* for all topics and each query expansion scheme are illustrated. Approximately from the 15th expanded term, our approach improves the *tfidf* results.

4.5 Summary

In this chapter, the Gauss model, a novel methodology to improve the document relevance evaluation in information retrieval applications is proposed. The Gauss model is based on a compressed representation of word positions in a document collection, based on two statistical parameters: the measures of *center* and *spread*, which reduce the index size compared to full term position index structures. By analyzing the distributions of query terms in the initial search results, the ranking can be optimized without any relevance feedback cycle. Furthermore, the *semantic distance* concept was extended to develop a query expansion methodology supporting the user in the query refinement process.

An evaluation of the Gauss model using the TREC-8 collection has exhibited a performance gain of 6.6% over the usual *tfidf* weighting scheme without applying query reformulation methods. This improvement represents 58% of the TREC-8 participants's performance improvements implementing relevance feedback techniques. Further analyses have shown that the Gauss model promotes documents having a wider query term distribution and thus minimizes term *agglutination* and *predominance* effects in the top-ranked documents.

5

The Fourier Model

5.1 Introduction

The Fourier model is based on an abstract description of the term positions in a document, represented by the Fourier series expansion of a rectangular function describing the term positions in the document. In addition, a document ranking optimization procedure, based on *objective query functions* determining a user defined document region, is proposed as an alternative to the well-known term frequency metrics. Furthermore, a query expansion algorithm is introduced. It is based on overlapping the distributions of query terms in the top-ranked documents. Experimental results obtained for the TREC-8 document collection demonstrate that the proposed approach is superior to state-of-the-art relevance feedback techniques such as *Rocchio* and *Divergence from Randomness* models [128, 4].

Part of the material presented in this chapter has been published in [58].

5.2 Term Distribution Analysis Using Fourier Series

Fourier analysis is based on the idea that functions can be approximated by a sum of sine and cosine waves at different frequencies. The more sinusoids are included in the sum, the better the approximation. There are several applications of Fourier analysis in the field of information retrieval (IR), such as audio-IR [32], image-IR [49], and in text-IR [116].

Consider a function $f(x)$ that is defined for $x \in [0, L]$. A Fourier series expansion is an expansion

$$f(x) = \frac{a_0}{\sqrt{L}} + \sqrt{\frac{2}{L}} \sum_{k=1}^{\infty} \left[a_k \cos\left(\frac{2\pi k x}{L}\right) + b_k \sin\left(\frac{2\pi k x}{L}\right) \right] \quad (5.1)$$

where the coefficients a_k and b_k have to be determined. If the sum over k is restricted to

$k \leq n$, the Fourier series gives an approximation $f_n(x)$ to the function $f(x)$ called the n-th order Fourier approximation of $f(x)$.

Consider a document D containing L terms. To characterize the distribution of a particular term t within the document, the set of positions of all occurrences of t in D is denoted as $\mathcal{P}_t$, where all terms are enumerated starting with 1 for the first term in the document and so on.

As exemplified in Figure 5.1, $\mathcal{P}_t = \{3, 8\}$ represents the fact that the two instances of the term t in the document D are located in the third and the eighth position of the document body.

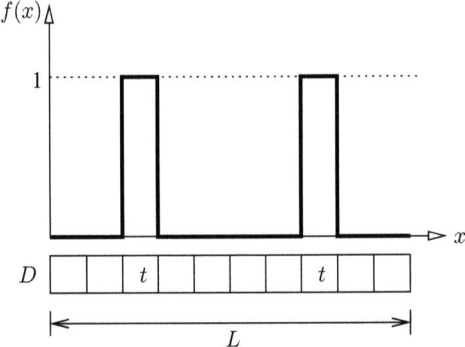

Figure 5.1: Distribution of the term t in document D, represented by a rectangular function.

The cardinality $|\mathcal{P}_t|$ of $\mathcal{P}_t$ is the total number of occurrences of t in the document. The characteristic function

$$f^{(t)}(x) := \begin{cases} 1 & \text{for } x \in [p-1, p] \text{ if } p \in \mathcal{P}_t \\ 0 & \text{otherwise} \end{cases} \quad (5.2)$$

is assigned to $\mathcal{P}_t$ for $x \in [0, L]$. The Fourier coefficients of $f^{(t)}$ are given by

$$a_0 = \frac{|\mathcal{P}_t|}{\sqrt{L}} \quad (5.3)$$

and for $k > 0$

$$a_k = \sqrt{\frac{L}{2}} \frac{1}{k\pi} \sum_{p \in \mathcal{P}_t} \left[\sin\left(2\pi k \frac{p}{L}\right) - \sin\left(2\pi k \frac{p-1}{L}\right) \right] \quad (5.4)$$

$$b_k = -\sqrt{\frac{L}{2}} \frac{1}{k\pi} \sum_{p \in \mathcal{P}_t} \left[\cos\left(2\pi k \frac{p}{L}\right) - \cos\left(2\pi k \frac{p-1}{L}\right) \right] \quad (5.5)$$

Figure 5.2 shows the Fourier representation of the step function $f^{(t)}(x)$ for the positions $\mathcal{P}_t = \{3, 8\}$ of the term t in document D, calculated for different Fourier orders $n = 2, 4, 6, 8$.

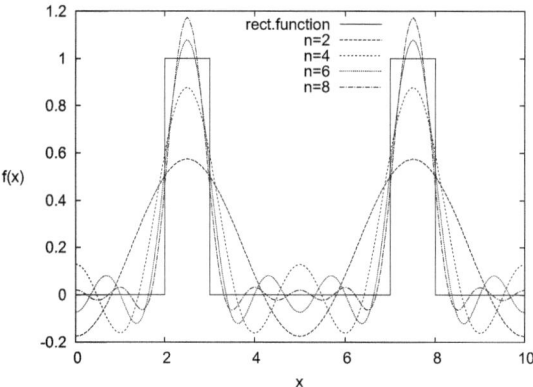

Figure 5.2: Fourier distribution of $\mathcal{P}_t = \{3, 8\}$ in document D, using different Fourier orders n.

5.3 Comparing Term Distributions

The underlying concepts of the proposed approach are:

- The positions of content terms in a document influence its relevance evaluation in the retrieval process.

- If two content term distributions are similar, then the corresponding terms are located in a similar document region, implying some semantic relationship between them [79, 7, 147].

- The algorithm to compare two term distributions has to be computationally simple such that it can be performed under realistic conditions.

It is noticeable that finite order Fourier approximations provide a systematic way to characterize and analyze the positions of terms. Applying a Fourier approximation of order n reduces the data necessary to describe the term distribution to $2n + 1$ real numbers.

In addition, the finite approximation allows to exploit the broadening effect on the original function (Figures 5.2, 5.3), defining a certain neighborhood around each term position. This broadening effect provides an instrument for estimating the similarity between terms within a document.

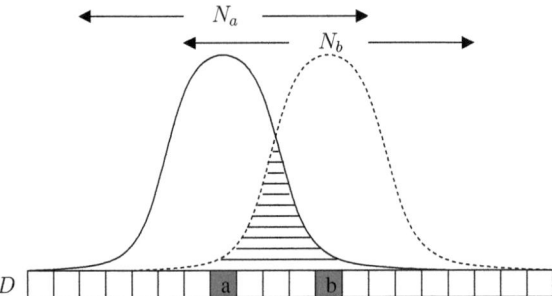

Figure 5.3: The broadening of the approximated term distributions, defining the term neighborhoods N_a and N_b and the corresponding overlapping region.

5.3.1 Comparing the Term Distribution Functions

In this section, the notion of *similarity* of two term distributions is defined. For a term distribution $f(x)$, the n-th order Fourier approximation $f_n(x)$ is considered and its Fourier coefficients are used to form the $2n + 1$ dimensional real vector $\vec{f}_n = (a_0, a_1, b_1, \ldots, a_n, b_n)$.

The similarity of two term distributions can be related to the overlap integral

$$\langle f_n, f_n' \rangle = \int_0^L f_n(x) f_n'(x) \, dx \qquad (5.6)$$

The overlap integral measures in which regions of the integration range both functions are large (see Figure 5.3). An important property of the Fourier expansion (5.1) is that the overlap integral can be easily expressed by the spectral vectors $\vec{f}_n$ and $\vec{f}_n'$:

$$\langle f_n, f_n' \rangle = a_0 a_0' + \sum_{k=1}^{n} (a_k a_k' + b_k b_k') = \vec{f}_n \cdot \vec{f}_n' \qquad (5.7)$$

i.e. the overlap integral is just the scalar product of the spectral vectors [143]. Since the functions f and f' can represent terms from documents of different lengths, the overlap integral (5.6) is not used directly to define the similarity of term distributions, but instead the overlap of the *normalized term distributions* $f_n/\sqrt{\langle f_n, f_n \rangle}$ is used. It is simply the cosine of the angle between the spectral vectors:

$$\mathrm{sim}(f_n, f_n') = \cos\theta = \frac{\vec{f}_n \cdot \vec{f}_n'}{|\vec{f}_n||\vec{f}_n'|} \qquad (5.8)$$

Here, the length of the spectral vector is given by

$$|\vec{f}_n| = \sqrt{a_0^2 + \sum_1^n (a_k^2 + b_k^2)} = \sqrt{\langle f_n, f_n \rangle}$$

5.3 Comparing Term Distributions

5.3.2 Relevance Ranking Optimization

The document ranking problem can be stated as an optimization problem that is based on the query term distribution function $f_{q,d}$ and a *user defined objective function* f_o representing the optimal query term distribution in the document body:

$$Maximize\{\text{sim}(f_{q,d}, f_o)\} \qquad \forall f_{q,d} \in A \qquad (5.9)$$

where A represents the set of query term distributions in an initial document ranking, $f_{q,d}$ is the query term distribution function for query q in document d, and f_o is a user defined *objective function*, representing the *optimal* query term distributions for the documents in the ranking.

For queries consisting of multiple terms, the distribution function is the sum of the single query term distributions.

Applying expression (5.9), a new sorted set of documents with a *maximum* similarity between each document distribution $f_{q,d}$ and the objective function f_o is obtained. In other words, we get a new ranking in which the searched terms are distributed similarly to the optimal query term distribution described by f_o.

Figure 5.4 illustrates several basic objective functions to identify documents where query terms are distributed in particular document regions. The following nomenclature is used to define an objective function:

Definition 13 *The expression "$f_o : X|Y$" represents an objective function to evaluate the relevance of documents with respect to the position of specific terms. Each document is divided into Y equally sized sections of length $\frac{L}{Y}$. The terms situated in the Xth section increase the document's relevance in the ranking.*

For example, the objective function $f_o : 1|1$ can be used to search for documents in which content terms (keywords) are distributed within the whole document body. It allows to identify so-called *topical* documents [81], where multiple keyword instances (*topical terms*) represent the intensity with which a concept is treated within the document.

More sophisticated objective functions, such as $f_o : 1|2$ and $f_o : 1|3 + 3|3$, can be used if the user is interested in documents where the contents of the first, or the first and the last section is more relevant. An example is the search for scientific papers where the abstract, the introduction (first sections) and the conclusion (last section) typically contain the most condensed document information. Another example might be a newspaper article, where readers expect to find the most relevant information at the top of the document.

Comparing the term distribution of our sample document D (Figure 5.1) to Figure 5.4, it can be observed that D will be only considered as relevant if the applied objective function resembles the pattern $f_o : 1|3 + 3|3$.

Algorithmic Complexity and Index Representation

Each term distribution function (i.e. their Fourier coefficients) can be obtained using an algorithm with a complexity of $O(\eta)$, where $\eta = termFrequency * fourierOrder$, and it will typically be executed in indexing time.

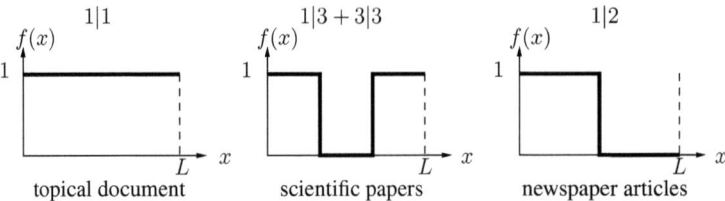

Figure 5.4: Examples of objective functions

The most efficient index structure for text query evaluation is the *inverted file*: a collection of lists (one per term) recording the identifiers of the documents containing that term [9]. An inverted file index consists of two main components: a *vocabulary* and a set of *inverted lists*. The *inverted lists* are represented as sequences of $<d, \nu_{d,t}>$ pairs, where $\nu_{d,t}$ is the frequency of term t in document d. This is the standard document-level index in which term positions within documents are not recorded. In the proposed approach, this index is augmented with Fourier coefficients:

$$<d, a_0^{(t)}, a_1^{(t)}, b_1^{(t)}, \ldots, a_n^{(t)}, b_n^{(t)}> \qquad (5.10)$$

where n is a predefined Fourier order and $a_k^{(t)}, b_k^{(t)}$ are the Fourier coefficients representing the positions of term t in document d. Note that from (5.3), the component $a_0^{(t)}$ corresponds to the term frequency $\nu_{d,t}$.

The Fourier coefficients are computed by the indexing process. It should be emphasized that at query time these coefficients will be used to evaluate the similarity score between terms, by applying a simple scalar product calculation. We call this method Fourier Vector Scoring (FVS).

An Example

Let us consider three arbitrary documents from the TREC-8 document collection containing the term "*brasil*". The corresponding term distribution functions will now be compared with different objective functions, simulating two particular ranking criteria.

In Table 5.1, the similarity for each document using the Fourier order $n = 3$ is shown. The applied objective function directly influences the ranking configuration, obtaining the documents FT944-15312 and FT931-11717 with the higher similarity (relevance) values for $f_o : 1|2$ and $f_o : 1|1$, respectively.

Figure 5.5 indicates how documents whose term distribution approximates the applied objective function obtain a higher similarity value. For example, document FT944-15312 with $f_o : 1|2$ obtains a similarity value of 0.9314, while the same document evaluated with $f_o : 1|1$ has a similarity value of 0.6067, lowering its relevance in the ranking.

Table 5.1: Similarity and ranking for the query *"brasil"* and three arbitrary TREC documents using the objective functions: $f_o : 1|2$ and $f_o : 1|1$.

document	$f_o : 1\|2$		$f_o : 1\|1$	
	sim	rank	sim	rank
FT944-15312	0.9314	1	0.6067	2
FBIS3-10730	0.5950	2	0.6053	3
FT931-11717	0.5277	3	0.6594	1

5.3.3 Query Expansion

Query expansion (or term expansion) is a process of supplementing the original query (q) with additional terms, with the aim of improving retrieval performance [42, 13]. The use of query expansion strategies such as automatic local analysis typically has positive effects on the retrieval performance. Based on this observation, a new approach for query expansion is proposed, considering the *top-r* documents $D = \{d_1, d_2, \ldots, d_r\}$ of an initial ranking process.

The function $f_{q,d}$ represents the distribution of the query term q for each document $d \in D$. The set of terms T_q whose elements t maximize the expression $\text{sim}(f_{q,d}, f_{t,d})$ is computed. Using this expression, the terms for all documents in D that have a similar distribution as the query, i.e. terms positioned near the query in the top ranked documents, are obtained.

Taking a look at the term positions of a typical TREC-8 document (see Figure 5.6), it can be observed how the similarity criterion reflects the location properties of *distant* and *neighboring* terms (see Figure 5.7). To order $n = 3$, the term *"brasil"* and its neighbor term *"portuguese"* have a high similarity value of 0.9490, while its similarity value with respect to the more distant term *"chile"* decreases to 0.0533, which is about 20 times smaller. Thus, the proposed method is quite sensitive with respect to the location properties of terms.

The expanded query is the set

$$T_q^k = \{\tau_1, \tau_2, \ldots, \tau_k\} \qquad (5.11)$$

consisting of the k best related query terms in D, obtained by ranking the terms according to the expression

$$\text{sim}(f_{q,d}, f_{\tau_i,d}), \ \forall d \in D, \ \tau_i \neq q \qquad (5.12)$$

The maximization process requires a simple comparison using the scalar product and norm of the corresponding Fourier coefficients, i.e. the algorithm to calculate the expanded query terms has a computational complexity of $O(\eta)$, where $\eta = |D|\, m + m \log m$, and m is the number of terms in each document in D.

5.4 Experimental Results

The TREC-8 document collection has been used to measure the performance of the proposed approach. The goal of this evaluation is to determine how well the algorithm is able

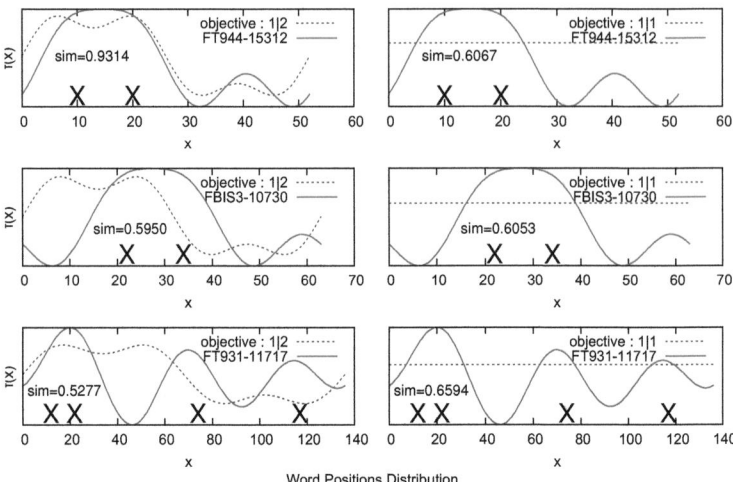

Figure 5.5: The distribution of the term "*brasil*" in three TREC documents, applying the objective functions: f_o : 1|2 (left) and f_o : 1|1 (right). The solid and dashed curves represent the approximations of order = 3 of the word distribution and the objective function, respectively.

to identify documents based on a predetermined objective function, and to compare the proposed query expansion approach with some of the state-of-the-art models.

The evaluation framework consists of the following components: (a) the Ad hoc Test Collection containing 556,077 documents (2.09 Gigabytes) corresponding to the Tipster disks (3 and 4), (b) the Topics and Relevance Judgments (qrels), (c) our approach consisting of 4 Java modules for indexing, search, graphical evaluation and configuration tasks, and (d) the results analysis where the effectiveness of our approach will be estimated.

All experiments were carried out using the third Fourier order.

5.4.1 Objective Function Runs

In this experiment, it will be analyzed how the query terms are distributed in the *top-10* ranked documents for three different ranking schemes: (a) tfidf (baseline) and two objective functions: (b) f_o : 1|3 and (c) f_o : 3|3.

To measure how the developed ranking algorithm follows the proposed objective functions, the skewness [102] of the term position distributions is calculated and their asymmetry is compared with the *tfidf* scheme. To obtain relevant statistical results, only topics that

5.4 Experimental Results 109

```
<DOC>
<DOCNO> FBIS3-10730 </DOCNO>
<HT> "drlat048_n_94005" </HT>
<HEADER>
<AU> FBIS-LAT-94-048 </AU>
Document Type:Daily Report
<DATE1> 11 Mar 1994 </DATE1>
</HEADER>
<F P=100> Chile </F>
<H3><TI> Brazil's Franco Completes Schedule
Despite Flu </TI></H3>
<F P=102> PY1103004294 Brasilia Voz
do Brasil Network in Portuguese
2200 GMT 10 Mar 94 </F>
<F P=103> PY1103004294 </F>
<F P=104> Brasilia Voz do Brasil Network </F>
<TEXT>
Language: <F P=105> Portuguese </F>
Article Type:BFN
[Text] Although he has the flu and a fever of 38 degrees
centigrade, President Itamar Franco is carrying out all
commitments included on the agenda of his visit to Chile.
</TEXT>
</DOC>
```

Figure 5.6: A typical TREC-8 document.

return more than 10 document hits were considered.

The results are shown in Figure 5.8, in which the horizontal axis corresponds to the terms given by the TREC topics 401 to 450.

The first graph of Figure 5.8 depicts the skewness of the query terms positions. In the *tfidf* ranking, the term positions have a skewness of around zero, i.e. the terms are evenly distributed. Applying both objective functions, it can be observed how in the optimized ranking the query terms approximate the corresponding objective function: the ranking based on $f_o : 1|3$ shows a positive skewness, demonstrating that terms are mainly situated in the header of the ranked documents. On the other hand, applying $f_o : 3|3$ generates a document ranking where query terms are predominantly distributed at the document's bottom (negative skewness).

The last two graphs of Figure 5.8 show the percentage of query terms fitting the proposed objective functions. For example, the $f_o : 1|3$ function applied to *topic* 420 produces a document ranking where 68% of the query terms are situated inside the objective function region, while the *tfidf* ranking returns only a fitting rate of 26%. Analyzing all experimental results, it can be observed that by applying the proposed approach to TREC-8, about 67% of the query terms (from the top ranked documents) are positioned inside the defined objective function region.

Therefore, it is evident that the ranking process can be flexibly optimized without affecting the index structure. This provides new possibilities to express the information need of the user.

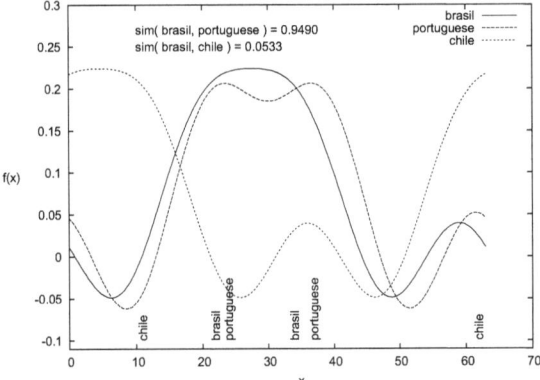

Figure 5.7: Term neighborhood analysis for a typical TREC-8 document for Fourier order $n = 3$.

5.4.2 Query Expansion Runs

Our query expansion experiments are based exclusively on the search results. No external knowledge structure was used to leverage the re-ranking procedure.

In the group of runs described in the following, the proposed query expansion model based on the query terms distribution (f_q) is evaluated.

Using the top-n ranked documents, the query distribution function f_q for each ranked document is obtained, and the terms having a similar distribution as f_q are calculated. Based on equation (5.12), the first k candidate terms $T_q^k = \{\tau_1, \tau_2, \ldots, \tau_k\}$ for query reformulation are obtained and the new ranking using our test collection is evaluated.

The query reformulation and ranking procedure consists of the following steps:

1. Calculate the expanded query terms T_q^k based on the top-n documents from the *tfidf* ranking.

2. Using T_q^k, calculate the expanded query

$$q_e = \{w_0 q,\ w_1 \tau_1,\ w_2 \tau_2,\ \ldots,\ w_k \tau_k\} \qquad (5.13)$$

where w_i is a weighting factor corresponding to the similarity between the original query q and the term τ_i.

3. Perform the *tfidf*-search with q_e.

Using the top-10 ranked documents and the first 40 terms having the highest query similarity, the proposed Fourier Vector Scoring (FVS) query expansion method for $w_i = 1$ is compared with eight state-of-the-art query-expansion methods: Rocchio for $\beta = 0.2, 0.4$,

5.5 Summary

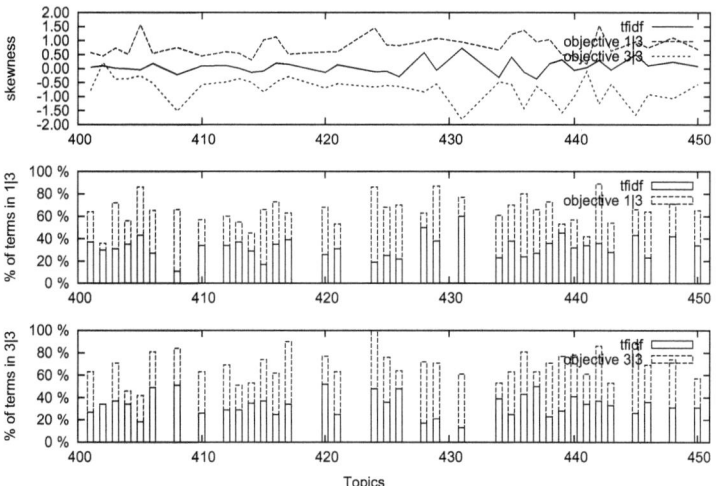

Figure 5.8: The first graph represents the skewness of the query terms distributions for *tfidf* and two different ranking schemes: $f_o : 1|3$ and $f_o : 3|3$. The last two graphs show the percentage of query terms in the proposed objective function regions.

0.6, 0.8, 1.0 (Ro.2, Ro.4, Ro.6, Ro.8, Ro1) [128], Bose-Einstein 1 (Bo1), Bose-Einstein 2 (Bo2) [4] and Kullback-Leibler (KL) [35]. For the query expansion experiments, the Terrier [106] platform was used.

Considering the measures of *relevance precision* and *precision at 10 documents*, it can be observed from Figure 5.9 that FVS outperforms all other query expansion methods.

Table 5.2 shows the most relevant expanded terms, listed in descending relevance order, for eight arbitrary topics from the test collection. The same term sets were also used in the query expansion runs.

5.5 Summary

In this chapter, the Fourier model based on term distribution analysis using Fourier series expansion has been proposed as a novel methodology to improve document relevance evaluation in information retrieval applications. The proposed approach is based on a Fourier series representation of the term positions in a document collection, by calculating the corresponding expansion coefficients. By using query objective functions for predetermined document regions, the approach provides new ways to define or refine queries. Further-

5 The Fourier Model

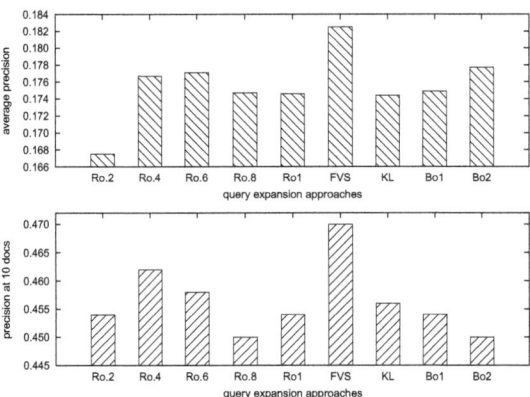

Figure 5.9: Ranking improvements using query expansion. FVS represents the proposed Fourier Vector Scoring.

more, a novel query expansion methodology has been presented to support the user in the query refinement process.

An evaluation of our proposal using the TREC-8 collection has demonstrated that 67% of the query terms are positioned inside the user defined objective function region. A further analysis has shown that using the proposed approach to generate expanded query terms leads to a performance gain over state-of-the-art query expansion models such as Rocchio and *Divergence from Randomness* models.

Table 5.2: Examples of query expansion terms for some arbitrary TREC-8 Topics.

Topic	Title Query	Terms for Query Expansion
403	osteoporosis	bone, women, calcium, health, risk, study, claim, research
406	Parkinson's disease	brain, research, cells, london, drug, symptoms, alzheimer, fetal
408	tropical storms	july, disaster, area, caribbean, hurricane, texas, georgia, temperatures
417	creativity	people, mental, illness, scientists, part, human, children, depression
421	industrial waste disposal	management, facilities, hazardous, radioactive, solid, company, state, site
427	UV damage, eyes	radiation, rays, sunglasses, protect, adhesive, patch, exposure, children
429	Legionnaires' disease	nosocomial, hyph, infection, control, patients, prevention, pneumonia
431	robotic technology	robot, manufacturing, industrial, system, company, human, industry

6
The Hilbert Model

6.1 Introduction

The Hilbert model synthesizes the main concepts of the term position paradigm, providing a general mathematical basis for the previously proposed term position models.

The Hilbert model is based on the basic metrics of Hilbert spaces, i.e. an abstract vector space possessing the structure of an inner product that allows length and angle to be measured and provides the tools to operate within n-dimensional vectors. Thus, transforming term positional information into n-dimensional vectors permits us to efficiently operate on term positional data, making it possible to optimize search results at query evaluation time.

Because the proposed Hilbert model is not limited to a specific function, two particular cases corresponding to the Legendre and Laguerre polynomials will be analyzed, and some properties of the Fourier model introduced in the last chapter will also be reviewed.

Experimental results obtained for the TREC-8 document collection demonstrate that the Hilbert model is superior to state-of-the-art relevance feedback techniques such as *Rocchio* and *Divergence from Randomness* models [128, 4], and provides an efficient instrument to personalize search results based on *objective query functions*.

Part of the material presented in this chapter has been published in [59].

6.2 Analyzing Term Positions

In this section, a general mathematical model to analyze term positions in documents is presented, making it possible to effectively use the term-positional information at query evaluation time.

Consider a document D of length L and a term t that appears in D. The distribution of the term t within the document is given by the set $\mathcal{P}_t$ that contains all positions of t, where all terms are enumerated starting with 1 for the first term and so on. For example, a set $\mathcal{P}_t = \{2,6\}$ represents a term that is located at the second and sixth position of the document body. A characteristic function

$$f^{(t)}(x) = \begin{cases} 1 & \text{for } x \in [p-1,p] \text{ if } p \in \mathcal{P}_t \\ 0 & \text{otherwise} \end{cases}, \qquad (6.1)$$

defined for $x \in [0,L]$, is assigned to $\mathcal{P}_t$.

The proposed method consists of approximating this characteristic function by an expansion in terms of certain sets of functions. In order to do so, some concepts of functional analysis are introduced. Details can be found in the book of Yosida [168].

6.2.1 Expansions in Hilbert Spaces

A Hilbert space $\mathcal{H}$ is a (possibly infinite-dimensional) vector space that is equipped with a scalar product $\langle .,. \rangle$, i. e. two elements $f, g \in \mathcal{H}$ are mapped to a real or complex number $\langle f, g \rangle$. We only consider real scalar products here.

An example of a Hilbert space is the space $L_2([0,L])$ defined as the set of all functions f that are *square-integrable* in the interval $[0,L]$, i. e. functions for which $\int_0^L (f(x))^2 \, dx < \infty$. In this vector space, the addition of two functions f and g, and the multiplication of a function f by a scalar $\alpha \in \mathbb{R}$ are defined point-wise: $(f+g)(x) = f(x)+g(x)$, $(\alpha f)(x) = \alpha f(x)$. The scalar product in $L_2([0,L])$ is defined by

$$\langle f, g \rangle = \int_0^L f(x) g(x) \, dx. \qquad (6.2)$$

Two vectors with vanishing scalar product are called *orthogonal*.

The scalar product induces a *norm* (an abstract measure of length)

$$\|f\| = \sqrt{\langle f, f \rangle} \geq 0. \qquad (6.3)$$

With the help of this norm, the notion of *convergence* in $\mathcal{H}$ can be defined: A sequence $f_0, f_1, \ldots$ of vectors of $\mathcal{H}$ is said to converge to a vector f, symbolically $\lim_{n \to \infty} f_n = f$, if $\lim_{n \to \infty} \|f_n - f\| = 0$. This allows to define an expansion of a vector f in terms of a set of vectors $\{\varphi_0, \varphi_1, \ldots\}$. One writes

$$f = \sum_{k=0}^{\infty} \gamma_k \varphi_k, \qquad (6.4)$$

where the γ_k are real numbers, if the sequence $f_n = \sum_{k=0}^n \gamma_k \varphi_k$ of finite sums converges to f. This kind of convergence is called *norm convergence*.

Of particular importance are so-called complete, orthonormal sets $\{\varphi_0, \varphi_1, \ldots\}$ of functions in $\mathcal{H}$. They have the following properties: (a) The φ_i are mutually orthogonal and normalized to unity:

$$\langle \varphi_n, \varphi_m \rangle = \delta_{nm} = \begin{cases} 1 & \text{for } n = m \\ 0 & \text{for } n \neq m \end{cases} \qquad (6.5)$$

6.2 Analyzing Term Positions

(b) The φ_i are *complete*, which means that every vector of the Hilbert space can be expanded into a convergent sum of them.

Important properties of expansions in terms of complete orthonormal sets are: (a) The expansion coefficients γ_k are given by

$$\gamma_k = \langle \varphi_k, f \rangle. \tag{6.6}$$

(b) They fulfill

$$\sum_{k=0}^{n} \gamma_k^2 \leq \|f\|^2 \text{ for all } n, \text{ and } \sum_{k=0}^{\infty} \gamma_k^2 = \|f\|^2 \tag{6.7}$$

(Bessel's inequality and Parseval's equation).

Given two expansions $f = \sum_{k=0}^{\infty} \gamma_k \varphi_k$, $g = \sum_{k=0}^{\infty} \gamma'_k \varphi_k$, the scalar product can be expressed as

$$\langle f, g \rangle = \sum_{k=0}^{\infty} \gamma_k \gamma'_k. \tag{6.8}$$

If the expansion coefficients are combined into coefficient vectors $\vec{c} = (\gamma_0, \gamma_1, \ldots)$, $\vec{c}' = (\gamma'_0, \gamma'_1, \ldots)$, the preceding equation takes the form $\langle f, g \rangle = \vec{c} \cdot \vec{c}'$.

The Fourier expansions considered by Galeas et al. [58] are an example of such an expansion. The functions

$$\varphi_0^{\text{Fo}}(x) = \frac{1}{\sqrt{L}}, \; \varphi_{2k-1}^{\text{Fo}}(x) = \sqrt{\frac{2}{L}} \sin\left(\frac{2\pi k}{L}\right), \; \varphi_{2k}^{\text{Fo}}(x) = \sqrt{\frac{2}{L}} \cos\left(\frac{2\pi k}{L}\right) \tag{6.9}$$

($k > 0$) form a complete orthonormal set in $L_2([0, L])$, leading to an expansion

$$f(x) = \frac{a_0}{\sqrt{L}} + \sqrt{\frac{2}{L}} \sum_{k=1}^{\infty} \left[a_k \cos\left(\frac{2\pi k x}{L}\right) + b_k \sin\left(\frac{2\pi k x}{L}\right) \right], \tag{6.10}$$

where $a_0 = \gamma_0$ and $a_k = \gamma_{2k}$, $b_k = \gamma_{2k-1}$ for $k > 0$.

Another complete set of orthonormal functions of $L_2([0, L])$ is given by

$$\varphi_k^{\text{Le}}(x) = \sqrt{\frac{2k+1}{L}} P_k^*(x/L), \; k \geq 0, \tag{6.11}$$

where the $P_k^*(x)$ are so-called *shifted Legendre polynomials* [1]. These polynomials are of order k. The first few of them are $P_0^*(x) = 1$, $P_1^*(x) = 2x - 1$, $P_2^*(x) = 6x^2 - 6x + 1$, $P_3^*(x) = 20x^3 - 30x^2 + 12x - 1$. Fig. 6.1 (left) shows $\varphi_k^{\text{Le}}(x)$ for $0 \leq k \leq 4$ in the range $x \in [0, L]$ for $L = 1$.

Another example that will be used later is a complete set for the space $L_2(\mathbb{R}_+)$ (the space of square-integrable functions for $0 \leq x < \infty$):

$$\varphi_k^{\text{La}}(x) = \frac{e^{-x/(2\lambda)}}{\sqrt{\lambda}} L_k(x/\lambda), \; k \geq 0. \tag{6.12}$$

Here, λ is a positive scale parameter and the $L_k(x)$ are *Laguerre polynomials* [1], the first few of which are $L_0(x) = 1$, $L_1(x) = -x + 1$, $L_2(x) = x^2/2 - 2x + 1$, $L_3(x) = -x^3/6 + 3x^2/2 - 3x + 1$, see Fig. 6.1 (right).

6 The Hilbert Model

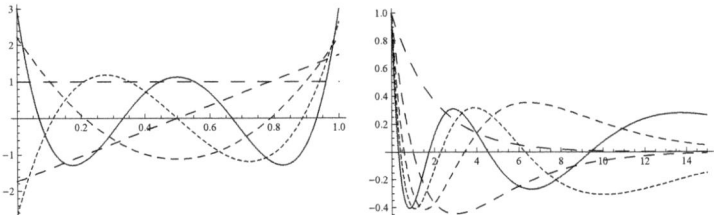

Figure 6.1: *Left*: Shifted Legendre polynomials $\varphi_k^{\text{Le}}(x)$ for $0 \leq k \leq 4$. *Right*: The expansion functions (6.12) for $0 \leq k \leq 4$ and $\lambda = 1$

6.2.2 Truncated Expansions of Term Distributions

As explained above, the finite sums $f_n = \sum_{k=0}^{n} \gamma_k \varphi_k$ converge to the function f in the sense of norm convergence. As a consequence of Bessel's inequality (6.7) they approximate f increasingly better for increasing n. An essential ingredient for the following discussion is to consider a truncated expansion, i. e. the mapping

$$P_n : f^{(t)} \mapsto f_n^{(t)}, \qquad (6.13)$$

which associates to a term distribution $f^{(t)}$ of the form (6.1) its finite-order approximation $f_n^{(t)}$ in terms of some complete orthonormal set for some order n.

Figure 6.2 shows an example for the Fourier expansion. One can observe the characteristic broadening effect generated by the reduction of the expansion order (truncation).

The L_2 scalar product of two truncated term distributions f_n and g_n,

$$\langle f_n, g_n \rangle = \int f_n(x) g_n(x) \, dx \qquad (6.14)$$

has the meaning of an *overlap integral*: The integrand is only large in regions in which both functions $f_n(x)$ and $g_n(x)$ are large, so that $\langle f_n, g_n \rangle$ measures how well both functions overlap in the whole integration range.

Given f_n and g_n, two truncated term distributions describing the term positions and their neighborhood in a certain document, we introduce the concept of *semantic interaction range*: Two terms that are close to each other present a stronger interaction because their truncated distributions have a considerable overlap. This semantic interaction range motivates the following definition of the *similarity* of two term distributions f and g: For some fixed order n, one sets

$$\text{sim}(f, g) = \langle f_n, g_n \rangle = \langle P_n f, P_n g \rangle . \qquad (6.15)$$

In this definition, the truncation $P_n : f \mapsto f_n$ is essential, because the original term distributions f and g are always orthogonal if they describe two different terms. This is so

6.2 Analyzing Term Positions

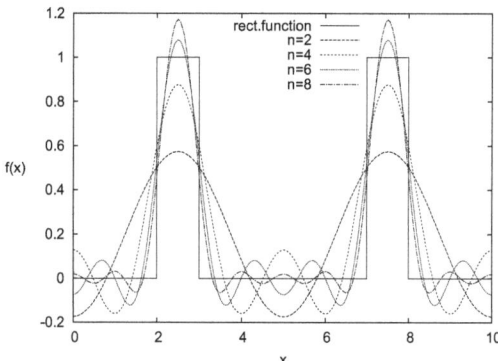

Figure 6.2: Fourier distribution of $\mathcal{P}_t = \{3, 8\}$ in document D, using different Fourier orders n.

because different terms are always at different positions within a document, so that their overlap always vanishes.

Definition (6.15) is only one possibility. In fact, any definition based on the scalar product $\langle f_n, g_n \rangle$ can be utilized. For example, in Galeas et al. [58] a cosine definition $\cos \vartheta = \frac{\langle f_n, g_n \rangle}{\|f_n\| \|g_n\|}$ has been used. Another choice is the norm difference

$$\|f_n - g_n\| = \left(\int (f_n(x) - g_n(x))^2 \, dx \right)^{1/2} = \sqrt{\|f_n\|^2 + \|g_n\|^2 - 2\langle f_n, g_n \rangle}. \quad (6.16)$$

Using different measures based on $\langle f_n, g_n \rangle$, no significant differences in the final retrieval results in several experiments were found.

The scalar product of the truncated distributions can be easily calculated using the coefficient vectors: If the original distributions f and g have the infinite-dimensional coefficient vectors $\vec{c} = (\gamma_0, \gamma_1, \ldots)$ and $\vec{c}' = (\gamma'_0, \gamma'_1, \ldots)$, respectively, then the truncated distributions f_n and g_n have the $(n+1)$-dimensional coefficient vectors $\vec{c}_n = (\gamma_0, \gamma_1, \ldots, \gamma_n)$ and $\vec{c}'_n = (\gamma'_0, \gamma'_1, \ldots, \gamma'_n)$, resp., and their scalar product is the finite sum

$$\langle f_n, g_n \rangle = \vec{c}_n \cdot \vec{c}'_n = \sum_{k=0}^{n} \gamma_k \gamma'_k. \quad (6.17)$$

6.2.3 The Semantic Interaction Range

In this section, a precise definition of the semantic interaction range is given.

In abstract terms, the truncation $P_n : f \mapsto f_n$ is a filtering or a *projection*: In the expansion $f(x) = \sum_{k=0}^{\infty} \gamma_k \varphi_k(x)$ the components φ_k for $k > n$ are filtered out, which amounts to a projection of f onto the components $\varphi_0, \ldots, \varphi_n$. Thus, P_n is a projection operator in the Hilbert space. To derive a closed expression for the operator P_n, one combines $(P_n f)(x) = f_n(x) = \sum_{k=0}^n \gamma_k \varphi_k(x)$, with (6.6) to obtain

$$(P_n f)(x) = \sum_{k=0}^n \left(\int \varphi_k(y) f(y) \, dy \right) \varphi_k(x) = \int \left(\sum_{k=0}^n \varphi_k(y) \varphi_k(x) \right) f(y) \, dy \,. \quad (6.18)$$

One can write the last expression as $\int p_n(y,x) f(y) \, dy$ with the *projection kernel*

$$p_n(y,x) = \sum_{k=0}^n \varphi_k(y) \varphi_k(x) \quad (6.19)$$

as an integral representation of P_n in the sense of a convolution. It has the advantage that one can study the properties of the truncation independently of the function f.

The width of $p_n(y,x)$ as a function of x is a lower bound for the width of a truncated expansion of a term located at y. Therefore, this width will be used as the semantic interaction range for a term at position y.

For the Fourier expansion, p_{2k} is given by

$$p_{2k}^{\text{Fo}}(y,x) = \frac{\cos(4\pi k(y-x)/L) - \cos(2\pi(2k+1)(y-x)/L)}{L(1 - \cos(2\pi(y-x)/L))} \,. \quad (6.20)$$

(We consider only even orders $n = 2k$, because for these orders the expansion consists of an equal number of sine and cosine terms, see (6.9).) The maximum of $p_{2k}^{\text{Fo}}(y,x)$ is at $x = y$ and the two zeros closest to the maximum are at $x = y \pm L/(2n+1)$. Thus, the semantic interaction range for a Fourier expansion of order n may be defined to be

$$\varrho_n^{\text{Fo}} = \frac{2L}{2n+1} \,. \quad (6.21)$$

Fig. 6.3 (left) shows $p_6^{\text{Fo}}(20,x)$ and $p_6^{\text{Fo}}(100,x)$ for $L = 200$.

For the expansions in terms of Legendre and Laguerre polynomials, the projection kernels can be calculated with the Christoffel-Darboux equation [1]. The results are

$$p_n^i(y,x) = \alpha_n^i \frac{\varphi_{n+1}^i(y)\varphi_n^i(x) - \varphi_n^i(y)\varphi_{n+1}^i(x)}{y-x} \,, \quad (6.22)$$

$i = $ Le, La, with $\alpha_n^{\text{Le}} = (L/2)(n+1)/(2n+1)$ and $\alpha_n^{\text{La}} = -\lambda(n+1)$. These kernels are no longer functions of $y - x$, meaning that the broadening of a term distribution depends on the position y of the term distribution within the document.

Fig. 6.3 (right) shows the projection kernel $p_6^{\text{La}}(y,x)$ for $y = 20$ and $y = 100$. One can see that the spatial resolution of the truncated expansion decreases for terms that are far away from the beginning of the document.

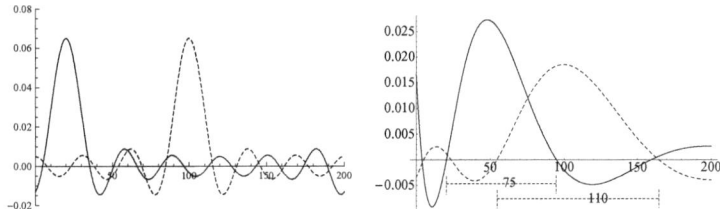

Figure 6.3: *Left*: Projection kernel for the Fourier expansion showing the semantic interaction range for two terms at the positions 20 and 100, for $n = 6$ and $L = 200$. *Right*: Projection kernel for the expansion in terms of Laguerre polynomials showing the semantic interaction range for two terms at the positions 20 and 100, for $n = 6$ and $\lambda = 15$.

6.3 Applications

The goal of our approach is to shift the complexity of processing the positional data from the query evaluation phase to the (not time critical) indexing phase, reducing the ranking optimization via term positions to a simple mathematical operation.

Hence, we propose to calculate the expansion coefficients γ_k of the term distributions in the indexing phase and to store this abstract term positional information in the index. This permits a considerably faster query evaluation, compared with methods that use the raw term-positional information.

Thus, the index contains an $(n + 1)$-dimensional coefficient vector $\vec{c}_n = (\gamma_0, \gamma_1, \ldots, \gamma_n)$ for each term and each document in the collection. The γ_k are calculated analytically via (6.6). To give an example of the complexity involved,

$$\gamma_k = \sum_{p \in \mathcal{P}_t} \sum_{j=0}^{k} \alpha_j \left[\left(\frac{p}{L}\right)^{j+1} - \left(\frac{p-1}{L}\right)^{j+1} \right] \quad (6.23)$$

with $\alpha_j = \sqrt{(2k+1)L}\, a_j/(j+1)$ is the expression for the expansion coefficients in the case of the expansion in terms of Legendre polynomials, cf. (6.1). (The a_j are the polynomial coefficients of the shifted Legendre polynomial of order k.) Calculations of this kind can be easily performed in the indexing stage.

The investigated retrieval scenarios are: (a) ranking optimization based on *user-defined objective functions* and (b) *query expansion based on term-positional information* [58], and (c) cluster analysis of terms in documents. They all involve a calculation of the similarity of term distributions.

6.3.1 Ranking Optimization

The first scenario states document ranking as an optimization problem that is based on the query term distribution function $f_{q,d}$ and a user-defined objective function f_o representing the optimal query term distribution in the document body:

$$Maximize\{\text{sim}(f_{q,d}, f_o)\} \quad \forall f_{q,d} \in A \quad (6.24)$$

where A represents the query term distributions in a document set, $f_{q,d}$ is the query term distribution function for query q in document d, and f_o is a user-defined objective function, representing the optimal query term distributions for the documents in the document ranking.

6.3.2 Query Expansion

The second scenario considers the *top-r* documents $D = \{d_1, d_2, \ldots, d_r\}$ of an initial ranking process and the functions $f_{q,d}$ with $d \in D$. The set of terms T_q whose elements t maximize the expression $\text{sim}(f_{q,d}, f_{t,d})$ is computed. It contains the terms for all documents in D that have a similar distribution as the query, i.e. terms positioned near the query in the top ranked documents. This set T_q is used to expand q.

6.3.3 Cluster Analysis of Terms in Documents

Given a document, one may ask whether there are groups (clusters) of terms whose elements all have similar distributions. One may then infer that all terms inside a cluster describe related concepts [7]. In this section, some properties of the proposed method will be explained that may be useful for the analysis of term clusters.

Consider a document of length L. Since at every position within the document a particular term may either be present or not, there are in total $N = 2^L$ possible term distributions. Each of these distributions is mapped to a point in an $(n+1)$-dimensional Hilbert space. If the norm difference (6.16) is used as the similarity criterion, then clusters of similar term distributions are just Euclidean point clusters in the Hilbert space.

We will now investigate the geometrical structure of the set of all possible term distributions. Let us first calculate the center $\bar{f}(x) = (1/N) \sum_{\nu=1}^{N} f^{(\nu)}(x)$ of all term distributions (here $f^{(\nu)}(x)$, $\nu = 1, \ldots, N$, is an enumeration of distributions of the form (6.1)). At any position x, half of all N distributions have a term present ($f^{(\nu)}(x) = 1$) and the other half does not ($f^{(\nu)}(x) = 0$), so that $\bar{f}(x) = 1/2 = \text{const}$ for all $x \in [0, L]$. This average distribution is mapped to a non-truncated, in general infinite-dimensional coefficient vector $\vec{c}$, whose length $|\vec{c}|$ is given by the norm $\|\bar{f}\| = [\int_0^L dx/4]^{1/2} = \sqrt{L}/2$. The squared distance between the center point and the coefficient vector $\vec{c}^{(\nu)}$ of a distribution $f^{(\nu)}$ is $|\vec{c} - \vec{c}^{(\nu)}|^2 = \|\bar{f} - f^{(\nu)}\|^2 = \int_0^L (1/2 - f^{(\nu)}(x))^2 dx$. Since $f^{(\nu)}(x)$ is either 0 or 1, it follows that $(1/2 - f^{(\nu)}(x))^2 = 1/4 = \text{const}$ for all $x \in [0, L]$, giving $|\vec{c}^{(\nu)} - \vec{c}| = \sqrt{L}/2$ for all ν. This means that the non-truncated coefficient vectors of all term distributions lie on the surface of a sphere with radius $\sqrt{L}/2$ whose center is at $\vec{c}$. Because $|\vec{c}| = \sqrt{L}/2$, this sphere touches the origin of the Hilbert space.

Bessel's inequality (6.7) leads to $|\vec{c}_n^{(\nu)} - \vec{c}_n| \leq \sqrt{L}/2$ for all ν for the coefficient vectors truncated to order n. Thus, the truncated vectors all lie *within* a sphere of radius

$$R_0 = \sqrt{L}/2 \quad (6.25)$$

6.3 Applications

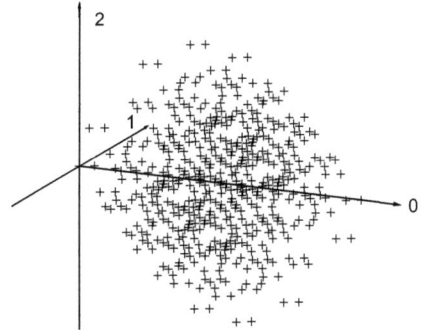

Figure 6.4: Three dimensional sphere of all 512 possible term distributions in a document of length $L = 9$ for the expansion in terms of Legendre polynomials.

in the $(n + 1)$-dimensional Hilbert space. The center of this sphere is at $\vec{c}_n$. If—as in the Fourier and Legendre cases—one of the expansion functions, say $\varphi_0(x)$, is constant, the vector $\vec{c}$ describing itself a constant function has only a non-vanishing zero component: $\vec{c} = \vec{c}_n = (\sqrt{L}/2, 0, 0, \ldots)$. Fig. 6.4 shows this term sphere in $n + 1 = 3$ dimensions for a document of length $L = 9$ and the expansion in terms of Legendre polynomials.

The fact that all possible truncated coefficient vectors $\vec{c}_n^{(\nu)}$ lie within a sphere whose radius and center are known is very useful for clustering analysis. First of all, it shows where in the Hilbert space to look for clusters. Secondly, assume one has found a cluster $K = \{\vec{k}_1, \ldots, \vec{k}_q\}$ of term distributions by some clustering algorithm (for an nth order truncation). The volume of this cluster can be estimated by calculating the standard deviation $R_K = [(1/q) \sum_{i=1}^{q} (\vec{k}_i - \vec{k})^2]^{1/2} = [(1/(2q^2)) \sum_{i,j=1}^{q} (\vec{k}_i - \vec{k}_j)^2]^{1/2}$ (here $\vec{k}$ is the center of the cluster) and approximating the cluster by a sphere of radius R_K. Since the volume of a sphere of radius R_K in $n + 1$ dimensions is proportional to R_K^{n+1}, the cluster occupies approximately a part $\xi = (R_K/R_0)^{n+1} = (2R_K/\sqrt{L})^{n+1}$ of the theoretically available space. A cluster would then be considered as significant only if $\xi \ll 1$. An analysis of this kind may be useful to generate an ontology of terms based on individual documents.

It has been conjectured that the use of quantum mechanical methods, in particular infinite-dimensional Hilbert spaces and projection operators, may be advantageous in IR [154]. The approach presented here goes into this direction, because constructing appropriate sets of orthogonal functions is a standard technique in quantum mechanics. Still, we emphasize that this approach is essentially classical, not quantum mechanical, since it does not use any of the interpretational subtleties of quantum mechanics.

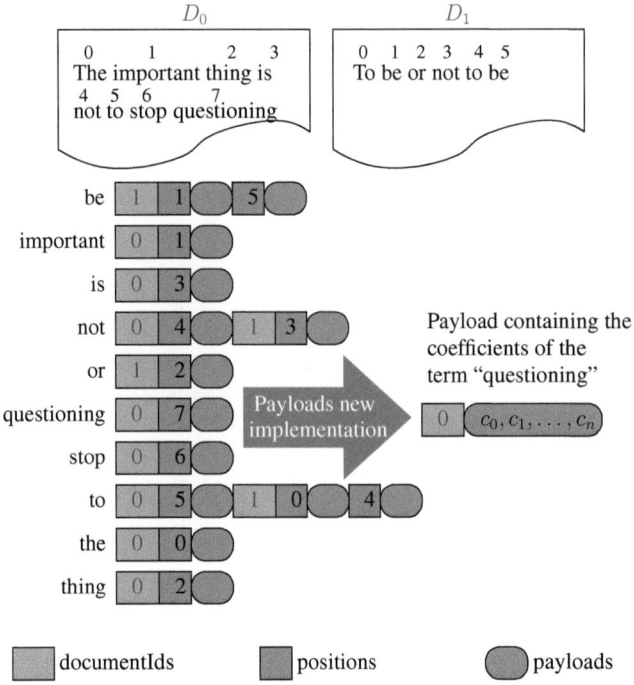

Figure 6.5: Lucene Payload structure

6.4 A Suitable Index Implementation

One of the main properties of our models is the abstract way to represent term positions information (using coefficients). This new data format will influence the structure of the database where term positions information is generally stored: the index. Consequently, the use of a suitable index structure is an important point to be considered in the design of an IR system that implements our approach.

As we began with the experimentation phase based on the Lucene platform, an extension of the index structure was not considered in the software model. But in the recent past, developers of Lucene proposed *Payloads*, a new data structure that permits this type of index manipulation. The Payloads model is an extension that adds the possibility to store arbitrary metadata together with each position of a term in its posting lists. In the actual development release of Lucene (2.9), Payloads are implemented as an arbitrary byte array stored at a specific position (i.e. a specific token/term) in the index (Figure 6.5). Payloads can be used to store weights for specific terms or things like part of speech tags or other semantic information [75].

The Payload structure offers a base for the implementation of our index model, but some important modifications have to be done. In an ideal index structure, we do not need to store the original term positional information, but only the corresponding coefficients containing an abstract representation of these term positions.

As illustrated in Figure 6.5, the term "questioning" in the original index structure contains the the value "7" corresponding to its position in the document D_0 plus the payload data, while in the proposed structure the original positional data was eliminated and the Payload field contains the coefficients representing the position of "questioning" in the document D_0.

Due to the very small number of sample documents in Figure 6.5, the necessary space to store the Payload information is bigger than the original position space. This effect vanishes in real documents containing hundreds or thousands of words.

Event though the implementation of an adapted Payload version for our data model requires some programming effort, we consider Payloads as the best alternative compared to the index models of actual open source IR platforms.

6.5 Implications Regarding the Document Length

One important aspect to be analyzed is how the length of document influences the similarity measures in the term position models. As shown in the expression 6.26, the vector model uses normalized vectors to calculate the similarity values between documents and the user query.

$$sim(d_j, q) = \frac{\vec{d_j} \cdot \vec{q}}{|\vec{d_j}| \times |\vec{q}|} \qquad (6.26)$$

Because the similarity measures with the Term Position models considers terms "*within*" the same document, a normalization process is not necessary. Nevertheless, there is an important effect by comparing term distributions "*between*" documents of different lengths. Using the Expansion Analyzer (Section 2.11.1) we examined a fixed term position configuration for two different document lengths: (a) a short document with $L = 24$, and (b) a long document with $L = 500$. Then, we compared the measures of similarity between the defined term distributions based on the scalar product and the cosine measures.

In Figure 6.6 (top), we observe the distribution of three different single terms at the positions $\{8, 12, 18\}$ represented by the functions: *Reference* (R), *Distribution 1* (D_1), and *Distribution 2* (D_2) respectively. If we compare these three functions in the main analysis window, we can observe a clear difference in the overlapping regions: $\text{Overlap}(R, D_1) > \text{Overlap}(R, D_2)$, particularly for low expansion orders. This difference can be confirmed in the scalar product and cosine measures from the Figure 6.6 (bottom): by low expansion orders ($order \leq 6$) the similarity values based on both measures reflex a high similarity between R and D_1, and a low similarity between R and D_2.

Using the same term position configuration and increasing the length of the document to $L = 500$, we obtain the results depicted in Figure 6.7 (top).

6 The Hilbert Model

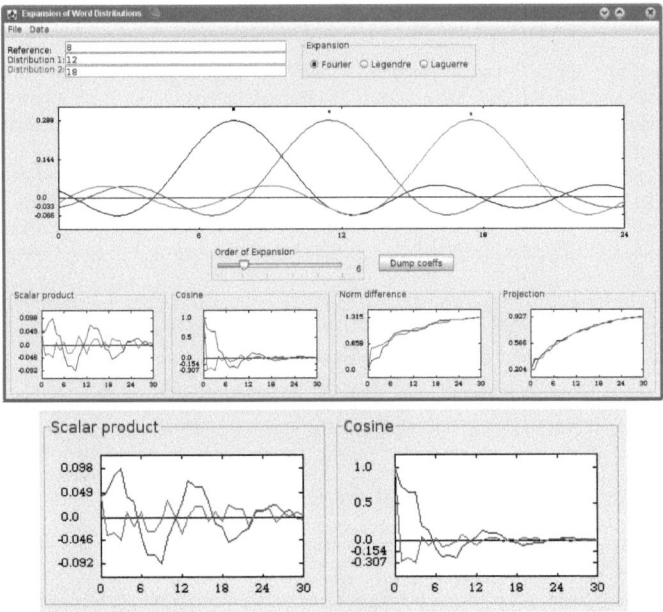

Figure 6.6: *Top*: The Expansion Analyzer illustrating three single terms at the positions $\{8, 12, 18\}$ in a document of length $L = 24$ with the Fourier model. A clear difference between the overlapping regions is shown: Overlap($Reference, Distribution_1$) > Overlap($Reference, Distribution_2$). *Bottom*: In the scalar product and cosine graphics, one can observe (by low expansion orders) a high similarity between R and D_1, and a low similarity between R and D_2.

Here one can observe that all functions (R, D_1, and D_2) present almost the same pattern and the overlapping regions are very similar: Overlap(R, D_1) $\sim$ Overlap(R, D_2). This effect can be confirmed in the scalar product and cosine (Figure 6.7 (bottom)) where for low expansion orders, a high similarity between the distributions (D_1, D_2) and the reference (R) functions is illustrated.

Using the Semantic Interaction Range (SIR) concept (Section 6.2) to analyse the document length effect, one can confirm that variations in the document length affect the SIR measures, depending on the applied term positions model. For instance, in Figure 6.8, the SIR for the Fourier model (6th order) at the positions $\{50, 100\}$ is illustrated. Here, the SIR values for the positions 50 and 100 do not vary within the document boundaries, but they grow proportionally to the variation in the document length. On the other hand, if we use the Laguerre model with the same term positions configuration (Figure 6.9), one can

6.5 Implications Regarding the Document Length

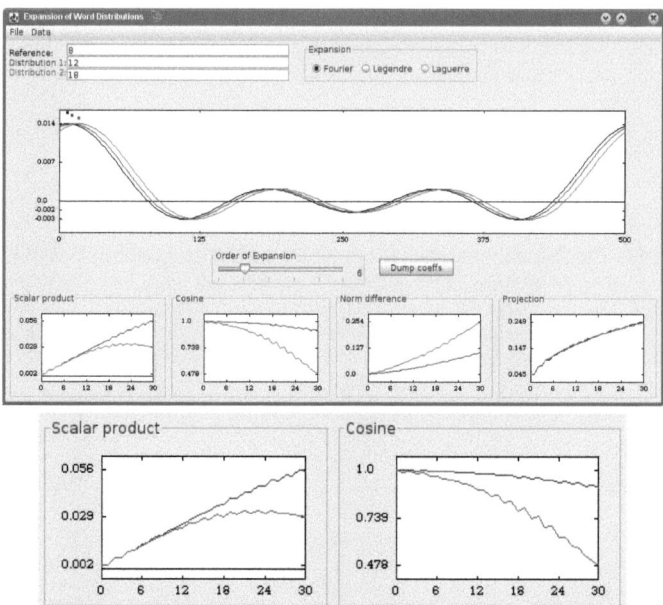

Figure 6.7: *Top*: The Expansion Analyzer illustrating three single terms at the positions $\{8, 12, 18\}$ in a document of length $L = 500$ with the Fourier model, having all distributions a similar term distribution pattern: $\text{Overlap}(Reference, Distribution_1) \sim \text{Overlap}(Reference, Distribution_2)$. *Bottom*: In the scalar product and cosine curves we observe, for low expansion orders, a high similarity between all term distribution representations.

observe that the SIR values lightly vary for term positions within the document, but they are not affected by variations of the document length.

Analyzing the document length effect in the proposed IR applications (Query Expansion and Ranking Optimization) we confirmed the following statements:

In Query Expansion : Due to the fact that the Semantic Interaction Range in a long document contains more terms than in a short document, long documents will contribute with more terms to the query expansion process than short documents. The level of influence depends directly on the applied term distribution model. In consequence, by the selection of the term distribution model one should consider the properties of the documents in the collection. For homogeneous collections where the document size does not vary considerably, the Fourier model will be probably the best alternative. The Laguerre model, due to its independence of the document length, will be the best

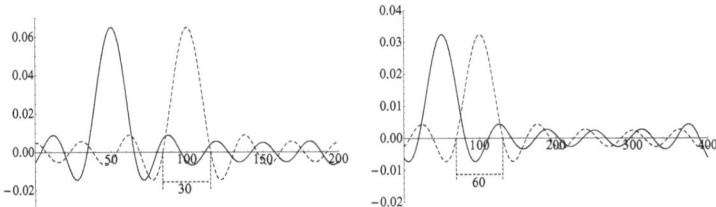

Figure 6.8: The Semantic Interaction Range ϱ^{Fo} for the Fourier expansion of order 6 does not vary within the positions of the document boundaries $\{50, 100\}$, but it grows proportionally to variations in the document length. For example, the term located at the position $\{100\}$ duplicates its interaction range from 30 to 60 terms, if the document length grows from 200 to 400 terms.

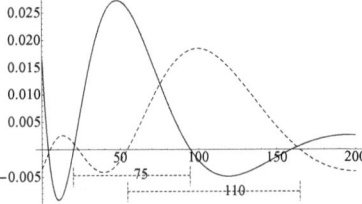

Figure 6.9: The Semantic Interaction Range ϱ^{La} for the Laguerre polynomial of order 6 is independent of the document length but lightly varies within the document boundaries.

choice in collections where the document length strongly varies.

In Ranking Optimization : The user defined objective function f_o (Expression 6.24) is always scaled to each processed document in the ranking, therefore the document length does not influence the proposed ranking optimization method.

6.6 Experimental Results

6.6.1 Software

During the development of the Hilbert model, we discovered the software Terrier [106] (see Section 2.11.3), a new platform for research and experimentation in text retrieval.

Unlike the Lucene platform, Terrier incorporates the modules necessary for experiments on the TREC collections, simplifying the evaluation and comparison of the different models.

To perform the experiments with the Hilbert model, the functionality of Terrier was extended, implementing new *Matching* and *QueryExpansion* classes for the Fourier and the polynomial models. In the same way, the necessary components to specify the properties of

6.6 Experimental Results

the term distribution models were also integrated in the Terrier modules.

6.6.2 Experiment 1: Varying the Query Expansion Parameters

First, a set of experiments to analyze the performance of all models by varying two basic variables of the query expansion methodology were performed: (a) the number of top-ranked documents to be considered in the pseudo relevance set (*expansion.documents*), and (b) the number of the highest weighted terms from the pseudo relevance set to be added to the original query (*expansion.terms*).

Recent studies in search engine user behavior [119, 25] demonstrate that 68% of search engine users click a search result within the first page of results, and a full 92% of search engine users click a result within the first three pages of search results. Based on this information, the proposed query expansion models were evaluated, assuming that the users are principally interested in the first page of the results. This corresponds approximately to the first 10 documents of the ranking, which is also equivalent to the well known measure in IR *precision at 10 documents* (P.10).

The goal of this experiment is two fold; first, we analyze how these two variables affect the retrieval performance of the models, and second, because the comparison of the models requires fixed values of *expansion.documents* and *expansion.terms*, we use the experimental data to estimate a common initial configuration where all models present a suitable retrieval performance, avoiding an unfair comparison.

Figure 6.10 shows the retrieval performance for different values of *expansion.documents* and *expansion.terms* applied to two groups of models: (a) the term position models on the left column, and (b) the state-of-the-art query expansion models on the right column.

Term Position Models   State-of-the-art Models

- Fourier
- Legendre
- Laguerre

- Rocchio 0.8
- Kullback-Leibler (KL)
- Bose-Einstein 1 (Bo1)

The x-axis corresponds to the number of expansion documents, the y-axis is the number of expansion terms, and the z-axis represent the Precision at 10 documents (P.10).

Figure 6.10 shows that all models increase their performance between 5 an 10 expansion documents. All state-of-the-art models present an optimal performance between 10 and 15 documents and they also drastically decrease their performance from the 15st document. The Fourier model, on the other hand, increases its performance directly proportional to the number of documents in the analyzed range (5 to 20 documents). The Legendre model initially presents a performance similar to the Fourier model, but decreases slightly its efficiency from the 15st document. Finally, the Laguerre model improves its performance uniformly with the number of expanded documents and terms.

Query Expansion Boundaries

Analyzing the numerical results of the experiments, we can argue that the performance reduction in the state-of-the-art models (described above) is highly influenced by the methodology used to process the documents in the first iteration of the query expansion.

All tested models use the *tfidf* weighting scheme to generate the initial ranking, but how these ranked documents are later processed distinguishes the proposed models from the traditional query expansion models.

$$Q_{i+1} = \alpha Q_i + \beta \sum_{relevant} \frac{D_i}{|D_i|} - \gamma \sum_{non-relevant} \frac{Di}{|D_i|} \qquad (6.27)$$

In the Rocchio formula (equation 6.27), the number of relevant documents obtained from the first iteration plays a fundamental role in the selection of the expanded terms, because the term frequency is here the main criterion to select the expansion terms. If one selected document from this iteration is irrelevant or contains terms that are not related to the original query, unwished noise (bad terms) will be added to the expanded query harming the performance of the model. This behavior affects all state-of-the-art models and it can be observed in the precision values calculated for different query expansion configurations in Table 6.1: In the last two rows, the performance of the Rocchio, KL and Bose-Einstein (Bo1) models drops drastically.

Table 6.1: Performance drops by the state-of-the-art query expansion models from the 15th document.

QE Config.		Precision at 10 documents (P_{10})					
		Models					
Terms	Docs	Rocchio	KL	Bo1	Fourier	Legendre	Laguerre
40	5	0.4340	0.4500	0.4480	0.4420	0.4580	0.4500
40	10	0.4580	0.4560	0.4540	0.4700	0.4620	0.4540
40	15	0.4640	0.4540	0.4580	0.4720	0.4740	0.4680
40	20	0.4340▽	0.4320▽	0.4360▽	0.4720	0.4580	0.4680

On the other hand, the term position models select the expansion terms using the query neighborhood, avoiding to include possible noisy terms from other regions of the document. This effect permits to increase the number of documents considered in the expansion process which are the source of relevant expansion terms, and minimizes the existence of irrelevant terms in the expanded query.

In the term position models, the Fourier and Laguerre models present the best performance, due to the high number of documents used in the expansion process that contribute to new relevant terms. We assume that this effect is a result of the symmetry of the expansion, specially in the case of the Fourier model that permits to obtain well defined regions around the query terms on the analyzed documents and thus more reliable neighbor terms.

With regard to the number of expansion terms, we observed that in all state-of-the-art models the increment of expansion terms (between 20 and 50 terms) scarcely affects

6.6 Experimental Results

their performance, while all term position models are more sensitive to a variation of this parameter.

6.6.3 Experiment 2: Using Fixed Query Expansion Parameters

Based on the results of Experiment 1, we conclude that a good trade-off for the performance of all models is between 10 and 15 expansion documents and between 30 and 40 expansion terms. In the query expansion experiments, all models will be evaluated for the proposed document and term ranges, which correspond to the combinations presented in Table 6.2:

Table 6.2: Query expansion experiments for different *expansion.documents* and *expansion.terms* configurations. The experimental results are displayed in the graph referenced in the column "Figure".

Run	expansion.documents	expansion.terms	Figure
QE.1	10	30	6.11
QE.2	10	40	6.12
QE.3	15	30	6.13
QE.4	15	40	6.14
QE.5	20	50	6.15

From Figures 6.11, 6.12, 6.13, 6.14, and 6.15 we can observe that the term position models outperform the state-of-the-art models in all tested query expansion configurations, where the Fourier model has the best general performance.

To measure the benefits of the term position models, a last query expansion run was performed using a configuration of 20 documents and 50 terms. As shown in Figure 6.15, the clearly superior performance of the term position models becomes evident.

6.6.4 Experiment 3: Comparing the Query Expansion Terms

To obtain a clear picture about the query expansion process, the expansion terms generated by the state-of-the-art models and the term position models are analyzed below.

As shown in the example of Table 6.3, 77% of the expansion terms generated by the Rocchio, Kullback-Leibler and Bose-Einstein-1 models are identical. Only a slight difference in the associated weighting coefficients can be observed. These weighting coefficients define the grade of importance of each term in the expanded query.

A similar situation can be observed in Table 6.4; about 92% of the expansion terms produced by the term position models are identical.

For this reason, it was decided to organize the results in two groups: The group "A" containing the expansion terms calculated with the state-of-the-art-models, and the group "B" containing the expansion terms generated with the term distribution models.

Table 6.5 shows the expansion terms for six arbitrary TREC-8 Topics, calculated with the algorithms of the group "A" (Rocchio, Kullback-Leibler, and Bose-Einstein-1) and with the algorithms of the group "B" (Fourier, Laguerre, and Legendre). The terms in bold represent the differences in the calculated sets.

Table 6.3: Query expansion terms for Topic 429, calculated with the state-of-the-art models, where 77% of the generated expansion terms are identical.

| Topic 429 : legionnaires disease ||||||
| Rocchio || Kullback-Leibler || Bose-Einstein 1 ||
term	weight	term	weight	term	weight
legionella	0,63	legionella	0,64	legionella	0,65
nosocomi	0,54	nosocomi	0,53	nosocomi	0,53
pneumonia	0,34	legionellosi	0,37	legionellosi	0,41
legionellosi	0,33	hospit	0,26	pneumophila	0,28
pneumophila	0,31	pneumophila	0,25	pneumonia	0,24
infec	0,20	water	0,24	spp	0,23
patient	0,20	pneumonia	0,22	hospit	0,20
prevent	0,19	spp	0,21	water	0,16
hyph	0,18	hyph	0,21	outbreak	0,16
spp	0,17	case	0,16	patient	0,15
infect	0,15	patient	0,16	infec	0,15
hospital	0,15	outbreak	0,15	epidemiolog	0,15
risk	0,15	preven	0,14	preven	0,14

Table 6.4: Query expansion terms for the Topic 429, calculated with the term distribution models, where 92% of the generated expansion terms are identical.

| Topic 429 : legionnaires disease ||||||
| Fourier || Legendre || Laguerre ||
term	weight	term	weight	term	weight
infec	0,27	pneumonia	0,28	pneumonia	0,34
nosocomi	0,27	nosocomi	0,26	system	0,32
pneumonia	0,26	system	0,26	infec	0,32
hospit	0,26	report	0,26	control	0,31
control	0,25	hospit	0,25	hospit	0,30
report	0,25	water	0,24	legionella	0,29
system	0,25	infec	0,24	health	0,29
preven	0,24	control	0,24	water	0,28
health	0,24	health	0,23	report	0,28
legionella	0,23	legionella	0,23	nosocomi	0,27
legionellosi	0,20	preven	0,21	preven	0,25
epidemiolog	0,19	legionellosi	0,20	legionellosi	0,22
water	0,19	laboratori	0,17	patient	0,21

In Table 6.5, it is shown that the state-of-the-art models produce quite different expansion terms than the term position models. For example, 83% of the generated terms for Topic 417 "creativity" are different in both groups.

Considering the results of the TREC-8 experiments shown in Figures 6.11, 6.12, 6.13, 6.14, 6.15 and the information contained in Table 6.5, the term position models seem to produce better expansion terms than the state-of-the-art models (at least subjectively).

6.6.5 Experiment 4: Objective Function with Term Position Models

In the fourth group of experiments, the effectiveness of a ranking based on the user defined objective function f_o for all term position models is measured.

For this purpose, the search results for two fictitious users having quite different information needs are analyzed. The first user (User$_A$) is searching for scientific papers having the query terms close to the *Abstract* and the *Introduction* sections, that is approximately, in the first third of the document. The second user (User$_B$), is interested in papers having the query terms in the *Conclusion* section, almost at the bottom (last third) of the document.

Using the document collection of TREC-8 and the corresponding 50 query sets (topics), the query term positions in the top-20 documents based on the objective functions $f_o = 1|3$ and $f_o = 3|3$ were analyzed, representing the information needs of User$_A$ ($f_o = 1|3$ means first third of the documents) and User$_B$ ($f_o = 3|3$ means last third of the documents), respectively. Both objective functions were evaluated using polynomials of 6th order for the Fourier, Legendre and Laguerre models.

Figures 6.16, 6.17, and 6.18 show the distribution of query terms after ranking optimization using the *interquartile range* (IQR), a robust measure of statistical dispersion that defines the difference between the 75th and 25th percentiles of a variable [101, 102]. The bounds around the □ symbol (square) define the positions of the query terms for $f_o = 1|3$, while the bounds around the ○ symbol (circle) define the positions of the query terms for $f_o = 3|3$.

The results demonstrate the high accuracy obtained by the Fourier and Legendre models. For example, in Figure 6.16, 50% of the topics produce a ranking where 100% of the query terms are located in the range defined by the objective function ($f_o = 3|3$). Many of the remaining topics have an equivalent query term distribution within the second half of the documents. As illustrated in the Legendre graph (Figure 6.17), the ranking shows a similar performance. Finally, due to the logarithmic component of the Laguerre polynomial, some difficulties to recognize search terms located at the bottom of the documents ($f_o = 3|3$) become obvious (Fig. 6.18).

6.7 Summary

In this chapter, relevance evaluation using truncated Hilbert space expansions has been presented. The proposed approach is based on an abstract representation of term positions in a document collection which induces a measure of proximity between terms (semantic interaction range) and permits their direct and simple comparison. Based on this abstract

Table 6.5: Query expansion stems for TREC-8 Topics. The column "A" contains a set of expansion stems calculated using the state-of-the-art query expansion algorithms (Rocchio, Kullback-Leibler, Bose-Einstein-1) and the column "B" contains a set of the expansion stems computed with the term distribution algorithms (Fourier, Laguerre, Legendre). The terms in bold indicate the differences in the calculated sets.

| 417: creativity || 427: uv damage, eyes || 421: industrial waste disposal ||
A	B	A	B	A	B
compute	artist	exposur	agenc	dump	compani
csikszentmihalyi	column	irradi	cancer	gorleben	countri
depres	design	lamp	effect	hazard	environ
dress	first	nm	exposur	inciner	facil
experi	human	protec	human	landfil	financi
gaultier	imagin	radiat	increas	municip	futur
idea	individu	rai	light	nirex	govern
ideafish	number	resist	measur	nuclear	hazard
ill	peopl	skin	product	plausibl	kingdom
manic	person	spectrum	protec	practic	london
mental	process	spf	radiat	quantiti	manag
mihali	product	sunglass	recent	radioact	method
peopl	start	sunscreen	research	sea	nuclear
practic	studi	ultraviolet	state	sellafield	power
research	think	uva	studi	site	sellafield
scientist	univers	uvgi	system	solid	water
studi	world	wavelength	wavelength	state	
think	writer			wastewat	

| 431: robotic technology || 408: tropical storms || 429: legionnaires disease ||
A	B	A	B	A	B
autom	assembl	atlant	associ	case	control
abb	autom	augusta	atlant	epidemiolog	epidemiolog
assembl	compani	carolina	brief	hospit	health
autom	control	coast	center	hyph	hospit
control	develop	depres	coast	infec	infec
demark	europ	flood	column	legionella	laboratori
develop	factori	floodwat	downgrad	legionellosi	legionella
engelberg	includ	gulf	forecast	nosocomi	legionellosi
handl	industri	hattera	hurrican	outbreak	nosocomi
hannov	intern	hurrican	intern	patient	patient
industri	manufactur	lili	least	pneumonia	pneumonia
machin	research	louisiana	mexico	preven	preven
odet	scienc	miami	miami	risk	report
satellit	system	nation	nation	spp	system
sensor		rain	peopl	water	water
space		remnant	press		
system		saturdai	report		
weld		shigehara	servic		
		weather	south		
		wind	staff		
		wire	weaken		

6.7 Summary

representation, it is possible to shift the complexity of processing term-positional data to the indexing phase, permitting the use of term-positional information at query time without significantly affecting the response time of the system. Three applications for IR were discussed: (a) ranking optimization based on a user-defined term distribution function, (b) query expansion based on term-positional information, and (c) a cluster analysis approach for terms within documents.

134 6 The Hilbert Model

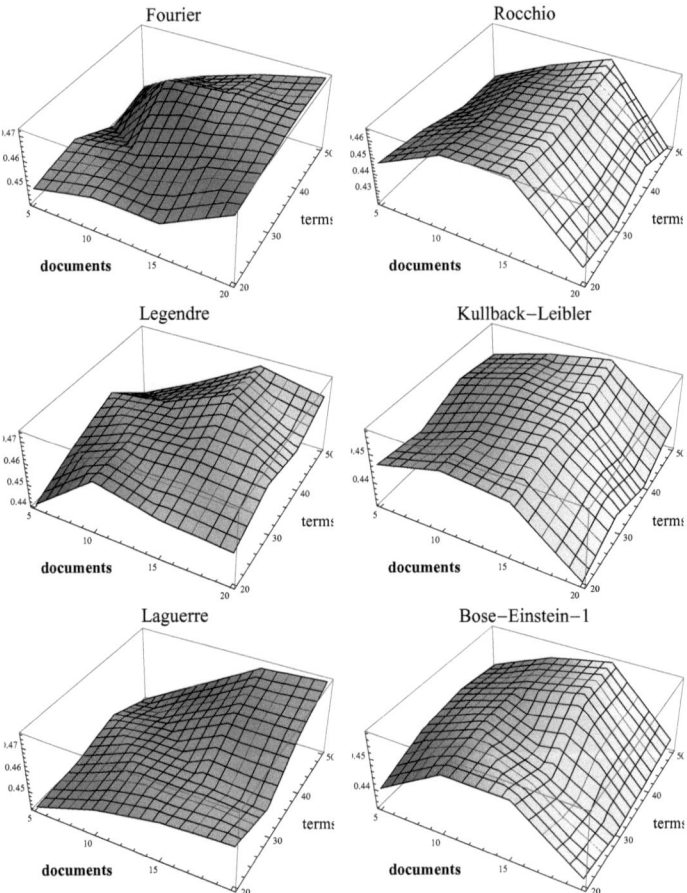

Figure 6.10: Precision at 10 documents for term positional models and three other models, using different query expansions configurations. The axes labeled documents and terms correspond to $|D|$ and $|T_q|$, respectively. The term position models (left column) differ from the state-of-the-art models (right column) because the former tend to increase the retrieval performance by incrementing the number of expansion documents and expansion terms, while the state-of-the-art models present an important drop in the performance from the 15th expansion document.

6.7 Summary

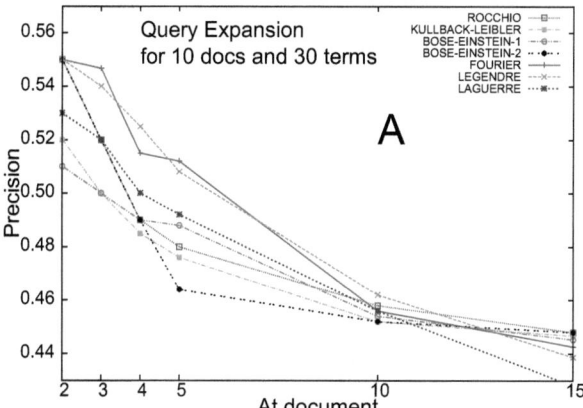

Figure 6.11: Comparing the query expansion performance for the term distribution models (Fourier, Legendre and Laguerre) and the state-of-the-art models, using three configurations of 10 expanded documents and 30 expanded terms.

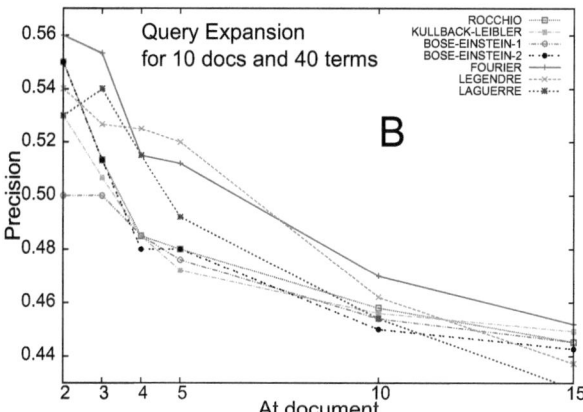

Figure 6.12: Comparing the query expansion performance for the term distribution models (Fourier, Legendre and Laguerre) and the state-of-the-art models, using three configurations of 10 expanded documents and 40 expanded terms.

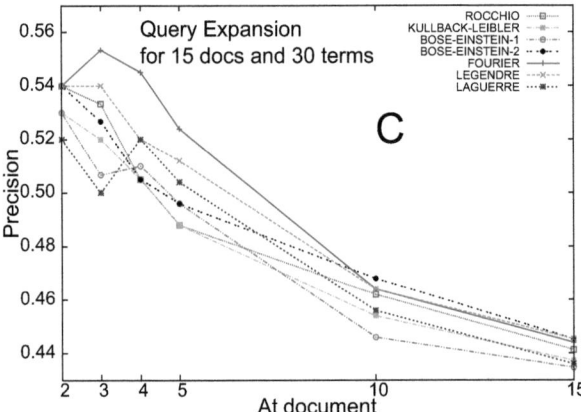

Figure 6.13: Comparing the query expansion performance for the term distribution models (Fourier, Legendre and Laguerre) and the state-of-the-art models, using three configurations of 15 expanded documents and 30 expanded terms.

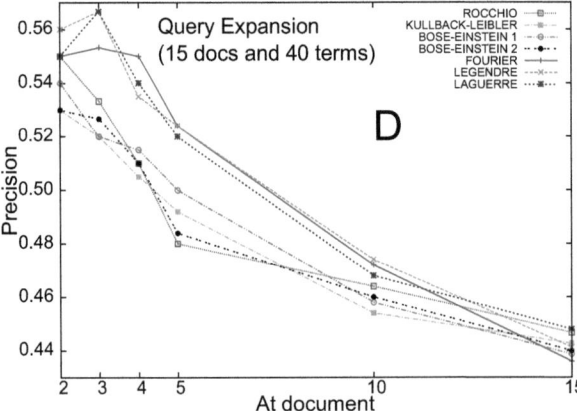

Figure 6.14: Comparing the query expansion performance for the term distribution models (Fourier, Legendre and Laguerre) and the state-of-the-art models, using three configurations of 15 expanded documents and 40 expanded terms.

6.7 Summary

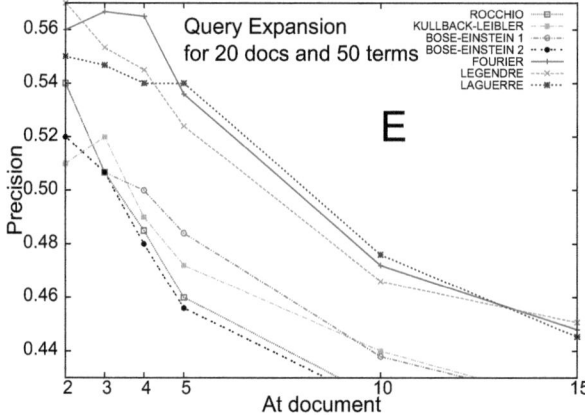

Figure 6.15: Comparing the query expansion performance for the term distribution models (Fourier, Legendre and Laguerre) and the state-of-the-art models, using three configurations of 20 expanded documents and 50 expanded terms. In this diagram the clear performance superiority of the term position models over the traditional models can be observed.

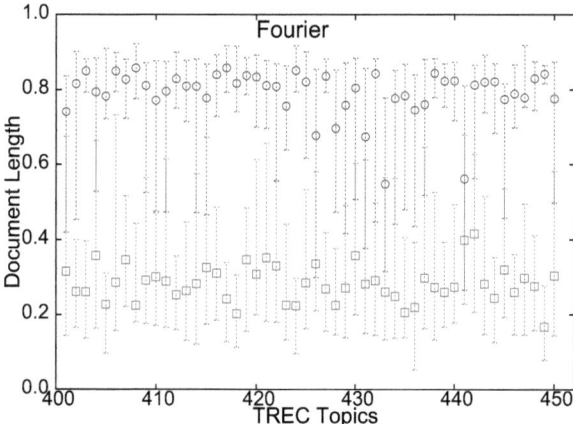

Figure 6.16: Distribution of the query terms for the top-20 TREC-8 documents ranked with the Fourier model and two different objective functions: $f_o = 1|3$ and $f_o = 3|3$.

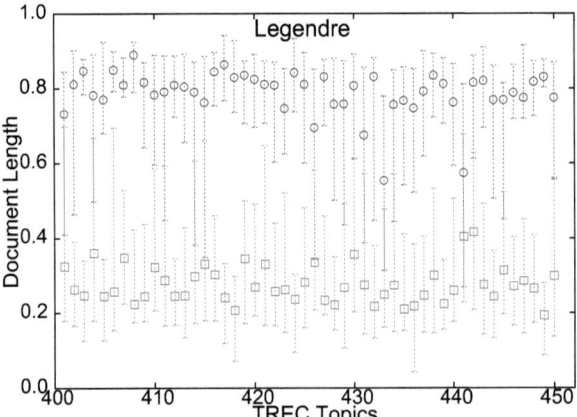

Figure 6.17: Distribution of the query terms for the top-20 TREC-8 documents ranked with the Legendre model and two different objective functions: $f_o = 1|3$ and $f_o = 3|3$.

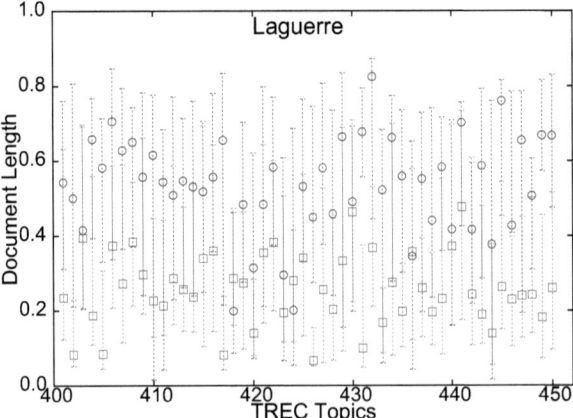

Figure 6.18: Distribution of the query terms for the top-20 TREC-8 documents ranked with the Laguerre model and two different objective functions: $f_o = 1|3$ and $f_o = 3|3$.

7
Conclusions

7.1 Summary

The main contribution of the thesis is the application of statistical, signal processing and functional analysis techniques in the field of information retrieval in order to capture positional information of terms in documents for improving the relevance of search results. It has been shown that the use of term positional information is an effective means to improve keyword based retrieval models, since it considers the terms in the context where they appear (neighborhood). Furthermore, the positions of other terms help to determine the relevance of a given term.

Different approaches to generate an abstract representation of term positional information have been investigated, starting from simple statistical models to refined polynomial representations that permit to construct a viable infrastructure to be applied in the IR process. Furthermore, the performed experiments provide the guidelines for implementing such models in real IR systems.

7.1.1 Term Position Models

The Gauss model has been the first attempt to incorporate term positional information in the IR process using simple statistical measures of center and spread. Using this model, it could be demonstrated that algorithms considering query term positions outperform algorithms based only on term frequency. In particular, documents containing query terms in neighborhood regions are more relevant than documents containing distant query terms. Using this criterion, two optimization methodologies based on the *semantic distance* concept have been proposed: ranking optimization without relevance feedback, and a query expansion methodology.

With the aim of improving the initial statistical representation of term positions, a novel model based on Fourier series has been proposed. The Fourier model provides a more precise representation of the term positions and allows us to control the resolution of the term representations (Fourier order). Experimental results have demonstrated that by using low Fourier orders (e.g. 6) accurate term position representations can be generated, providing a basis for reliably estimating the relevance of documents.

In the newly proposed Hilbert model, a mathematical basis for the term position paradigm has been defined. It considers the use of orthogonal polynomials to describe the term position functions, and the Fourier model is a special case of this model. The Legendre and Laguerre polynomials have been proposed as further representational functions.

One can misleadingly think that the use of mathematical instruments such as Fourier series or orthogonal polynomials could decrease the speed of the retrieval system. On the contrary, all necessary calculations to generate the abstract term position representations are executed and stored in the indexing phase, which does not interfere with the time-critical phases of the IR process. The simplicity of the computed positional data permits an efficient execution of the corresponding term position operations at query evaluation time, without increasing the response time of the system.

Several experiments conducted on the TREC-8 collection have demonstrated the superiority of the models using term positional information over term frequency approaches.

7.1.2 Query Expansion

It has been demonstrated experimentally that the performance of query expansion strategies is highly influenced by the number of documents and terms considered in the expansion process. The use of term positional information constitutes a key element for selecting expanded terms, because it allows to increase the amount of analyzed data (documents), improving the quality of the expanded terms.

Query expansion methods based only on term frequency are susceptible to incorporate noisy or irrelevant terms in the expanded query, particularly if many documents are considered in the expansion process. This behavior affects all state-of-the-art models, as confirmed in Figure 6.10, and the *precision* values calculated for different query expansion configurations (Table 6.1).

In contrast, the term position models select the expansion terms using the neighborhood of the query, avoiding to include possible noisy terms from other irrelevant document regions. This property allows us to increase the number of documents considered in the expansion process that are the source of relevant expansion terms, and minimizes the addition of irrelevant terms in the expanded query.

7.1.3 User Objective Functions

The proposed objective function concept represents a novel methodology in IR. Experiments on the TREC collection have confirmed that relevance ranking can be improved by defining particular document regions (Section 6.6, Run 3), but it is very likely that an even better performance can be obtained by processing collections of documents having homogeneous structures such as forms, papers, questionnaires, etc.

Due to the symmetry properties of the Fourier and Legendre models, they show the best performance in recognizing the document regions defined as relevant by the user. On the other hand, the logarithmic component of the Laguerre model mislead the representation of terms at the bottom of documents, harming its overall performance.

7.1.4 Document Length

As shown in Section 6.5, variations in the document length can influence the measures of neighborhood in the term position models. That is, the neighborhood of a term is directly proportional to the document length. This effect is harmless by term operations within the document boundaries, but it could be problematic if we want to compare term distributions among different documents.

A clear example is the proposed query expansion algorithm, where long documents contribute with more expansion terms than short documents. In this case, the selection of the term position model is fundamental for adequate query expansion performance: for homogeneous collections where the document size does not vary considerably, the Fourier model will probably be the best choice, while the Laguerre model, due to its independence of the document length, will be a better alternative in heterogeneous collections. In other words, the selection of a suitable term position model regarding the properties of the document collection minimizes the negative effect induced by variations in the document length.

7.2 Future Work

There are several issues for future work, as outlined below:

7.2.1 Document Structure

It would be interesting to study the possibility of generating optimized objective functions by training the proposed approach with particular document categories such as medical, juridical, scientific papers, etc. Such document categories generally have well defined structures that are interesting for specialized searchers. For instance, scientific papers always contain three main elements in their structure: the abstract (at the top of the document), the body, and the conclusions (at the end of the document). By using objective functions, the retrieval model can be easily optimized to promote such essential regions and help the user to refine results or specify individual information needs.

7.2.2 Index Size

A further topic to be investigated is how an abstract representation of term positions will influence the size of the index. Depending on the number of coefficients defined in the model, the space required to save positional data is smaller than the positional data itself, except for terms of very low frequency. An experimental analysis of such variables is an interesting area to be investigated.

7.2.3 Other Applications

Since this work is based on functional representations, one can easily extend it to cover areas other than text. For example, sound and images could be represented in an index with their coefficients (sound as one-dimensional and images as two-dimensional signals). Retrieving them would be as easy as presenting portions of the sound or image that we want.

7.2.4 Clustering

Document clusters that are based on term frequency could be an interesting area for using positional information. As mentioned in Section 6.3.3, the model provides a graphical representation of the term position space that could be used as the basis for a graphical analysis of document collections.

7.2.5 Software Platform

Regarding the index structure and the term positions representation, the use of the Lucene platform currently offers the best alternative to implement the proposed models – on the one hand, due to the newly proposed Payloads approach (Section 6.4), and on the other hand because its increasing popularity, permanent improvements, and active support. However, the implementation of the proposed models based on term positional information in other information retrieval platforms should also be considered in future work.

Bibliography

[1] M. Abramowitz, I. Stegun, M. Danos, and J. Rafelski. *Pocketbook of Mathematical Functions*. H. Deutsch, 1984.

[2] E. S. Adams. *A study of trigrams and their feasibility as index terms in a full text information retrieval system*. PhD thesis, George Washington University, Washington, DC, USA, 1992.

[3] J. Allan. Relevance feedback with too much data. In *SIGIR '95: Proceedings of the 18th Annual International ACM SIGIR Conference on Research and Development in Information Retrieval*, pages 337–343, New York, NY, USA, 1995. ACM.

[4] G. Amati and C. J. V. Rijsbergen. Probabilistic models of information retrieval based on measuring the divergence from randomness. *ACM Trans. Inf. Syst.*, 20(4):357–389, 2002.

[5] A. Arthur, editor. *Ukolug Quick Guide to Online Commands*. UK Online User Group, 2nd edition, April 1989.

[6] R. Attar and A. Fraenkel. Experiments in local metrical feedback in full-text retrieval systems. *Information Processing and Management*, 17(3):115–126, 1981.

[7] R. Attar and A. S. Fraenkel. Local feedback in full-text retrieval systems. *Journal of the ACM*, 24(3):397–417, 1977.

[8] R. Baeza-Yates and B. Ribeiro-Neto. *Modern Information Retrieval*. Addison Wesley, 1999.

[9] R. A. Baeza-Yates and B. Ribeiro-Neto. *Modern Information Retrieval*. Addison-Wesley Longman Publishing Co., Inc., Boston, MA, USA, 1999.

[10] D. Beeferman, A. Berger, and J. Lafferty. Text segmentation using exponential models. In *In Proceedings of the Second Conference on Empirical Methods in Natural Language Processing*, pages 35–46, 1997.

[11] M. Beigbeder and A. Mercier. An information retrieval model using the fuzzy proximity degree of term occurences. In *SAC '05: Proceedings of the 2005 ACM Symposium on Applied Computing*, pages 1018–1022, New York, NY, USA, 2005. ACM.

[12] M. Berry, S. Dumais, and G. O'Brien. Using linear algebra for intelligent information retrieval. *SIAM Review*, 37(4):573–595, 1994.

[13] B. Billerbeck, F. Scholer, H. E. Williams, and J. Zobel. Query expansion using associated queries. In *CIKM '03: Proceedings of the 12th Int. Conference on Information and Knowledge Management*, pages 2–9, New York, NY, USA, 2003. ACM Press.

[14] R. C. Bodner and F. Song. Knowledge-based approaches to query expansion in information retrieval. In *AI '96: Proceedings of the 11th Biennial Conference of the Canadian Society for Computational Studies of Intelligence on Advances in Artificial Intelligence*, pages 146–158, London, UK, 1996. Springer-Verlag.

[15] A. Bookstein, S. Klein, and T. Raita. Clumping properties of content-bearing words. *Journal of the American Society for Information Science*, 49(2):102–114, 1998.

[16] C. L. Borgman. The user's mental model of an information retrieval system: an experiment on a prototype online catalog. *Int. J. Man-Mach. Stud.*, 24(1):47–64, 1986.

[17] S. Brin and L. Page. The anatomy of a large-scale hypertextual web search engine. *Computer Networks*, 30(1-7):107–117, 1998.

[18] C. Buckley, G. Salton, and J. Allan. The effect of adding relevance information in a relevance feedback environment. In *17th Annual International ACM-SIGIR Conference on Research and Development in Information Retrieval*, pages 292–300, London, July 1994.

[19] C. Buckley, G. Salton, J. Allan, and A. Singhal. Automatic query expansion using smart: TREC-3. In *Overview of the 3rd Text Retrieval Conference*, pages 69–80. NIST Special Publication, 1995.

[20] F. J. Burkowski. An algebra for hierarchically organized text-dominated databases. *Inf. Process. Manage.*, 28(3):333–348, 1992.

[21] F. J. Burkowski. Retrieval activities in a database consisting of heterogeneous collections of structured text. In *SIGIR '92: Proceedings of the 15th annual international ACM SIGIR conference on Research and development in information retrieval*, pages 112–125, New York, NY, USA, 1992. ACM.

[22] V. Bush. As we may think. *Interactions*, 3(2):35–46, 1996.

[23] D. Cai, S. Yu, J.-R. Wen, and W.-Y. Ma. Block-based web search. In *SIGIR '04: Proceedings of the 27th Annual International ACM SIGIR Conference on Research and Development in Information Retrieval*, pages 456–463, New York, NY, USA, 2004. ACM Press.

[24] J. P. Callan. Passage-level evidence in document retrieval. In *SIGIR '94: Proceedings of the 17th annual international ACM SIGIR conference on Research and development in information retrieval*, pages 302–310, New York, NY, USA, 1994. Springer-Verlag New York, Inc.

[25] N. Carroll. Search engine optimization and user behavior. Technical report, Encyclopedia of Library and Information Sciences, 2009.

[26] T. Cawkell and E. Garfield. Institute for scientific information. *Information Services and Use*, 21(2):79–86, 2001.

[27] T. Chunqiang, S. Dwarkadas, and Z. Xu. On scaling latent semantic indexing for large peer-to-peer systems. In *SIGIR '04: Proceedings of the 27th Annual int. conference on research and development in information retrieval*, pages 112–121, New York, NY, USA, 2004. ACM Press.

[28] C. L. A. Clarke and G. V. Cormack. Shortest-substring retrieval and ranking. *ACM Trans. Inf. Syst.*, 18(1):44–78, 2000.

[29] C. W. Cleverdon and M. Keen. Aslib cranfield research project - factors determining the performance of indexing systems; volume 2, test results. Technical report, Aslib Cranfield Research Project, 1966.

[30] K. Coffman and A. M. Odlyzko. The size and growth rate of the internet. *First Monday*, 3(10), 1998.

[31] K. G. Coffman, K. G. Coffman, A. M. Odlyzko, and A. M. Odlyzko. Growth of the internet. In *Utility, Utilization, and Quality of Service, Tech. Rep. 99-08, DIMACS*, pages 17–56. Academic Press, 2001.

[32] M. D. Cooper, U. Nam, and J. Foote. Audio retrieval by rhythmic similarity. In *3rd International Conference on Music Information Retrieval*, 2002.

[33] K. D. Corbitt and E. Kaplan. Calvin N. Mooers Papers (CBI 81). Charles Babbage Institute, University of Minnesota, Minneapolis, 1992.

[34] G. V. Cormack, C. L. A. Clarke, C. R. Palmer, and S. S. L. To. Passage-based query refinement (multitext experiments for trec-6). *Inf. Process. Manage.*, 36(1):133–153, 2000.

[35] T. M. Cover and J. A. Thomas. *Elements of Information Theory*. Wiley-Interscience, August 1991.

[36] W. B. Croft and J. Xu. Corpus-specific stemming using word form co-occurrence. In *Fourth Annual Symposium on Document Analysis and Information Retrieval*, pages 147–159, 1995.

[37] C. J. Crouch and B. Yang. Experiments in automatic statistical thesaurus construction. In *SIGIR '92: Proceedings of the 15th annual international ACM SIGIR conference on Research and development in information retrieval*, pages 77–88, New York, NY, USA, 1992. ACM.

[38] O. de Kretser and A. Moffat. Locality-based information retrieval. In *10th Australasian Database Conference*, pages 177–188, Auckland, New Zealand, January 1999.

[39] S. C. Deerwester, S. T. Dumais, T. K. Landauer, G. W. Furnas, and R. A. Harshman. Indexing by latent semantic analysis. *JASIS*, 41(6):391–407, 1990.

[40] S. Dumais. Latent semantic indexing (lsi): Trec-3 report. In *Proceedings of the Text Retrieval Conference (TREC-3)*, pages 219–230, 1995.

[41] E. Efthimiadis. *Interactive query expansion and relevance feedback for document retrieval systems*. PhD thesis, City University, London UK, 1992.

[42] E. Efthimiadis. Query expansion. *Annual Review of Information Science and Technology (ARIST)*, (2):121–187, 1996.

[43] E. Efthimiadis and P. Biron. Ucla-okapi at TREC-2: Query expansion experiments. In *Proceedings of the 2nd Text Retrieval Conference (TREC-2)*, pages 279–290. NIST Special Publication 500-215, 1994.

[44] P. Elias. Universal codeword sets and representations of the integers. *Information Theory, IEEE Transactions on*, 21(2):194–203, 1975.

[45] W. Fan, M. Luo, L. Wang, W. Xi, and E. Fox. Tuning before feedback: combining ranking discovery and blind feedback for robust retrieval. In *SIGIR '04: Proceedings of the 27th Annual International ACM SIGIR Conference on Research and Development in Information Retrieval*, pages 138–145, New York, NY, USA, July 2004. ACM.

[46] C. H. Fenichel. Online searching: Measures that discriminate among users with different types of experiences. *Journal of the American Society for Information Science*, 32(1):23–32, Januar 1981.

[47] M. Fernandez, É. Villemonte de La Clergerie, and M. Vilares. Knowledge acquisition through error-mining. In *Proc. of International Conference on Recent Advances in Natural Language Processing (RANLP'07)*, pages 220–229, Borovets, Bulgaria, 2007.

[48] L. Finkelstein, E. Gabrilovich, Y. Matias, E. Rivlin, A. Solan, G. Wolfman, and E. Ruppin. Placing search in context: the concept revisited. *ACM Transactions on Information Systems*, 20(1):116–131, January 2002.

[49] A. Folkers and H. Samet. Content-based image retrieval using fourier descriptors on a logo database. In *ICPR '02: Proceedings of the 16 th International Conference on Pattern Recognition (ICPR'02) Volume 3*, page 30521, Washington, DC, USA, 2002. IEEE Computer Society.

[50] E. Fox. Characteristics of two new experimental collections in computer and information science containing textual and bibliographic concepts. Technical Report 83-561, Department of Computer Science, Cornell University, Ithaca, NY, 1983.

[51] W. B. Frakes and R. Baeza-Yates. *Information Retrieval Data Structures & Algorithms*. Prentice Hall PTR, June 1992.

[52] W. N. Francis and H. Kucera. Frequency analysis of english usage: Lexicon and grammar. *Journal of English Linguistics*, 18(1):64–70, April 1985.

[53] W. N. Francis, H. Kučera, and A. W. Mackie. *Frequency analysis of English usage : lexicon and grammar*. Houghton Mifflin, 1982.

[54] V. I. Frants and C. B. Brush. The need for information and some aspects of information retrieval systems construction. *Journal of the American Society for Information Science*, 39(2):86–91, March 1988.

[55] V. J. Frants, V. G. Voiskunski, and J. Shapiro. *Automated Information Retrieval: Theory and Methods*. Academic Press Inc, London, August 1997.

[56] M. Fuller, L. Kelly, and G. Jones. Applying contextual memory cues for retrieval from personal information archives. In *PIM 2008 - Proceedings of Personal Information Management, Workshop at CHI 2008*, Florence, Italy, 2008.

[57] P. Galeas and B. Freisleben. Word distribution analysis for relevance ranking and query expansion. In *Computational Linguistics and Intelligent Text Processing*, number 4919 in Lecture Notes in Computer Science, pages 500–511. Springer Berlin / Heidelberg, 2008.

[58] P. Galeas, R. Kretschmer, and B. Freisleben. Document relevance assessment via term distribution analysis using fourier series expansion. In *JCDL '09: Proceedings of the 2009 ACM/IEEE-CS Joint International Conference on Digital Libraries*, pages 277–284, New York, NY, USA, 2009. ACM.

[59] P. Galeas, R. Kretschmer, and B. Freisleben. Information retrieval via truncated Hilbert space expansions. In *Proceedings of the 9th IEEE International Conference on Computer and Information Technology*, page (accepted for publication). IEEE Press, 2010.

[60] E. Garcia. The classic vector space model. Information Retrieval Intelligence: http://www.miislita.com/term-vector/term-vector-3.html, 2006.

[61] J. Gemmell. Capture, archival & retrieval of personal experiences. Internet, May 2007. http://www.sigmm.org/Members/jgemmell/CARPE.

[62] S. W. Golomb. Run-length encodings. *IEEE Transactions on Information Theory*, 12(3):399–401, 1966.

[63] O. Gospodnetic and H. Hatcher. *Lucene In Action*. Manning Publications Co., 1st edition, 2005.

[64] D. A. Grossman and O. Frieder. *Information Retrieval. Algorithms and Heuristics*. Springer Netherlands, 2nd edition, January 2005.

[65] C. D. Gull. Historical note: Information science and technology: From coordinate indexing to the global brain. *Journal of the American Society for Information Science*, 38(5):338–366, 1987.

[66] Z. Gyöngyi and H. Garcia-Molina. Spam: It's not just for inboxes anymore. *Computer*, 38(10):28–34, 2005.

[67] C. Hamilton, R. Kimberley, and J. Rowley, editors. *Text Retrieval: Directory of Software*. Gower Publishing Ltd, 3rd edition, July 1990.

[68] S. P. Harter. *Online Information Retrieval: Concepts, Principles, and Techniques*. Academic Press, Inc., Orlando, FL, USA, 1986.

[69] M. Hearst and G. Pedersen. Reexamining the cluster hypothesis: scatter/gather on retrieval results. In A. Press, editor, *Proceedings of International ACM SIGIR Conference on Research and Development in IR*, pages 76–84, New York, 1996.

[70] M. A. Hearst. Multi-paragraph segmentation of expository text. In *Proceedings of the 32nd annual meeting on Association for Computational Linguistics*, pages 9–16, Morristown, NJ, USA, 1994. Association for Computational Linguistics.

[71] M. A. Hearst and C. Plaunt. Subtopic structuring for full-length document access. In *SIGIR '93: Proceedings of the 16th annual international ACM SIGIR conference on Research and development in information retrieval*, pages 59–68, New York, NY, USA, 1993. ACM.

[72] S. Hodges, L. Williams, E. Berry, S. Izadi, J. Srinivasan, A. Butler, G. Smyth, N. Kapur, and K. R. Wood. Sensecam: A retrospective memory aid. In *Ubicomp*, pages 177–193, 2006.

[73] X. Huang and Y. Huang. Using contextual information to improve retrieval performance. In *Proceedings of 2005 IEEE International Conference on Granular Computing*, pages 474–481, Beijing, China, July 2005.

[74] E. Ide. *The SMART Retrieval System Experiments in Automatic Document Processing*, chapter Relevance Feedback in Information Retrieval, pages 337–354. Prentice Hall, 1971.

[75] G. Ingersoll. Getting started with payloads. Website, Aug. 2009. http://www.lucidimagination.com/blog/2009/08/05/getting-started-with-payloads.

[76] A. Jerri. The shannon sampling theoremits various extensions and applications: A tutorial review. In *Proceedings of the IEEE*, pages 1565–1596, Nov 1977.

[77] K. S. Jones and C. V. Rijsbergen. Information retrieval test collections. *Journal Of Documentation*, 32(1):59–75, 1976.

[78] K. S. Jones and K. van Rijsbergen. Report on the need for and provision of an 'ideal' information retrieval test collection. *BL R&D REPORT*, 1(5266), 1975. Computer Laboratory, University of Cambridge.

[79] M. Kaszkiel and J. Zobel. Passage retrieval revisited. In *SIGIR '97: Proceedings of the 20th annual international ACM SIGIR conference on Research and development in information retrieval*, pages 178–185, New York, NY, USA, 1997. ACM.

[80] M. Kaszkiel and J. Zobel. Effective ranking with arbitrary passages. *J. Am. Soc. Inf. Sci. Technol.*, 52(4):344–364, 2001.

[81] S. M. Katz. Distribution of content words and phrases in text and language modelling. *Natural Language Engineering*, 2(1):15–59, 1996.

[82] E. M. Keen. The use of term position devices in ranked output experiments. *J. Doc.*, 47(1):1–22, 1991.

[83] E. M. Keen. Some aspects of proximity searching in text retrieval systems. *J. Inf. Sci.*, 18(2):89–98, 1992.

[84] J. Kleinberg. Authoritative sources in a hyperlinked environment. *Journal of the ACM*, 46(5):604–632, September 1999.

[85] R. R. Korfhage. *Information Storage and Retrieval*. Wiley, June 1997.

[86] G. J. Kowalski and M. T. Maybury. *Information Storage and Retrieval Systems. Theory and Implementation*. Springer US, 2nd edition, September 2000.

[87] M. Krajewski. Zettelwirtschaft. die geburt der kartei aus dem geist der bibliothek. Internet, February 2003. http://www.kunsttexte.de/ download/ bwt/ Kuehl.PDF.

[88] R. Krovetz. Viewing morphology as an inference process. In *SIGIR '93: Proceedings of the 16th annual international ACM SIGIR conference on Research and development in information retrieval*, pages 191–202, New York, NY, USA, 1993. ACM.

[89] R. Krovetz and W. B. Croft. Word sense disambiguation using machine-readable dictionaries. *SIGIR Forum*, 23(SI):127–136, 1989.

[90] F. W. Lancaster. *Information retrieval systems: Characteristics, testing, and evaluation*. Wiley, 1979.

[91] T. Landauer and M. Littman. Fully automatic cross-language document retrieval using latent semantic indexing. In *Proceedings of the 6th Annual Conference of the UW Centre for the New Oxford English Dictionary and Text Research*, pages 31–38, Waterloo Ontario, 1990. UW Centre for the New OED and Text Research.

[92] J. Li, M. Guo, and S. Tian. A new approach to query expansion. In *Machine Learning and Cybernetics*, pages 2302–2306, August 2005.

[93] X. Liu and W. B. Croft. Passage retrieval based on language models. In *CIKM '02: Proceedings of the eleventh international conference on Information and knowledge management*, pages 375–382, New York, NY, USA, 2002. ACM.

[94] R. Losee. Probabilistic retrieval and coordination level matching. *American Society for Information Science*, 38(4):239–244, 1987.

[95] J. B. Lovins. Development of a stemming algorithm. Technical report, Massachusetts Institute Of Technology Cambridge Electronic Systems Lab, June 1968.

[96] H. P. Luhn. The automatic creation of literature abstracts. *IBM Journal of Research and Development*, 2(2), 1958.

[97] H. P. Luhn. Key word-in-context index for technical literature (kwic index). *American Documentation*, 11(4):288–295, 1960.

[98] M. E. Maron and J. L. Kuhns. On relevance, probabilistic indexing and information retrieval. *J. ACM*, 7(3):216–244, 1960.

[99] S. Miyamoto. *Fuzzy Sets in Information Retrieval and Cluster Analysis*. Kluwer Academic Publishers Group, 1990.

[100] A. Moffat and J. Zobel. Self-indexing inverted files for fast text retrieval. *ACM Trans. Inf. Syst.*, 14(4):349–379, 1996.

[101] D. Moore and G. McCabe. *Introduction to the Practice of Statistics*. W H Freeman and Co, 1nd edition, 1989.

[102] D. S. Moore. *The Basic Practice Of Statistics*. W H Freeman, 3rd edition, 2003.

[103] G. Navarro and R. Baeza-Yates. Proximal nodes: a model to query document databases by content and structure. *ACM Trans. Inf. Syst.*, 15(4):400–435, 1997.

[104] G. O'Brien. Information management tools for updating an svd-encoded indexing scheme. Technical report, University of Tennessee, Knoxville, TN, USA, 1994.

[105] A. S. of Indexers. How information retrieval started. Internet, October 2005. http://www.asindexing.org/site/history.shtml.

[106] I. Ounis, G. Amati, V. Plachouras, B. He, C. Macdonald, and C. Lioma. Terrier: A high performance and scalable information retrieval platform. In *Proceedings of ACM SIGIR'06 Workshop on Open Source Information Retrieval (OSIR 2006)*, 2006.

BIBLIOGRAPHY 151

[107] R. Papka and J. Allan. Why bigger windows are better than smaller ones. Technical report, Department of Computer Science, University of Massachusetts, 1997.

[108] L. A. F. Park. *Spectral Based Information Retrieval*. PhD thesis, Department of Electrical and Electronic Engineering, The University of Melbourne, December 2003.

[109] L. A. F. Park, M. Palaniswami, and K. Ramamohanarao. Internet document filtering using fourier domain scoring. In *PKDD '01: Proceedings of the 5th European Conference on Principles of Data Mining and Knowledge Discovery*, pages 362–373, London, UK, 2001. Springer-Verlag.

[110] L. A. F. Park, K. Ramamohanarao, and M. Palaniswami. Fourier domain scoring: A novel document ranking method. *IEEE Trans. on Knowl. and Data Eng.*, 16(5):529–539, 2004.

[111] J. W. Perry. In *Encyclopedia of library and information science*, volume 22, pages 66–68. New York: Marcel Dekker, Inc., 1977.

[112] J. M. Ponte and W. B. Croft. Text segmentation by topic. In *ECDL '97: Proceedings of the First European Conference on Research and Advanced Technology for Digital Libraries*, pages 113–125, London, UK, 1997. Springer-Verlag.

[113] M. F. Porter. An algorithm for suffix stripping. *Readings in information retrieval*, pages 313–316, 1997.

[114] Y. Qiu and H.-P. Frei. Concept based query expansion. In *SIGIR '93: Proceedings of the 16th annual international ACM SIGIR conference on Research and development in information retrieval*, pages 160–169, New York, NY, USA, 1993. ACM.

[115] N. Ramakrishnan. From the area editor: Frontiers of search. *Computer*, 38(10):26–27, 2005.

[116] K. Ramamohanarao, M. Palaniswami, and L. A. Park. Fourier domain scoring: a novel document ranking method. *Transactions on Knowledge and Data Engineering*, 16(5):529–539, May 2004.

[117] Y. Rasolofo and J. Savoy. Term proximity scoring for keyword-based retrieval systems. In *Advances in Information Retrieval*, volume 2633/2003 of *Lecture Notes in Computer Science*. Springer Berlin / Heidelberg, 2003.

[118] M. A. Razek, C. Frasson, and M. Kaltenbach. Context-based information agent for supporting intelligent distance learning environment. In *Proc. of the Twelfth International World Wide Web Conference, WWW03*, page 968, Budapest, Hungary, 2003. Springer-Verlag.

[119] C. Reed. Blended search results studyblended search results study. Technical report, Iprospect, Apr. 2008.

[120] J. C. Reynar. An automatic method of finding topic boundaries. In *Proceedings of the 32nd annual meeting on Association for Computational Linguistics*, pages 331–333, Morristown, NJ, USA, 1994. Association for Computational Linguistics.

[121] A. Reynolds and P. W. Flagg. *Cognitive Psychology*. Wintrop Publishers, 1977.

[122] K. Richmond, A. Smith, and E. Amitay. Detecting subject boundaries within text: a language independent statistical approach. In *2nd Conference on Empirical Methods in Natural Language Processing*, pages 47–54, Providence, Rhode Island, USA, Aug 1997.

[123] C. V. Rijsbergen. A theoretical basis for the use of cooccurrence data in information retrieval. *Journal of Documentation*, 33(2):106–119, 1977.

[124] S. Robertson and K. S. Jones. Relevance weighting of search terms. *American Society for Information Sciences*, 27(3):129–146, 1976.

[125] S. Robertson, M. Porter, and C. van Rijsbergen. New models in probabilistic information retrieval. Technical report, Computer Laboratory, Cambridge University, 1980.

[126] S. E. Robertson and K. Sparck Jones. Relevance weighting of search terms. pages 143–160, 1988.

[127] S. E. Robertson, S. Walker, M. Hancock-Beaulieu, A. Gull, and M. Lau. Okapi at TREC. In *TREC*, pages 21–30, 1992.

[128] J. Rocchio. Relevance feedback in information retrieval. In G. Salton, editor, *The SMART Retrieval System: Experiments in Automatic Document Processing*, pages 313–323, Englewood Cliffs, NJ, 1971. Prentice-Hall.

[129] G. Salton. *Automatic Information Organization and Retrieval*. McGraw Hill Text, 1968.

[130] G. Salton. *The SMART Retrieval System - Experiments in Automatic Document Processing*. Prentice Hall Inc, Englewood Cliffs. NJ, 1971.

[131] G. Salton, J. Allan, and C. Buckley. Approaches to passage retrieval in full text information systems. In *SIGIR '93: Proceedings of the 16th annual international ACM SIGIR conference on Research and development in information retrieval*, pages 49–58, New York, NY, USA, 1993. ACM.

[132] G. Salton, J. Allan, and A. Singhal. Automatic text decomposition and structuring. *Inf. Process. Manage.*, 32(2):127–138, 1996.

[133] G. Salton and C. Buckley. Term weighting approaches in automatic text retrieval. Technical report, Ithaca, NY, USA, 1987.

BIBLIOGRAPHY 153

[134] G. Salton and M. E. Lesk. The smart automatic document retrieval systems - an illustration. *Commun. ACM*, 8(6):391–398, 1965.

[135] G. Salton and M. E. Lesk. The smart automatic document retrieval systems an illustration. *Commun. ACM*, 8(6):391–398, 1965.

[136] G. Salton and M. J. McGill. *Introduction to Modern Information Retrieval*. McGraw-Hill, Inc., New York, NY, USA, 1986.

[137] G. Salton, A. Singhal, M. Mitra, and C. Buckley. Automatic text structuring and summarization. *Inf. Process. Manage.*, 33(2):193–207, 1997.

[138] G. Salton, A. Wong, and C. S. Yang. A vector space model for automatic indexing. *Communications of the ACM*, 18(11):613–620, 1975.

[139] G. Salton, C. S. Yang, and C. T. Yu. A theory of term importance in automatic text analysis. Technical report, Ithaca, NY, USA, 1974.

[140] X. Shen and C. Zhai. Exploiting query history for document ranking in interactive information retrieval. In *26th Annual International ACM-SIGIR Conference on Research and Development in Information Retrieval*, pages 377–378. ACM Press, 2003.

[141] A. Singhal, C. Buckley, and M. Mitra. Pivoted document length normalization. In *SIGIR '96: Proceedings of the 19th annual international ACM SIGIR conference on Research and development in information retrieval*, pages 21–29, New York, NY, USA, 1996. ACM.

[142] S. Soy. Class lecture notes: H. p. luhn and automatic indexing – references to the early years of automatic indexing and information retrieval. Internet, 2003. http://www.gslis.utexas.edu/ ssoy/organizing/l391d2c.htm.

[143] M. R. Spiegel. *Schaum's Outline of theory and problems of Fourier analysis*. McGraw Hill, New York, 1 edition, 1974.

[144] C. Stanfill and D. L. Waltz. Statistical methods, artificial intelligence, and information retrieval. pages 215–225, 1992.

[145] J.-T. Sun, Z. Chen, H.-J. Zeng, Y.-C. Lu, C.-Y. Shi, and W.-Y. Ma. Supervised latent semantic indexing for document categorization. In *ICDM '04: Proceedings of the Fourth IEEE International Conference on Data Mining*, pages 535–538, Washington, DC, USA, 2004. IEEE Computer Society.

[146] R. Sun, C.-H. Ong, and T.-S. Chua. Mining dependency relations for query expansion in passage retrieval. In *SIGIR '06: Proceedings of the 29th Annual International ACM SIGIR Conference on Research and Development in Information Retrieval*, pages 382–389, New York, NY, USA, 2006. ACM Press.

[147] T. Tao and C. Zhai. An exploration of proximity measures in information retrieval. In *SIGIR '07: Proceedings of the 30th annual international ACM SIGIR conference on Research and development in information retrieval*, pages 295–302, New York, NY, USA, 2007. ACM.

[148] M. Taube. *Studies in coordinate indexing*. Washington Documentation Incorporated, 1953.

[149] S. Teasdale. *Flame and Shadow*, volume 591. Project-Gutenberg, 1996.

[150] S. Tellex, B. Katz, J. Lin, A. Fernandes, and G. Marton. Quantitative evaluation of passage retrieval algorithms for question answering. In *SIGIR '03: Proceedings of the 26th annual international ACM SIGIR conference on Research and development in informaion retrieval*, pages 41–47, New York, NY, USA, 2003. ACM.

[151] J. W. Tukey. *Exploratory Data Analysis*. Series in Behavioral Science. Addison-Wesley, Juni 1977.

[152] H. Turtle and J. Flood. Query evaluation: strategies and optimizations. *Inf. Process. Manage.*, 31(6):831–850, 1995.

[153] C. J. van Rijsbergen. *Information Retrieval*. Butterworths, London, 2nd edition, 1979.

[154] C. J. van Rijsbergen. *The Geometry of Information Retrieval*. Cambridge University Press, New York, NY, USA, 2004.

[155] P. Vaswani and J. Cameron. The national physical laboratory experiments in statistical word associations and their use in document indexing and retrieval. Technical report, National Physical Laboratory, Teddington, 1970.

[156] E. Voorhees and D. Harman. *Trec: Experiment and Evaluation in Information Retrieval*. The MIT Press, 1st edition, 2005.

[157] H. H. Wellisch. *Indexing from A to Z*. Niso Press, April 1996.

[158] W. J. Wilbur and K. Sirotkin. The automatic identification of stop words. *J. Inf. Sci.*, 18(1):45–55, 1992.

[159] R. Wilkinson. Effective retrieval of structured documents. In *Proceedings of the 17th Annual International ACM-SIGIR Conference on Research and Development in Information Retrieval. Dublin, Ireland, 3-6 July 1994 (Special Issue of the SIGIR Forum)*, pages 311–317. ACM/Springer, 1994.

[160] R. Wilkinson and P. Hingston. Using the cosine measure in a neural network for document retrieval. In *SIGIR '91: Proceedings of the 14th annual international ACM SIGIR conference on Research and development in information retrieval*, pages 202–210, New York, NY, USA, 1991. ACM.

BIBLIOGRAPHY 155

[161] R. V. Williams. Chronology of information science and technology. Internet, 2002. http://www.libsci.sc.edu/ BOB/ istchron/ ISCNET/ ISCHRON.HTM.

[162] R. V. Williams and M. E. Bowden. Chronology of chemical information science, abstracts, reviews, compilations, and indexes stored and retrieved using electronic computers, 2000. http://www.chemheritage.org/ explore/ timeline/ MACHINE.HTM.

[163] I. H. Witten, A. Moffat, and T. C. Bell. *Managing Gigabytes: Compressing and Indexing Documents and Images*. Morgan Kaufmann Publishers, San Francisco, CA, 1999.

[164] J. Xu and W. Croft. Query expansion using local and global document analysis. In *Proceedings of the 19th Annual International ACM SIGIR Conference on Research and Development in information Retrieval*, pages 4–11, New York, August 1996. ACM Press.

[165] J. Xu and W. Croft. Improving the effectiveness of information retrieval with local context analysis. *ACM Transactions on Information Systems*, 18(1):79–112, 2000.

[166] J. Xu and W. B. Croft. Query expansion using local and global document analysis. In *SIGIR '96: Proceedings of the 19th annual international ACM SIGIR conference on Research and development in information retrieval*, pages 4–11, New York, NY, USA, 1996. ACM.

[167] Y. Yaari. Segmentation of expository texts by hierarchical agglomerative clustering, 1997.

[168] K. Yosida. *Functional Analysis*. Springer, 1980.

[169] S. Yu, D. Cai, J. Wen, and W. Ma. Improving pseudo-relevance feedback in web information retrieval using web page segmentation. In *Proceedings of the 12th International Conference on World Wide Web*, pages 11–18, Budapest, 2003. ACM Press.

[170] J. Zobel and A. Moffat. Exploring the similarity space. *SIGIR Forum*, 32(1):18–34, 1998.

[171] J. Zobel, A. Moffat, R. Wilkinson, and R. Sacks-Davis. Efficient retrieval of partial documents. *Inf. Process. Manage.*, 31(3):361–377, 1995.

Die VDM Verlagsservicegesellschaft sucht für wissenschaftliche Verlage abgeschlossene und herausragende

Dissertationen, Habilitationen, Diplomarbeiten, Master Theses, Magisterarbeiten usw.

für die kostenlose Publikation als Fachbuch.

Sie verfügen über eine Arbeit, die hohen inhaltlichen und formalen Ansprüchen genügt, und haben Interesse an einer honorarvergüteten Publikation?

Dann senden Sie bitte erste Informationen über sich und Ihre Arbeit per Email an *info@vdm-vsg.de*.

Sie erhalten kurzfristig unser Feedback!

VDM Verlagsservicegesellschaft mbH
Dudweiler Landstr. 99   Telefon +49 681 3720 174
D - 66123 Saarbrücken   Fax   +49 681 3720 1749
www.vdm-vsg.de

Die VDM Verlagsservicegesellschaft mbH vertritt

Printed by Books on Demand GmbH, Norderstedt / Germany